Management for Professionals

More information about this series at http://www.springer.com/series/10101

Moshe Kress

Operational Logistics

The Art and Science of Sustaining Military Operations

Second Edition

 Springer

Moshe Kress
Department of Operations Research
Naval Postgraduate School
Monterey, CA, USA

ISSN 2192-8096   ISSN 2192-810X   (electronic)
Management for Professionals
ISBN 978-3-319-22673-6   ISBN 978-3-319-22674-3   (eBook)
DOI 10.1007/978-3-319-22674-3

Library of Congress Control Number: 2015947261

Springer Cham Heidelberg New York Dordrecht London
© Springer International Publishing Switzerland 2002, 2016

Printed on acid-free paper

Springer International Publishing AG Switzerland is part of Springer Science+Business Media (www.springer.com)

Preface

The term *management* is seldom used in the context of military operations, yet several aspects of modern warfare lend themselves to common management disciplines. *Information management* is needed to control, filter, process, and route the flow of data and information to and from the battlefield. The role of *manpower management* becomes more important as more specialized personal qualifications and training are needed to operate and maintain advanced weapons. *Movement management* is applied throughout a campaign to accumulate and deploy military forces. The term *management* is used occasionally even in combat operations in the context of *fire control*. As more advanced, effective and expensive combat systems enter the battlefield, *efficiency* must be considered, along with the more traditional *effectiveness* objective. Attaining efficiency depends on good management.

However, the broadest, the most complex, and probably the oldest of all the managerial aspects of warfare is logistics – the *management of combat means and resources*. This book is about the management of warfare logistics – planning, implementing, and controlling processes that sustain military operations.

Before we proceed to describe the scope of this second edition of the book, we start with a few quotes concerning logistics.

Few Quotes on Logistics...

About 250 years ago Benjamin Franklin composed the following lines, which have become since a motto for logisticians:

> For the want of a nail the shoe was lost,
> For the want of a shoe the horse was lost,
> For the want of a horse the rider was lost,
> For the want of a rider the battle was lost.

This well-known maxim expresses allegorically a chain of events that is so common in combat situations. A seemingly marginal and local "maintenance" fault initiates a cascade of events that leads to the ultimate military failure – defeat.

As a response to the plans and instructions of General George Marshall, the US Chief of staff during WWII, Admiral Ernest J. King – Chief of Naval Operations at that time – was quoted to say [1]:

> I don't know what the hell this "logistics" is that Marshall is always talking about, but I want some of it.

Even the light "virtual wink" that may have probably accompanied this statement does not blunt the lack of logistic understanding that is embedded in it. The message implied from this statement, which is so prevalent to commanders throughout history, is: "Don't bother me with this thing that is called logistics, simply make sure that we have all we need…"

In November 1984 the *Washington Post* published an article about the US National War College. In that article there was also a reference to the Industrial College of the US Armed Forces. The following is an excerpt from that article.

> The [National War] College is supposed to teach strategy to 'The thinkers'… and the Industrial College is supposed to teach logistics to the nuts-and-bolts types.

This citation implies two superficial and misguided beliefs: (a) strategy and logistics are two separate disciplines, and (b) logistics has nothing to do with thinking – it is just a collection of technical and dull skills.

Finally, it seems appropriate to cite General Julian Thompson who concluded, at the end of the preface to his book *The Lifeblood of War [2]*, that:

> I have no reason to believe that logistics will ever have much military sex-appeal, except to serious soldiers, but this book is written in the hope that I am wrong.

This book has been written with the same hope.

Perception

The historical experience in warfare since the military expeditions of Alexander the Great to the Iraq and Afghanistan wars teaches us that logistics is an important and inseparable part of warfare. Logistics facilitates movement, fire, and sustaining of the impetus and vitality of combat forces along time and space. Despite this evident "truth," some of the quotations above indicate that logistics has been treated as a second rate subject compared to "pure" tactics and strategy. It is probably the lack of glamor and, as Thompson describes it, the lack of sex appeal that is associated with slow moving convoys of trucks – as compared to charging tank columns and swift infantry operations – that led to this perception.

Also, the misled notion that logistics is low risk (close to 500 supply personnel and close to 700 maintenance personnel were killed during Israel wars) affected this perception. Commanders tended to concentrate on maneuvers and fire, while the logisticians were supposed to worry about moving supplies, maintaining the equipment, and evacuating the injured. The logisticians were expected not to bother their chiefs with mundane problems such as stalled convoys, overflowing maintenance areas, blown-up ammunition dumps and the like.

However, from talking to commanders and military scholars in Israel and the USA, it seems that this perception is changing. The claims and statements regarding the central role of logistics in the making of war do not need any more proof or justification. Exploring the causes for this perceptual leap is beyond the scope of this book; it may deserve an analysis of its own. We only point out here that technological changes in the battlefield and lessons learned from wars in the past 50 years – lessons that only relatively recently have been studied and analyzed in depth [3, 4, 5, 6, 7, 8] – are probably the main reasons for that change.

This change of perception, and the enhanced interest in logistics that this change may generate, are the main motivation for this book

Literature

There are three categories of books and monographs on Military Logistics. The first category comprises historical accounts of wars and military operations, as viewed from the logistics angle. One of the first books in this category, and probably the most cited one, is that by Van Creveld [9]. This class of history monographs provides detailed descriptions of logistics processes and events in past wars, along with some analyses of these phenomena.

The second category of logistics literature includes doctrinal publications and manuals – published mostly by military organizations. The US Field Manuals are typical examples of this category. These publications include doctrinal principles, rules and instructions that are designated mainly for commanders and logistics practitioners.

The third category of logistics publications includes theoretical essays that probe into the intricate structure and essence of logistics. These monographs attempt to reveal intrinsic properties, processes, and general rules that govern logistics. Such essays have appeared in few books and in journals such as *Military Review*, *Parameters*, and *Army Logistician*. An important monograph on the theoretical foundation of logistics is that of Admiral Eccles, [10] which first appeared in 1959. The link between strategy and logistics is discussed by Brown [11] in an essay from 1987. A more recent book is that by Foxton [12] (1993). This book is an excellent review of the components, structure, and general doctrinal aspects of contemporary logistics. Another book of this type is by Sarin [13] (2000).

Objectives

As implied from its title, this book belongs to the third category of logistics texts and its goal is to explore the theoretical foundations of operational logistics. This effort has two dimensions. The first dimension applies to the "artistic" or qualitative aspects of contemporary logistic issues within the context of the operational level of war. These aspects include principles, imperatives, and tenets, which are stated and analyzed. The second dimension – the "scientific" one – comprises formal representation, by a network model, of operational logistics.

To the best of my knowledge, this book is a first attempt to bridge the gap between the artistic and scientific aspects of military operational logistics. Specifically, the main thrust of the book is to study – both qualitatively and quantitatively – the interactions between the logistic system in the theater of operations and the principles of operational level of war.

The book is intended for logisticians, commanders, and military scholars. Operations research analysts, who are interested in large-scale logistic systems, may also find interest in the models presented in the last four chapters. Except for Chap. 12, and parts of Chaps. 9, 10 and 11, no quantitative background is needed.

Finally, while most of the content in this book is universal and apply to any military scenario – aerial, naval, or land operations, the focus is on land operations, arguably the most complex and challenging logistically.

Book Overview

This second edition has 12 chapters. Besides refreshing all the chapters from the first edition, the three major changes are:

- A new chapter on insurgency and counterinsurgency logistics (Chap. 7).
- A new chapter on military logistic intervention in humanitarian relief operations (Chap. 8).
- Chapter 12 (formerly Chap. 10) has been completely rewritten. The model has been simplified but also modified to account for uncertainties.

  Chapter 1 is a general introduction to Logistics. The term _logistics_ is discussed in its military context and a new general definition is proposed by drawing an analogy between warfare and production systems. The chapter concludes with a historical review of the three logistic options and a discussion regarding their impact on modern warfare.

  Chapter 2 discusses the structure and characteristics of logistics and describes its three levels – _strategic, operational,_ and _tactical._ Basic terminology is defined, which is used in subsequent chapters. Quantitative tools and models that are utilized for analyzing and planning logistics are reviewed.

  Chapter 3 focuses on the main theme of this book – _Operational Logistics_ _(OpLog)._ A brief introduction to the operational level of war is followed by a discussion on the cognitive, functional, and practical aspects of _OpLog._ Next, the main functional areas of _OpLog_ are reviewed and _OpLog_ principles are discussed. We show that the set of principles can be viewed as a union of two sets of properties – _cognitive properties_ and _operational and structural properties._

Chapter 4 deals with *OpLog* planning. Following a brief discussion on planning at the strategic and tactical levels, the main body of the chapter is focused on the operational level. First, the term *responsiveness* is defined and described by two visual models. Then, the two cycles of logistic planning – the *macro-logistics* cycle and the *micro-logistics* cycle – are described and demonstrated.

Chapter 5 addresses the issue of logistic information. First, we describe the information needs and then define the logistic information network. The structure and features of the information flow through the network are described. Finally, various types of logistic information are identified and analyzed.

Chapter 6 deals with forecasting logistic needs. It discusses battlefield uncertainties and their impact on estimating attrition and logistic consumption. It concludes with an outline of a methodology for logistics forecasting.

Chapter 7 is devoted to insurgency and counterinsurgency (COIN) operations. This type of armed conflicts has been prevalent and drew much attention since the early 2000s. The chapter discusses special logistic characteristics and challenges associated with both insurgents and COIN operations.

Chapter 8 is about humanitarian relief operations. The chapter describes the types of situations that trigger humanitarian aid and the types of responses applied. It discusses the civilian environment in which *OpLog* capabilities are implemented, and the challenges this environment imposes on military operations.

Chapter 9 introduces a logistic network model. This model is a descriptive-visual tool that provides an abstract display of logistic deployments and *OpLog* operational–structural properties defined in *Chap. 3*. This model – called *Visual Network* (VN) – may be used as a planning aid in the *macro-logistics* planning phase described in *Chap. 4*.

Chapter 10 addresses one of the most important *OpLog* properties – *Flexibility.* In this chapter, the basic definition and brief qualitative discussion given in *Chap. 3* are elaborated further. Quantitative metrics for measuring the two types of flexibility – intrinsic and structural – are described.

Chapter 11 discusses two major functions in *OpLog* practice: *Force accumulation* (also called *mobilization*) and *medical treatment and evacuation*. Both functions are complex and rely on efficient management of *time*. Some optimization issues related to these functions are discussed.

Chapter 12 presents an inter-temporal optimization model based on the logistic network model introduced in *Chap. 9*. The network optimization model optimizes the deployment of *OpLog* resources in the theater of operations.

Monterey, CA, USA   Moshe Kress

References

1. US GAO, *Welcome to the Logistics and Communication Division*, Washington DC, GPO, 1974
2. Thompson, J., *The Lifeblood of War - Logistics in Armed Conflict*, Brassey's (UK), 1991.
3. Ohl, J. K., *Supplying the Troops - General Somervell and American Logistics in WWII*, Northern Illinois University Press, DeKalb Ill, 1994.
4. Lynn, J. A., *Feeding Mars - Logistics in Western Warfare from the Middle Ages to the Present*, Westview Press, 1993.
5. Pagonis, W. G., *Moving Mountains - Lessons in Leadership and Logistics from the Gulf War*, Harvard Business School Press, Boston Mass. 1992.
6. Stucker, J. P., and I. M. Kameny, *Army Experiences with Deployment Planning in Operation Desert Shield*, RAND, Arroyo Center, 1993.
7. Shrader, C. R., *Communist Logistics in the Korean War*, Greenwood Press, Westport CN, 1995.
8. Wandall, R. S., *US Army Logistics: The Normandy Campaign, 1944*, Greenwood Publication Group, 1994.
9. Van Creveld, M., *Supplying War*, Cambridge University Press, Cambridge Mass, 1977.
10. Eccles, H. E., *Logistics in the National Defense*, Greenwood Press, Westport CN, 1981.
11. Brown, K. N., *Strategics, The Logistics-Strategy Link*, A National Security Essay, National Defense University Press, Washington DC, 1987.
12. Foxton, P. D., *Powering War: Modern Land Force Logistics*, Brassey's (UK), 1993.
13. Sarin, P., *Military Logistics – The Third Dimension*, Manas Publications, New Delhi, 2000.

Contents

Chapter 1
Introduction

The term *Operational Logistics* has different meanings according to the context in which it is being used. In the business world this term typically describes a collection of processes and actions aimed at supplying demands in an effective way. Large organizations have logistics departments in charge of daily operations such as transportation and maintenance, production plants require logistic support for handling inventories and shipping goods, and new products may be effectively marketed only if the manufacturer provides proper long-term service, which is manifested in efficient operational logistics.

In the military context *operational logistics* not only describes processes and actions but also indicates the level of military operations at which the logistics is being planned and executed. This level typically represents military campaigns, prolonged combat operations, and large-scale operations other than war (e.g., humanitarian relief).

There are profound differences between military logistics and its business-world counterpart. The differences are in the scope and scale of operations as well as the environment in which the two systems operate. There are very few, if any, business or public organizations that control and manage such a vast assortment of supplies, equipment, and personnel. Just the variety of supply items – ammunition, fuel, spare-parts, medical, food, construction, etc. – are in the hundreds of thousands if not millions of items. These supplies need to reach many customers – combat and combat support units – that may vary considerably in their needs and demands. Moreover, the scale of logistic operations – the tonnage that needs to be transported and distributed – is huge compared to any commercial operation. Finally, the highly uncertain, quite often malevolent and dangerous, environment in which military logistics operates is in stark contrast to the routine, largely peaceful, business environment.

Before we proceed to discuss the theory, and analyze the applications of operational logistics – which constitute the core of this book – it would be useful to look first at the broader area of logistics. This wider look provides the basic

© Springer International Publishing Switzerland 2016
M. Kress, *Operational Logistics*, Management for Professionals,
DOI 10.1007/978-3-319-22674-3_1

terminology and concepts underlying the theory, and facilitates a better understanding of the way the two terms – operational and logistics –merge to form *Operational Logistics*. From now on the use of the term *logistics* is narrowed down to military and military-related settings.

The first two chapters (Chaps. 1 and 2) discuss the term *logistics* in general, while thereafter the focus further narrows to *operational logistics*. Chapter 3 provides a brief introduction to the concept of operational level of war, thereby setting the stage for the remainder of the book.

In this introductory chapter we examine the term *logistics* from a historical perspective and analyze its features by drawing some useful analogies from general production systems. Based on this examination, a new and concise definition of the term *logistics* is proposed. The chapter concludes with a brief discussion on the three generic options for implementing logistics.

1.1   The Need for Logistics

Logistics is multidimensional and complex. It constitutes one of the most important and essential components of military operations. However, similar to other intangible and complex terms such as *economics, strategy, policy,* and *intelligence*, the term *logistics* is difficult to define, or even explain, in a few simple words. In the most general (and not very useful) language, one could say that logistics is a complex mix of physical entities, processes, and rules – a *system* – governed by mostly abstract concepts and principles, aimed at physically supporting military operations. This complex mix is, however, a critical ingredient in any attempt to conduct military operations, and therefore needs to be thoroughly studied. Throughout history many military leaders had not realized the essence and importance of logistics and failed to appreciate its impact on the battlefield. They paid dearly for their negligence. George Washington in the American War of Independence, Napoleon in Spain and in Russia, General Ludendorff in WWI, Fieldmarshal Montgomery in WWII and General MacArthur in the Korean War are just a few examples of commanders who excelled in combat planning and execution, but whose disregard of logistics resulted in grave operational consequences.

1.1.1   The Purpose of Logistics

Notwithstanding the elusiveness of its definition, the purpose of logistics is quite clear: to support military operations and sustain the troops who take part in it. In particular, the purpose of logistics is to

- Facilitate movement and fire
- Treat and evacuate casualties

- Deploy and position human resources
- Supply the troops with food and other personal needs

Logistics also fulfills a psychological function by affecting the morale of the troops. As a provider of military resources, logistics play an important role in unifying the force, preserving its motivation and strengthening the moral authority of its commanders.

1.1.2   Realizing Logistics Objectives

Logistics objectives are not easily attained in the uncertain reality typical to battlefields. Some military scholars characterize the combat environment by the terms *friction* [1] and, even chaos [2] – two characteristics that seriously hinder the implementation of any structured process. There are inherent difficulties in sustaining military operations when the means that are needed to do so may be vulnerable to enemy hostilities and are subject to attrition by the elements. Moreover, the impact of incomplete information, misunderstanding, and confusion, combined with the effect of variable consumption rates and attrition, is significant, and makes it extremely hard to respond adequately to demands in the area of operations.

Thus, although the purpose of logistics is quite clear and simple, its realization is shrouded with problems and uncertainties. Hence, the treatment of logistics must start by focusing on its essence – its internal structure and the ways in which this structure is implemented in the theater of operations. In particular, there is a need to develop analytical tools that can help formalize and analyze logistic concepts and principles. The first step towards this end is to formally define the term *logistics* and describe its content.

1.2   What Is Logistics?

Probably the oldest source for the word *logistics* is Greek. The adjective *logisticos* applies to someone who is skilled in calculating or reckoning. In a military context, these activities refer to managing battlefield resources – adding-up consumption of materials, calculating supply rates, estimating travel time, etc. This quantitative interpretation represents the "mathematical" or "scientific" aspect of logistics. Another historical source for this term, with a somewhat more qualitative orientation, is the French "*maréchal de logis*" in Louis XVI's army. The French word *logis* means lodging or quarters, thus the *maréchal de logis* was, in today's terms, the quartermaster general responsible for managing camps and organizing billets and marches. This designation was removed from the French Army jargon after the French revolution but the term *Logistique* remained in use.

1.2.1   Jomini's Definition

The first formal and functional definition of the term, albeit not exactly in the sense that we would use it today, was given by Jomini [3]. According to his definition:

> Logistics is the art of moving armies. It comprises the order and details of marches and camps, and of quartering and supplying troops; in a word, it is the execution of strategic and tactical enterprises.

Later on in his book, when he discusses logistics in detail, it becomes apparent that Jomini's interpretation of the term is much wider than what it appears to be from the above definition. It is closer to what we would call today general staff work.

1.2.2   Other Definitions

A definition in the same spirit of Jomini's is given in the US Field Manual 100-16 - *Operational Support* [4]:

> Logistics is the process of planning and executing the movement and sustainment of operating forces in the execution of military strategy and operations. It is the foundation of combat power – the bridge that connects the nation's industrial base to its operating forces.

The British use the term "Administration," to designate a function whose key activities relate to the movement and maintenance of armed forces [5]. Similarly, NATO defines logistics as the science of planning the movement and maintenance of forces.

1.2.3   So, What Is It?

Some of the definitions given above are too general, blurry and cumbersome and others are partial and not very informative. However, the many attempts to define this term indicate a need to describe an existing and real entity, which is indeed difficult to define. A possible approach for defining abstract concepts is to find an analogous context in which corresponding definitions may be obtained more easily. It seems that for the purpose of defining *logistics* it would be useful to draw an analogy between war and a general production system.

1.3   War as a Production System

War is associated with terms such as attrition, annihilation, conquest, and defeat, and its conduct is dictated, to a large extent, by intangible terms such as leadership and morale. Yet, from economic and engineering points of view, it is possible to treat war as a production system. In other words, war can be viewed as a system, operating in a hostile environment, which produces outputs from inputs through a process called warfare or combat.

1.3.1   Production System

A production system is a collection of entities and processes that consumes inputs to produce one or more outputs of higher value than the inputs. The principal component of this system is *processing* – the physical transformation of inputs into outputs. Inputs of a production system are typically divided into two sets: *means of production* or in short – *means*, and *production resources* or in short – *resources*. The means of a classical production system are labor, capital, and knowledge that are manifested in manpower and machines. The resources are raw materials and services. For example, the means in an automobiles manufacturing plant are engineers, technicians, production-line workers, robots, welding machines, molds, presses, and the like. The resources are raw materials such as steel, plastic, glass, and rubber, and services such as personnel management, catering, computer system, transportation, and maintenance. Figure 1.1 depicts schematically a production system. Intangible inputs such as technology and financial strength are embodied in the tangible inputs.

1.3.2   Outputs and Inputs in Combat

The outputs of war are its outcomes. The outputs may be tangible, such as capturing territory, annihilating the enemy, and gaining control over natural resources, or intangible, such as attaining operational goals and achieving strategic or political objectives. The process in this "production system" is the act of war, comprised of fire-fights, maneuver, and other hostile engagements. As in a production system, the inputs to the "war process" are divided into two main groups: *means* and *resources*.

   The means in combat are manpower, weapons, and combat support systems. Manpower comprises combatants of various types (army, navy, air force, etc.) who

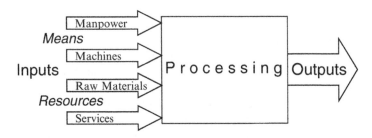

Fig. 1.1 A production system

actively participate in the act of war. Weapons are typically fire producing equipment, such as machine guns, tanks, missile launchers, aircraft, destroyers, and artillery pieces. Combat support systems are entities such as surveillance, detection, command and control, and communication systems. The combat *resources* are consumables such as ammunition, fuel, food, and water, and services such as medical, maintenance, recovery, and transportation. These inputs facilitate the execution of the military production system.

The distinction made earlier, regarding a general production systems, between means and resources applies also in the military context. The first type – means – cannot operate and produce any output without adequate inputs of the second type – resources. To demonstrate this analogy we present a few historical examples.

1.3.3 From the Stone Age to the Iron Age

Typical battles in the period between the Stone Age and the Bronze Age were quite simple. Warriors from small tribes and clans fought each other to gain land, food, and women. They moved around on foot, carrying only minimum amount of food and were equipped with weapons such as improvised clubs and stones – means that were available in their immediate surroundings. The *outputs*, as it is referred to above, were controlled over limited pieces of land, food, water sources, and women. The battles – the combat *processes* – were usually series of fundamental one-on-one duels.

Following a significant leap in technology, the Iron Age introduced new weapons, equipment, and war-fighting techniques that changed the conduct of war. Some of the weapons, such as arrows and spears, dictated modes of operation that used up these weapons, which had to be replenished. Also, horses pulling chariots appeared on the battlefield. The horses needed fodder and the chariots needed maintenance and repair. Thus, the input set had expanded considerably: the *means* comprised, besides warriors, also bows, lances, horses, and chariots. The *resources* needed to sustain this type of combat were arrows, spears, food, water, fodder, and maintenance units.

1.3.4 Alexander the Great

One thousand years after the Iron Age, Alexander the Great embarked on his long campaigns, which reached as far as the river Hyphasis in India – over 18,000 km away from Macedonia. The *processes* in his campaign were long conquest expeditions, naval warfare, and combined combat of infantry, cavalry, and chariots. Accordingly, the *means* that were used included soldiers, horsemen, seamen, horses, ships, and weapons such as swords and bows. The *resources* were the basic necessities, such as food, water, fodder, personal belongings, and money, but also, for the first time, sea-based lines of communications and maritime means of transportation. These resources were essential for the long-distance campaigns conducted by Alexander.

1.3.5   The Twentieth Century

The beginning of the twentieth century brought about significant changes in military operations. These changes affected the way war was conducted and the inputs that were required for the war-making process. The development of new and effective fire-producing weapons prompted a vast increase in ammunition expenditure, which, in turn, resulted in a need for many more means of transportation. Moreover, an all-mechanized and motorized army replaced horses, mules, and oxen. Fodder was replaced by vast amounts of fuel, and maintenance meant having on hand stocks of spare parts and special-purpose tools. Advances in medicine enabled better and more effective treatment of combat-injured soldiers thus prompting the establishment of medical support units. The set of *means* expanded to include tanks, armored vehicles, aircraft, and long-range artillery pieces. The *resources* mix had been reshaped to include ammunition, fuel, land lines of communication, and means of transportation, as its major components.

The military interpretations of the production theory terms *means* and *resources* are utilized next to obtain a new, unified, and concise definition of the term *logistics*.

1.4   Logistics – A Definition

Following the discussion and examples given in Sect. 1.3, we define:

> **Logistics:** *A discipline that encompasses the* **resources** *needed to keep the* **means** *of a military* **process** *(operation) going in order to achieve its desired* **outputs** *(objectives). It includes planning, managing, treating, operating and controlling these resources.*

1.4.1   The Evolution of Resources

The set of military resources has been modified throughout history. From a small set of basic resources such as locally available food and water, it has expanded into a huge gamut of ammunition, fuel, maintenance, medical facilities, and means of transportation. This collection of resources is still in a state of change. The introduction of high-tech weapons onto the battlefield necessitates skilled personnel with adequate equipment and tools to service and maintain those systems. For example, Precision Guided Missiles (PGM) are relatively new, efficient, and costly weapons. Their high kill rate, coupled with their high price tag, may reduce the total tonnage of such ammunition shipments sent to the battlefield. The apparent relative scarcity of these high-tech missiles imposes a logistic challenge to optimally allocate them in the theater of operations.

The concrete content of logistics and its typical problems depend on the functional level of military operations – strategic, operational or tactical –, and on the context in which it is considered. These issues are addressed in Chap. 2.

1.5   Art or Science?

As noted in Sect. 1.2, the earliest source of the term logistics – the Greek word *logisticos* – implies a quantitative and formal connotation. Indeed, logistics is one of the more tangible components of warfare. Its implementation is based upon physical factors, quantitative relations among parameters, formal rules, and a lot of data. This is the *"scientific"* facet of logistics. However, the scientific knowledge that forms the formal foundation of logistics cannot be applied only in a purely technical and prescriptive manner. The volatile and uncertain battlefield environment requires a creative and flexible approach – beyond the rigid framework of strict prescriptive rules. It also needs leadership in times of crisis. The creative and nonformal attributes needed to run logistics include common sense, experience, imagination, the ability to improvise, and intuition –factors that represent the *artistic* facet of logistics. Throughout history logistics has been viewed as part of the art of war. Alexander the Great's original logistics' solutions (see Sect. 1.6.2) and the mobility capabilities of Hannibal in crossing the Alps are examples of creative application of that art.

1.5.1   The Scientific Facet

Since World War II and until recently, logistics has been regarded by many as a purely quantitative discipline detached, in many respects, from the "artistic" side and fuzzy reality at the battlefield. This notion has been amplified by the evolution of the area of Operations Research and the advent of computer technology.

Indeed, logistics is abundant with quantitative aspects. Typical logistic parameters and problems include:

- Physical parameters such as volume of fuel, tonnage of ammunition, and number of spare-parts.
- Time parameters such as force accumulation time and order-and-ship time.
- Forecasting attrition and projecting demands for resources.
- Optimization of logistic processes such as transportation, inventory, distribution, and storage.

All of these factors are quantitatively oriented and lend themselves to computation and mathematical modeling. The scientific facet of logistics is manifested in concrete logistic plans, based on hard data, that contain quantities and time parameters. By applying quantitative methods and algorithms that merge requirements and capabilities, a coherent logistics plan is achieved. A review of such methods and models is presented in Chap. 2. Applications of mathematical modeling in logistics are given in Chaps. 10, 11 and 12.

1.5.2   The Artistic Facet

Besides the quantitative components of logistics, there are many qualitative ones representing aspects of logistics not readily quantifiable. Properties such as creativity, intuition, insight, determination, and mental flexibility are important ingredients in the cognitive process underlying logistic decision-making. These properties enable the logistician to express his artistic side and help him handle the uncertainties in the battlefield.

While arguably the artistic facet of logistics has very few formal and no quantitative aspects, it is not necessarily void of order and structure. Any form of art incorporates within it elementary principles that form the basis of the artist's creativity. Classical music adheres to solid principles of counterpoint, harmony, and rhythm, and paintings embody principles of color, composition, balance, and perspective. Likewise, the artistic facet of logistics is generated by principles such as improvisation, anticipation, synchronization, and continuity that are well defined (see Chap. 3) but cannot be always formalized. By utilizing these "soft" principles, the logistician, together with the operational commander, can create the appropriate logistics "picture".

1.5.3   Pure Logistics and Applied Logistics

Thorp [6] proposes a similar distinction to that made between the science and art of logistics, but from a different point of view. He draws a distinction between two separate areas of logistics: *Pure Logistics* and *Applied Logistics*. Pure logistics is concerned with the research of theoretical aspects of logistics and with its role in military theory. This research examines the boundaries of logistics, analyzes its properties, and studies its organizational components. Applied logistics implements the insights and conclusions gained from the study of pure logistics. It utilizes these insights for building up the logistic system, and effectively deploying and employing it in the theater of operations.

1.6   The Three Logistic Options

From the times of Neanderthal man's battles, through the Napoleonic era campaigns, to the Operation Iraqi Freedom, combat operations have always been sustained by utilizing one or more of the three basic logistic options.

(a) *Obtain* the needed resources in the battlefield.
(b) *Carry* the resources with the troops.
(c) *Ship* the resources from the rear area and distribute it to the forces in the battlefield.

Throughout history, the choice of a logistic option has been dictated by the nature of war, logistic requirements, and available capabilities.

1.6.1 Obtain in the Battlefield

Water and food were essentially all the resources needed for battles in ancient times. These resources were found along the way to a skirmish and could be obtained by foraging, looting civilians or, if successful, by capturing the enemy's sources of water and food. The "fuel" for the means of transportation, i.e., fodder for animals, was also readily available almost anywhere. Thus, troops looked for cultivated areas and major trade routes to forage and loot. However, since the resources at any location were limited, and no replenishment was realistically possible, it was clear that the troops had to move in order to survive. Thus, sustaining an army then was easier when it was on the move. If the army stopped at a particular point for an extended period of time, it could exhaust the local resources. More recently, the sustainment of the German forces during WWII in Operation Barbarossa depended, to a large extent, on resources in the Russian theater of war. The unavoidable heavy reliance on this logistic option was one of the major reasons for the Germans' defeat there.

1.6.2 Carry with the Troops

When combat resources became more varied and specialized, and means of transportation became more widespread, troops started to carry their supplies to the battlefield. Probably one of the first practitioners of this mode of logistics was Alexander the Great of Macedonia. Alexander made extensive use of ships as floating supply depots. By leading his army along carefully selected routes, never too distant from the seashore, he could use these ships continuously as a source of supply. Almost 1500 years later, when firearms were introduced into the battlefield in the seventeenth and eighteenth centuries, ammunition use was so modest that in most cases a field army could pack all the ammunition it would require on its wagons. Thus, resources that would not be readily available at the battlefield could be carried with the troops.

In general, this mode of logistic implementation imposes a heavy burden on the troops since it creates a considerable logistic tail that may hinder the force's rate of advance.

1.6.3 Ship to the Forces

The first two options – *obtain* and *carry* – were the principal methods of supplying and sustaining the troops up until the middle of the nineteenth century. The Industrial Revolution that was taking place then set the stage for the emergence of the third option – *send*. In particular, trains, one of the significant results of this revolution, which were also employed for military uses, affected the way logistics was implemented. Supplies could now be sent from the rear area to the front over distances and at speeds never before possible. What was now possible soon became necessary, and armies rapidly became dependent on regular supplies sent from the rear.

The logistics revolution, however, occurred in the twentieth century when the third option predominated. Several factors contributed to this revolution, and to the new phenomena that have resulted from it on the battlefield. These factors were a combination of new needs and new technological capabilities.

1.6.4 New Needs

Two significant developments on the battlefield brought about respective changes in logistic needs. First, the appearance of new weapons in the theater of war, such as automatic machine guns, has resulted in an increase in the weight of ammunition – both conceptually and physically. The increased demand for ammunition and the heavier weight of shells and rounds required larger space for storage and appropriate means for transportation and handling. Combatants and weapons could no longer carry all the ammunition they needed to the battlefield. The ability to sustain a battle for extended periods became contingent on a regular and continuous supply of ammunition from depots at the rear area.

The second development was the introduction of mechanized weapons such as tanks, which replaced horses, mules, camels, and oxen. The implication of this transition was that traditional sources of energy needed for mobility – fodder and water – were replaced by another source of energy, not readily available at the battlefield – fuel. Fuel has to be produced, stored in appropriate facilities, transported in specially designed vehicles and distributed by tools such as pumps. According to a Soviet source [7], 50 % of the total weight of resources consumed in a mechanized attack is fuel products. Thus, handling fuel imposes a heavy logistic burden.

Another consequence of the technological advancement was the concomitant need for professional technical support – a requirement that meant both personal technological capabilities and specialized equipment and tools. The required resources were usually limited and could not be provided to each small mechanized-unit. Allocating the limited maintenance resources among the potential customers became a major logistic problem in the twentieth century and the solution was to send them when required, rather than to attach them to combat units.

1.6.5 New Capabilities

Technological advances in transportation, communication, and command and control improved the capability to effectively deliver resources. Moving resources from the rear area to the front could be performed more quickly and efficiently, and thus the response could meet battlefield demands more adequately. From the emergence of the train in the middle of the nineteenth century, through the trucks in World War II that connected the railheads and the troops, to the large transport aircraft and advanced load systems of today, means of transportation have become the basis for the logistic link between the rear area and the front. This basis has been complemented by long-range and reliable communication systems and advanced computerized information and decision support tools.

Matching the new needs with the new capabilities has resulted in the emergence of the third option – *send* – as the current principal method for logistic support. The adoption of this option, however, has three important implications that must be taken into account.

1.6.6 Implications of the Third Option

First, in order to facilitate a proper implementation of the *send* option, it is crucial to be able to maintain a continuous, effective, and secure line of communication (LOC) between the logistic bases at the rear area and the consumers at the front. This ability depends on the availability of means of transportation and their maintenance units, and on effective allocation and scheduling of these means on inter-theater and intra-theater routes. The more dynamic the combat posture becomes, the more difficult it is to carry out these activities. When troops are on the move, logistic units have to share the capacity of the LOCs with combat units. As a result, it may be impossible to fully realize the logistic potential available at the rear area because of clogged LOCs. The force accumulation phase in the Gulf War [8] is a good example where trade-off between sending first the "tooth" (combat units) or the "tail" (logistic assets) had to be considered in the presence of limited transportation (air and sea) capabilities. Moreover, the dynamic ever-changing, theater of operations is shrouded with uncertainties and "fog" that increase over time. Information may be fuzzy and partial. For example, coordination of meeting points between logistic convoys and combat service support (CSS) units in the theater may become extremely difficult. Thus, unlike ancient times when it was easier to sustain an army that was on the move, today modern and dynamic warfare imposes tight constraints on logistics.

Second, the vast quantities of resources needed to sustain warfare – ammunition, fuel, spare-parts, etc. – generate a continuous flow of supplies that are sent from the rear. This flow creates a huge theater-level logistic *tail*. In a forward-deployment scenario, long and slow moving convoys of trucks clog roads and thus may hinder the advancement of combat units. Moreover, transportation units need sustainment too and therefore consume logistic assets – in addition to the means and effort that they require to keep them safe and secure. Thus, a large logistic tail that extends from the theater of operations back to the logistic sources in the rear area may "wag" the body of the force in the theater – causing it more damage than providing help. Admiral Eccles [9] defines the phenomenon of uncontrollable increase in the logistic tail as the *Logistic Snowball*. He identifies it as one of the major causes for operational blunders.

Third, the dependence of forces at the front on supplies and services sent from the rear has a clear operational impact. For example, if a convoy of tankers carrying fuel is delayed, a combat unit that relies on that supply may not be able to execute its mission. If a certain maintenance unit that is required to fix a particular weapon is not available when needed, that weapon may become dysfunctional and may therefore affect the readiness and operational capabilities of the combat unit. In his book *Strategics*, Brown [10] claims that the growing dependency on specialized logistic support imposes new limitations on executing sustained military operations since there is no guarantee that this support will be available when needed. He suggests reducing the reliance on the third option, in particular with regards to maintenance, by training and equipping individuals to handle and maintain their own equipment independently. While this approach for a "versatile" soldier is still far from being realistic, some new technologies may pave the way towards this end. For example, the modular structure of modern weapons may ease the maintenance burden since replacing modules or major components is simpler and less technically demanding than fixing them.

1.6.7   Combining the Options

The third option – send the resources from the rear – is clearly the most efficient option from the combat forces' perspective. On the one hand, this logistic mode alleviates the need to "waste" combat time on looking for resources in the theater of operations, and on the other hand, the logistic tail of the tactical units is reduced to a minimum size, which facilitates higher tactical agility. However, the third option also depends on reliable means of transportation, secure lines of communication, and timely and accurate information. In short, it is the least robust of the three.

It follows that modern logistics must rely on a mix of all three options. Although some insurgencies still rely on looting and foraging (e.g., ISIS in Iraq. See also Chap. 7), modern manifestation of the first logistic option – to *obtain* resources in the theater of operations – is generally quite different. Looting and foraging, as a main source of sustainment, has been transformed into partial reliance on host nation's resources – in particular in power-projection situations. Resources that were provided to the Coalition forces in the Gulf War by Saudi Arabia is an example of obtaining logistic resources in the theater of operations.

Armies also heavily rely on the second option: carrying supplies with them. The "belly" of a unit, e.g., tank rounds carried in the tank, artillery shells hauled with the battery or fuel tankers that closely follow a battalion are particularly necessary when time is the scarcest resource. In the first stages of operation Desert Shield deployed units relied on their own resources until significant amounts of supplies arrived by sea to the theater of operations.

Finally, the only option that can sustain a modern army for a long period of time is the third option. Whether a forward-deployment posture or a power-projection one, armies will be able to operate and maintain their momentum only if a continuous logistic support chain is feeding the forces reliably and at a proper rate.

This latter logistic option – to send – is the core and backbone of operational logistics. Chapter 12 presents a mathematical model for optimizing the balance between the second and third options.

1.7   Summary

Logistics is a discipline that deals with the means of waging war and major operations, and the resources that these operations require. There are essentially three generic ways – or options – for implementing logistics: to obtain locally, to carry with the troops or to ship it from behind. Modern logistics relies primarily on the third option – with complementary capabilities that are provided by the first two older options.

The discussion about logistics in this chapter was general and somewhat abstract. In the next chapters the discussion becomes more concrete and focuses on *operational logistics*. The skeleton, organs, flesh, and arteries of operational logistics will be examined and analyzed in detail in the subsequent chapters.

References

1. Von Clausewitz C. On war. Princeton, NJ: Princeton University Press; 1976.
2. Dockery T, Woodcock AER. Models of Combat with Embedded C^3. II: Catastrophe theory and chaotic behavior. Int CIS J. 1988;2(4):17–51.
3. Jomini. The Art of War, translated by Cpt. G. H. Medel and Lt. W. P. Craighill, US Army. Westport:Greenwood Press; 1971. p. 69.
4. Department of the Army, FM 100-16 Army Operational Support, Headquarters, Dept. of the Army, Washington DC, 1995.
5. Foxton PD. Powering war—modern land force logistics. London: Brassey's; 1994. p. 3.
6. Thorp GC. Pure logistics. Washington, DC: National Defense University Press; 1986.
7. Donnelly CN. Rear Support for Soviet Ground Forces, TDRC 4567. Camberley: The British Army Staff College; 1978.
8. Pagonis WG. Moving mountains: lessons in leadership and Logisticsfrom the gulf war. Boston, MA: Harvard Business School Press; 1992.
9. Eccles HE. Logistics in the national defense. Westport Connecticut: Greenwood Press; 1981. p. 102.
10. Brown KN. Strategics: the logistics-strategy link. Washington, DC: National Defense University Press; 1987. p. p58.

Chapter 2
Structure, Terminology, and Analytic Tools

Following the definition of the term *logistics* in Chap. 1 and the description of its three generic implementations, this chapter sets the stage for analyzing logistics in general, and operational logistics in particular. We discuss the general structure of logistics, introduce terminology, and describe the tools and methodologies utilized for its analysis.

The first part of the chapter (Sects. 2.1–2.3) discusses the three levels of logistics: *strategic, operational,* and *tactical*. The focus here is on the two ends of the spectrum – strategic logistics and tactical logistics. We discuss the main issues typical to each one of these two logistics levels. The in-depth analysis of the middle layer – operational logistics – is presented in later chapters, after providing some theoretical background. In Sect. 2.4 we introduce some operational logistics terms that form the building blocks for any logistic paradigm at the operational level. The last section is a short review of formal methodologies and mathematical models that may be used for analyzing and evaluating operational logistics.

2.1 The Three Levels of Logistics

Similarly to the three levels of war – strategic, operational, and tactical – logistics too is separated into three corresponding levels: *strategic logistics, operational logistics,* and *tactical logistics*. These three levels are not necessarily disjoint; there are functional areas, sometimes quite substantial, that intersect two adjacent levels and constitute a link between processes in both levels. Moreover, it is argued [1, 2] that with the advent of information technology, logistic systems will be so integrated in the future that the three levels of logistics will in fact merge into a seamless entity - blurring the traditional distinction between strategic, operational, and tactical logistics. It is true that we are witnessing a revolution in information technology, and that it already has a remarkable consolidating and streamlining effect on logistics.

© Springer International Publishing Switzerland 2016
M. Kress, *Operational Logistics*, Management for Professionals,
DOI 10.1007/978-3-319-22674-3_2

Yet, there are serious doubts concerning the extent of its impact on logistics' basic three-level structure. The reason for these doubts lies in the nature of military operations, as explained next.

2.1.1   The Basic Hierarchy

There is an inherent hierarchy typical to any managerial or operational system. Such a hierarchy is especially notable in military organizations. This hierarchy, whether it is deep or shallow – as is the case in modern organizations – is fundamental and, to a large extent, invariant to changes in information technologies and capabilities. Advanced information systems can enhance the linkage among the levels in the hierarchy, but they cannot completely eliminate them. The following analogy to the business world may clarify this point.

2.1.2   An Analogy to a Production Company

A major industrial company usually comprises three main levels: board of directors, executive management, and the plant that includes the production lines, storage facilities, distribution centers, research and development labs, etc. The board of directors determines the long-term guidelines of the firm; it defines the strategic objectives, sets profit goals, selects market segments, and decides on strategic cooperation with other companies. The company's executives translate these guidelines into long-term and short-term plans that include marketing strategies, inventory policy, facility layout, seasonal production schedules, quality control processes, etc. The executive level also controls the implementations of the plans and is responsible to provide managerial solutions in unexpected situations that result in major deviations from the plans.

Actual operations are executed at the third level of the company. This level, which comprises production lines, R&D activities, acquisitions, inventory management, marketing, etc., implements the plans, policies, directives, and rules that are dictated by the executive level. The activities at this level are physical, mostly mundane, and directly translated into tangible terms like new products, production quota, quality standards, inventory levels, and transportation schedules. The plant gets a bundle of resources (input) whose size and mix are determined by the executives.

The three levels are not disjoint. The interface between each two adjacent levels determines the directors–executives and executives–mangers interactions. These interactions are necessary to facilitate effective and efficient operation of the company.

The division of the company into three distinct levels stems from structural as well as perceptual considerations. The executive management at the middle level bridges between the economic, strategic, financial, and technological resources of the firm that are essentially controlled by the board of directors, and the "tactical units" that are in charge of the daily operation of the company: production lines, laboratories, computer services, warehouses, and distribution facilities.

A similar rationale generates the three levels of military logistics. Specifically, operational logistics bridges between the macroscopic and aggregate economic foundation of the military might at the strategic level, and the actual executers of military operations – the tactical units. As it is the case in the business environment, the three-level hierarchy of logistics is deep rooted in the military organizational structure and probably will not be eliminated even if command, control, communication, and computer capabilities may enable it in theory.

2.2   Strategic Logistics

From many aspects, the issues considered at the strategic level of logistics are analogous to the decisions taken by the board of directors of a firm. At this level, military leadership is in charge of making major defense-related decisions that have long-lasting impact. These decisions, such as investments in research and development, procurement and replenishment policies, and decision issues related to the physical infrastructure, have significant and long-range economic and operational implications. In particular, economic constraints affect logistic capabilities, and both – economics and logistics – determine operational capabilities.

Example 2.1
In the early 60s, few years before the Six Days War, the Israel Defense Forces' (IDF) General Staff was deliberating the issue of logistic infrastructure. A heated debate between two generals, General Horev and General Peled, concerning the structure and deployment of the logistic system, was eventually resolved by the Chief of Staff at that time – General Itzhak Rabin. The decision was to consolidate the existing distributed logistic system into a few major logistic centers: ammunition center, ordinance center, POL center, etc.

Example 2.2
In the late 1990s the US Defense Logistics Agency (DLA) had been undergoing a major transformation that included infrastructure reduction and acquisition reform. The thrust of this reform was a shift to commercial practices, private sector partnerships, and profound reengineering and restructuring initiatives. Examples of these shifts were fuel privatization, joint ventures with commercial entities and reliance on premium commercial services such as FedEx.

2.2.1 Economic and Logistic Constraints

While limited economic resources have direct impact on the force structure and its composition (including the logistic infrastructure), logistic constraints affect the way this force may operate. For example, the number of advanced aircraft procured by the Air Force is restricted by the national budget, which is an economic factor. But the number of hours these aircraft can fly is limited by factors such as the amount of available fuel, which is a logistics factor. Figure 2.1 depicts this interrelationship.

Figure 2.1 demonstrates a central dilemma at the strategic level: the tradeoff between building the force and sustaining it. This tradeoff is discussed in more detail later on in this chapter.

2.2.2 Issues of Strategic Logistics

Strategic logistics is concerned with building up and maintaining the national military and military-related infrastructure. This infrastructure includes technology, industry, inventory, storage capacity, and transportation capabilities.

Technology

Technological infrastructure provides the capabilities needed to develop, improve and maintain weapons and other defense related equipment. As weapons become more technically specialized and technologically advanced, the need for these capabilities increases. Thus, the technological knowledge and capabilities of a nation directly contribute to its military power. Moreover, while in general nonmilitary (e.g., consumer goods) technology may be acquired from other sources, these

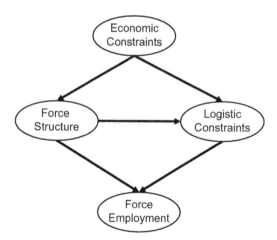

Fig. 2.1 Economic and logistic constraints

opportunities do not always exist for defense technologies, which are considered national assets that are not traded as easily as commercial technologies. These technologies are usually classified, and therefore must be developed internally – by a joint national effort.

Industry

The industrial infrastructure facilitates the actual implementation of available technologies. It provides the required means for producing and maintaining equipment and supplies needed during military operations. This infrastructure may include both civilian and military plants. Decisions supporting certain industries depend on economic considerations based on large-scale cost-benefit analyses and a broad view of national economic interests. But such decisions are also affected by social concerns (e.g., generating employment opportunities in remote underprivileged regions) and political considerations such as self-reliance in times of crisis and hedging against possible embargos.

Inventory

The national inventory of logistic resources comprises stockpiles of ammunition, fuel, spare-parts, medical supplies, food, and other military and military-related items. These stockpiles make up the resources bundle that is necessary for military operations. The size and mix of this bundle determine the type, intensity, and length of military operations that can be adequately sustained. There are two ways for generating national inventories of logistic resources: (a) acquisitions from other countries and (b) local production (see *Industry* above).

Determining the balance between these two sources – acquisition and production – is a major strategic decision. On the one hand, it may be more convenient, and even cheaper, to obtain resources from foreign sources than to produce it internally. This is true in particular when economies of scale have a significant effect on cost. However, on the other hand, total dependency on foreign sources may be too risky. At times of national emergency, political or other constraints may hinder the flow of supplies from abroad thus causing severe shortfalls in logistic capabilities. To avoid such situations it is sometimes necessary to maintain local capacity to produce these resources, even if this production is not justified economically. A related tradeoff is between investments in military-oriented industries and inventories of those industries' products.

Example 2.3
An effective capability to produce mortar shells in relatively short notice can reduce the size of the inventory of these shells. Such a reduction is desirable since inventories incur cost, require routine maintenance and may be subject to limited shelf life.

Storage Facilities

Storage facilities, such as arsenals, depots, and warehouses, are needed to keep and maintain the inventories of supplies in an adequate condition for the times when they are needed. Several factors affect decisions regarding locations of these storage facilities. The most important factors are operational considerations, which are derived from existing doctrine and strategic plans. Other factors are associated with the transportation infrastructure, locations of other military installations, population centers, and environmental considerations.

> **Example 2.4**
> Prepositioned US Navy ships based at Diego Garcia Island in the Indian Ocean provided supplies to deployed forces in Saudi Arabia at the early stages of operation Desert Shield in the early 90s'. These floating storage facilities enabled an effective response to the logistic needs of fast-deployed forces in a power-projection posture.

Transportation

The transportation infrastructure comprises two types of components –static components and dynamic components. The static components, which determine the physical attributes of the lines of communication (LOC), include the network of roads, railway systems, waterways, sea-lanes, aerial routes, seaports, and airports. The dynamic components are means of transportation such as cargo planes, ships, containers, trains, trucks, and transporters.

The static components comprise mostly nonmilitary entities used regularly by the state for public needs. All roads and railways are used for everyday routine transportation and, except for relatively few military installations, most seaports and airports are regularly serving civilian passengers and commercial cargo. However, when planning and designing these entities at the national level, military-strategic considerations must be taken into account too. For example, the force accumulation (mobilization) process at the beginning of a military operation is of concern at the strategic level. The effectiveness of this process depends on the quality, capacity, and location of the LOCs that lead from the rear area to the front. Any decision concerning these transportation assets must also take into account its influence on the rate of force-accumulation.

Unlike the static components, the dynamic components are predominantly military. There are specially designated cargo planes, supply ships, trucks, transporters, and containers. This fleet may be augmented during war by civilian means of transportation too, but the core of this dynamic part of the transportation system is clearly painted in military colors.

Other Strategic Issues

In addition to its main role of developing and maintaining logistic infrastructure, strategic logistics is also associated with a few operational issues.

Doctrine, training, and logistics-related combat development are operational issues dealt at the strategic level, where Field-Manuals (FMs), doctrinal directives, and training curricula are developed and distributed. Two other operational tasks that are typically handled at the strategic level are power-projection mobility – planning and executing large-scale transportation missions of combat and combat-support forces. Also, logistic coordination with foreign forces operating in a coalition in a certain theater is an operational issue handled at the strategic level.

In a power-projection scenario, such as the campaign of UK in the Falkland Islands and the US in Iraq and Afghanistan, large forces are transported over long distances – as far as thousands of kilometers from their home country. In such scenarios, it is necessary to project the right mix of forces and resources in the theater of operations as fast as possible. To achieve this goal, mobility must be at the focus of attention at the highest possible level of the military hierarchy; the task of managing, scheduling, and coordinating the force-accumulation process is clearly a strategic mission. Besides effective timing and proper allocation of transportation assets, there is also a need to secure the lines of communications, which may be subject to threats and hostile activities by the enemy.

When a campaign is a joint operation of several nations – as was the case in the Gulf war, Iraq, and Afghanistan – coordinating several, potentially different, logistic systems is a big challenge. Military forces in a coalition may be equipped with different weapons, utilize resources of different types, and may operate according to distinct doctrines and different standard operating procedures. In such situations it is essential to tune the various logistic systems such that they become as compatible as possible. Issues of standardization and interoperability become of utmost importance – as it is manifested in NATO's logistic doctrine [3].

2.2.3 Logistic Efficiency

A major consideration that affects the decisions at the strategic level is *efficiency*, which is a measure that takes into account the economic cost of effectiveness. Since economic resources are usually limited, decision-makers must weigh competing alternatives in the presence of constrained defense budget. Efficiency of an entity is generally measured in terms of the ratio between its benefits and its cost, or more generally, by the output/input ratio. The benefits (outputs) in the logistic setting are expected military effects as measured by the readiness of the supported military force. The costs (inputs) are measured by the various types of expenditure associated with bundles of logistic resources and capabilities. The efficiency objective is to maximize the output/input ratio.

A related term used at the strategic level is *tradeoff*. The tradeoff between two competing alternatives represents their relative merit with respect to utility and cost. In other words, the tradeoff between alternative A and B determines how many units of A are comparable to a single unit of B. Through tradeoff analysis, various alternative bundles are compared using quantitative and/or judgmental criteria. For example, there are tradeoffs between investments in weapons such as tanks and aircraft, and expenditure on resources such as advanced ammunition. Another common tradeoff prevails when evaluating alternative weapons in a process called Analysis of Alternatives (AoA).

A common question asked in this context concerns the tradeoff between an existing low-cost military system, with relatively limited capabilities, and a new, advanced and expensive system with improved performance. While the scope of this tradeoff question focuses at operational aspects, the answer relies heavily on cost factors (R&D, production, etc.) and logistic considerations such as life-cycle cost and maintenance expenditures.

In summary, the two factors – efficiency and tradeoff –incorporate economic aspects in strategic logistics decision-making. As such, the analysis of these two factors takes place at the strategic logistics domain.

2.2.4 The Strategic Decision Problem

Strategic logistics decisions are concerned with logistic infrastructure. A typical problem at this level comprises two stages:

- Distribution of the total budget among the various types of logistic infrastructure (see Sect. 2.2.2 above).
- Determining the best mix of resources within a certain area of logistic infrastructure.

The possible distributions of the budget among logistic areas and the various possible mixes of resources within an area are alternatives in a multi-criteria decision-making process. The criteria according to which one alternative is compared with another are either formal, quantitative, and "objective" measures, or judgmental inputs that are provided by subject-matter experts.

2.2.5 The Nature of Strategic Logistics

Strategic logistics is macroscopic, aggregative, and deals with national resources and capabilities. It is handled routinely during peacetime by well-structured working processes. Logistic decisions at this level are relatively stable over time and are insensitive to local and random changes in logistic demands. The picture that is drawn at this level is large and is characterized by broad strokes of colors.

It takes considerable time to draw this picture, and it takes even longer time to change the composition of its colors. Strategic logistic plans are robust and have long-lasting effect on military organizations and capabilities.

2.3 Tactical Logistics

Tactical logistics, which is placed at the other end of the logistics spectrum, is used to affect the battle in progress [4]. Using, once again, the industrial firm analogy described in Sect. 2.1.2, tactical logistics is implemented in an environment that is comparable to the physical environment of the production plant. Similarly to the features of a production floor, tactical logistics comprises basic and practical activities that facilitate the "production" of military outcomes. Tactical logistics sustains the troops, provides them with production material (ammunition and fuel) and maintains their equipment. These activities are technical, prescriptive, normative, and readily measurable by relatively simple and straightforward quantitative metrics. However, unlike the production plant that operates in relatively neutral, stable and certain conditions, tactical logistics supports a "plant" that is susceptible to disturbances by enemy actions, and that may change its course of action abruptly and unexpectedly. Supporting such an entity is a task far more complex and challenging than maintaining a relatively steady commercial production line.

Thus, contrary to the relatively stable working environment and macroscopic view that characterize strategic logistics, tactical logistics is implemented in a highly volatile setting and demands a microscopic approach.

2.3.1 Logistic Activities at the Tactical Level

The logistics main activities at the tactical level are technical and apply directly to the combat units. They are:

- Replenishing ammunition
- Refueling
- Fixing equipment
- Supplying rations and other personal needs
- Providing immediate medical aid and evacuating
- Treating POWs and civilian population
- Providing some construction and engineering services

The need for these activities, and their extent, are derived from the tactical activities of the combat units at the battlefield. This correspondence between "combat cause" and "logistic effect" has significant consequences on the erratic nature of tactical logistics. While strategic logistics is characterized by standardization, uniformity, and relative predictability that ensue simply because of its sheer size and the "law of large numbers," tactical logistics is unpredictable, variable, and sometimes even chaotic since it heavily depends on the random outcome of the tactical battle.

2.3.2 The Focus of Tactical Logistics

Tactical logistics is focused on three important characteristics of tactical warfare: *protection*, *mobility,* and *firepower*. At the tactical level, warfare is concrete, focused, and tightly constrained by fire, time, and space. Likewise, logistics at this level is specific and tailored to the given tactical posture. These features, coupled with the mechanistic and quantifiable properties discussed above, imply that tactical logistics is more of a technical and "scientific" trade than anything else. It is accounting, scheduling, transporting, and basic management.

While strategic logistics decisions are made in a multi-criteria environment where the leading criterion is *efficiency*, at the tactical level the leading criterion is *effectiveness.* The objective at the tactical level is to minimize two gaps: the *quantity gap* and the *time gap*. These gaps are minimized when the right quantity of supply (or other form of logistic support) reaches the tactical unit on time. Too little support may delay, alter, or even abort the execution of a tactical mission while supplying too much logistic support may cause overflow, waste, and possible shortages elsewhere on the battlefield. Unneeded supplies that cannot be unloaded may cause a severe under-utilization of means of transportation. Stalled loaded trucks become storage facilities rather than mobile entities that facilitate logistic flow. Similarly, delivering the supply to the unit too early may find it unprepared to receive it. Getting the support too late is probably the most severe gap since a combat unit may not be able to execute its mission as planned and may even be compelled to abort it. Recurring large quantity and time gaps may have severe operational effects on the campaign in the theater of operations.

2.4 Basic Operational Logistics Terms

The area of logistics is abundant with technical terms that describe *processes* and *entities*:

- *Processes:* consumption, movement, supply, traffic control, inventory control, maintenance, medical support.
- *Entities*: inventory, facilities, means of transportation, equipment.

Each one of the processes and entities above contains a rich technical terminology that is usually prevalent in logistics field-manuals and other technical and doctrinal documents. Such a terminology, however, is not needed for the discussion and analysis in this book, and therefore it is not presented here.

For the purpose of describing the logistic concepts and structures at the operational level, and analyzing their theoretical aspects, it is possible (and desirable) to limit the number of terms to a necessary minimum. The terms defined below represent physical as well as abstract components of an operational logistics (*OpLog*) system.

These terms are neither comprehensive nor representative of the logistics (applied) profession. Their sole purpose is to form the basis for an *OpLog* theory developed in the subsequent chapters.

Logistic Node is a location where any logistic activity may take place. Forward-area rearm/refuel point, brigade support area, ammunition supply point, port of debarkation, airfield, ammunition depot, and a home base are examples of logistic nodes. Logistic nodes are sometimes referred to as *terminals*.

Logistic Edge connects two logistic nodes. A road connecting a rear supply depot with a forward supply point, a railway connecting a maintenance depot with a port of embarkation and an air route between two airfields are examples of logistic edges.

Lines of Communication (LOC) are routes that connect military forces at the front of the theater of operations to logistic bases at the communication zone and the rear area. Along an LOC, supplies, equipment, and military forces move forward and evacuated personnel and equipment move backwards. An LOC is composed of a series of connected logistic edges.

Logistic Network is an ordered set of logistic nodes and edges. Lines of communication are *paths* in the logistic network. Generally speaking, a logistic network comprises *source nodes*, *intermediate nodes,* and *destination nodes*. The source nodes are home bases, strategic depots and ports of embarkation. The intermediate nodes are theater facilities (see definition below) such as intermediate support bases, theater ammunition dumps, and ports of debarkation. Intermediate nodes may be divided into two sets: rear and forward. The destination nodes are typically combat service support units of the tactical combat forces. Source nodes are connected with intermediate nodes by *external LOCs*, while intermediate nodes are connected to destination nodes by *internal LOCs*. Figure 2.2 presents a logistic network.

Note that some flow, such as evacuated casualties, damaged equipment, and POWs, may be directed backward – from the destination nodes to the source nodes.

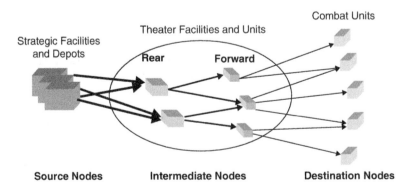

Fig. 2.2 Logistic network

Theater Facility is an intermediate node in the logistic network. Theater facilities, which are the backbone of the *OpLog* system, are usually end points of external LOCs, and/or starting points for internal LOCs. For example, during the Gulf War, Dhahran airport was a theater facility that was the end point of an aerial LOC and a starting point of a ground LOC. In some cases the set of theater facilities is divided into two subsets: *rear theater* facilities and *forward theater* facilities (see Fig. 2.2). The rear facilities are typically ports of debarkation while the forward facilities are major (Corps level) logistics centers in the theater of operations.

Logistic resources are entities – equipment, supply, and logistic personnel – that flow through the logistic network. Their common objective is to sustain and support the military operation. The logistic resources constitute a *flow* in the logistic network

Means of Transportation facilitate the flow of resources in the logistic network by carrying personnel, equipment, and supply. Typical means of transportation are mules, trucks, tankers, transporters, trains, ships, helicopters, and airplanes.

Logistic Deployment is a specific implementation of the logistic network. In particular, logistic deployment determines the size, composition, and location of the theater facilities. It also determines the lines of communication and affects the feasible flow rate and the mixture of the logistic flow that passes through the network.

Logistic Support Chain is a conceptual cyclic sequence of processes and events with the common objective of sustaining the military operation in progress. The chain comprises two main parts: the *demand part* and the *supply part*. At the demand part the tactical units present their requirements, which are passed on, through the command channels, to the logistic sources – operational or strategic. At the supply part, resources are transported through the logistic network from source or intermediate nodes to the tactical destinations. Evacuation of personnel and equipment retrograde are also part of the logistic support chain – constituting a reverse flow from the tactical nodes backwards.

2.5 Models and Analytic Tools

We have already seen in Chap. 1 that logistics is as much a science as an art. For example, at the strategic level logistics planners have to compute cost-effectiveness measures, calculate tradeoffs between alternative bundles of logistic resources, optimize the allocation of resources and efficiently deploy logistic facilities. At the operational level, as we shall see later on, problems of deployment, routing, location, allocation, and scheduling are abundant. At the tactical level, the logistician has to project consumption rates, forecast attrition, determine local schedules and select appropriate LOCs at his zone in the theater of operations. All these tasks require tools for analysis and decision support.

In the following we present a short list of the most common methodologies, models and Operations Research techniques that are used as tools for logistic analysis and decision support. These tools are not necessarily unique for military logistics. Most of them are widely used also in business logistics, in particular as decision aids for profit maximization organizations. Some of these models, which apply to certain types of operational logistics problems, will be discussed in more detail in later chapters.

2.5.1 Multiple Criteria Decision Analysis (MCDA) Models

MCDA models deal with decision situations where a set of well-defined alternatives is given or formed, out of which the "best" alternative is to be selected. The double quotation mark in "best" alludes to the fact that, unlike classical optimization models, the notion of optimality in MCDA problems is fluid and subjective. The alternatives are evaluated with respect to a set of predetermined criteria that may be measurable (i.e., evaluated objectively according to some standards or scales) or judgmental (i.e., based on subjective evaluations by subject matter experts and decision-makers). As a result of the evaluations, the alternatives are prioritized on each criterion. The final step in the MCDA process is scaling these evaluations by the weight of each criterion – weights that reflect the relevance and importance of each criterion regarding the decision problem.

For example, consider the problem of locating a new distribution center for a major retailer. The alternatives are possible locations that may have been chosen out from a larger set of potential locations, following a preliminary screening process. The criteria according to which these locations are evaluated are *operational* criteria, such as proximity to major highways and distance to potential markets, *economic* criteria, such as land value and construction costs, *social* criteria, and *environmental* criteria.

While MCDA Models are predominantly used for logistics decision problems at the strategic level, where competing projects or alternative systems must be carefully examined in view of several operational and economic criteria, this methodology may also apply to *OpLog* systems. The term used by the US Department of Defense for this type of alternative-selection problems is Analysis of Alternative (AoA).

2.5.2 Forecasting Methods

Logistics decisions, in particular supply related problems, rely on estimates of future consumption and attrition rates. The values of these parameters depend on military scenarios, combat situations, and battlefield outcome – factors that embody a considerable amount of uncertainty. These types of decisions are taken therefore in an uncertain environment where pertinent input data are subject to unpredicted variability that may hinder logisticians from reaching the right decisions. Moreover, absent solid input data, logistic planners may tend to make decisions based on intuition or, even worse, made-up inputs that have little or no bearing to the actual situation.

To alleviate the negative impact of uncertainty on logistics decisions, it is necessary to systematically forecast consumption and attrition rates. There are many forecasting methods that range from formal statistical models, such as linear regression and time-series, to group decision models that extract subjective assessments from subject matter experts and evaluate them methodically.

Thus, logistic forecasting is fundamental for logistics decision-making. This important issue is the topic of Chap. 6.

2.5.3   Attrition Models

Attrition is a major driver for logistic needs, and *attrition models* are a special class of warfare forecasting models that help estimate these needs. Evaluating attrition is essential in particular for planning of maintenance and medical services. Decisions regarding stocks of replacement-parts and medical supplies, and spatial deployment of maintenance and medical units depend on adequate projection of attrition in the various parts of the theater of operations.

There are two types of warfare attrition: *Technical* (*natural*) *attrition* and *combat attrition*. Technical attrition is caused by natural wear of the equipment or by accidents and mishaps that occur in the theater of operations. Technical attrition is estimated by methods from *Reliability Theory* [5, 6]. These methods are based on probability models and statistical techniques that produce estimates for the statistical distribution of the time between failures. A parameter commonly used in these models is *mean time between failures* (MTBF), which is estimated by breakdown and failure data collected over time.

Combat attrition is much more difficult to estimate because of the very limited available relevant data. Historical data of combat attrition are very sparse and not always reliable. Moreover, even the little data that exists on past wars may not be relevant to project future attrition in the presence of modern weapon systems, advanced command and control capabilities, new doctrines, and most importantly – new combat scenarios. Methods for assessing combat attrition are developed by combined efforts of military operations research analysts, who develop combat models, [7] and experienced military commanders who induce experts' evaluations. See also Chap. 6.

2.5.4   Transportation Models

There are several types of quantitative models associated with transportation problems in military logistic settings. They range from optimization models, where some measure of effectiveness (MOE) is maximized (or minimized), to probabilistic descriptive models that provide estimates for some transportation related metrics.

Routing Models

Vehicle routing models [8, 9] help to select routes for transporting supplies and services throughout the logistic network. The main objective is to find the fastest way for transporting resources from certain sources to certain destinations. Other objectives are to minimize interference with other concurrent transportation missions and to maximize the survivability of the moving vehicles in contested areas.

Scheduling Models

Scheduling models [10, 11] are used to set timetables for departures, and coordinate the passage of convoys that share common LOCs. The first objective here is to bring the military convoys to their destination on time. A second objective is to minimize the time the convoys spend en-route – thus minimizing their exposure to possible hostile actions by the enemy. The constraints that affect the optimal schedule are time constraints (e.g., readiness time) and capacity constrains of the logistic network (e.g., capacity of roads and intersections).

Distribution Models

Distribution Models (also called *Transportation Models*) [12] prescribe optimal ways to transport supplies from a set of origins to a set of destinations where the total cost of the transportation plan is minimized, and certain supply and demand constraints are satisfied.

Network Models

Routing, scheduling, and distribution models are optimization models where some MOEs are minimized or maximized, subject to certain constraints. A class of models that combine many of these models is *Network Models*. In Chaps. 9, 10, 11 and 12 we present network models and discuss their use in operational logistic modeling.

Descriptive Models

Another family of models includes descriptive models that use probability methods to represent transportation related phenomena. By applying such models, a transportation planner may get insights concerning the nature of the transportation process, and good estimates for the various parameters that govern it. These insights and estimates are important inputs for the aforementioned optimization models.

For example, it is important to estimate the length of time it takes a convoy to travel from a certain source node to a certain destination node. The time is measured from the moment the first vehicle starts moving until the moment the last vehicle in the convoy reaches the destination. There are several random elements in this process such as: acceleration rate, deceleration rate, individual response to road conditions, breakdowns, accidents, and hostile actions like roadside improvised explosive devices (IEDs). It is well known that a convoy is a dynamic entity that changes its shape and its road behavior over time. The relative positions of the vehicles in the convoy, the length of the convoy and its average velocity close to the destination point may be completely different than the values of these parameters at the start of the trip. Probability models may provide systematic time-dependent estimates for these travel parameters.

2.5.5 Inventory Models

Inventory models [13] are used to manage warehouses, depots, distribution centers, and similar logistic installations. These types of models help the logistician to set an ordering schedule and to determine the size and mix of orders. Important parameters in inventory models are capacities, lead (order-to-ship) times, demand rates, and various cost parameters.

2.5.6 Implementing the Models

The models and quantitative methods briefly discussed in this section are used as decision support tools for logistic planning and operation. By no means can these models replace logistic knowledge, operational insight, common sense, and, above all, experience. A logistician must have these four attributes in order to successfully plan and execute logistic operations. The formal models listed above and other quantitative methods are designated to provide analytic and computational support only in those technical areas where the human mind cannot encompass and evaluate effectively all the details of the situation, and when the computational power of the computer adds a significant value.

2.6 Summary

In this chapter we defined the three levels of logistics – strategic, operational, and tactical – and described the main features characterizing strategic logistics and tactical logistics. In particular, we pointed out the difference between the economics-oriented and efficiency-driven strategic logistics and the operations-oriented effectiveness-driven tactical logistics.

Many logistic issues – at all three levels – are of quantitative nature and therefore lend themselves to analysis by formal quantitative methods. A representative selection of such methods was briefly discussed at the end of the chapter.

This chapter concludes the first part of the book in which a general introduction to logistics has been provided. The remainder of the book focuses on the middle and most complex logistics level - *operational logistics* (*OpLog*).

References

1. Feris SP, Keithly DM. 21st-century logistics: joint ties that bind. Parameters, Autumn 1997, pp 38–49.
2. US Army FM 100-5 (Final Draft), August 1997, p 11–1.
3. NATO Logistics Handbook, Senior NATO Logisticians' Conference, Secretariat, NATO Headquarters, Brussels, 1997.
4. Pagonis WG, Krause MD. Operational logistics in the gulf war. The Institute of Land Warfare, Association of the United States Army, Arlington, VA, 1992, p. 2.
5. Barlow RE, Proscham F. Mathematical theory of reliability, society for industrial and applied mathematics, 1996.
6. Ebeling CE. An introduction to reliability and maintainability engineering. New York: McGraw Hill College Div; 1996.
7. Bracken J, Kress M, Rosenthal RE, editors. Warfare modeling. Alexandria, VA: MORS, J. Wiley & Sons; 1995.
8. Eibl PG. Computerized vehicle routing and scheduling in road transport. Aldershot: Ashgate Publishing Co; 1996.
9. Golden BL, Assad A. Vehicle routing: methods and studies. Amsterdam: Elsevier Science; 1988.
10. Kasilingam RG. Logistics and Transportation. Dordrecht: Kluwer; 1998.
11. Bramel J, Simchi-Levi D. The logic of logistics. New York: Springer; 1997.
12. Belenky AS. Operations research in transportation systems. Dordrecht: Kluwer Academic Publishers; 1998.
13. Zipkin PH. Foundations of inventory management. New York: McGraw Hill College Div; 2000.

Chapter 3
The Foundation of Operational Logistics

The term *Operational Level of War* or in short – *Operational Level* has emerged in the West in the 1982 revision of the US Army Field-Manual FM 100-5. This term was redefined in the 1986 version of that manual and since then it has been under continuous examination and review, and a source for debate amongst commanders and military scholars – in particular in conjunction with the related term: *Operational Art* [1]. The 1997 edition of that manual [2] introduced a new term – *Operational Level of Conflict* – and the 2012 edition [3] (now called ADRP 3-0) defines yet another term: *Unified Land Operations* as activities aimed at "seize, retain, and exploit the initiative to gain and maintain a position of relative advantage in sustained land operations through simultaneous offensive, defensive, and stability operations." The logistics that supports and sustains these operations is called *operational logistics* (*OpLog*).

Thus, *OpLog* is related to sustained operations and is usually associated with a certain theater of operations. In general, the missions of *OpLog* are to set up the logistic system in the theater of operations, operate this system, and forecast, analyze, and prioritize future demands for logistic assets according to the operational objectives.

In this chapter we lay the theoretical foundations of operational logistics, define its components, and explore its essence. To set the stage for this analysis, we start off with a brief discussion about the *operational level* in general.

3.1 The Operational Level

The depth and breadth of the terms *operational level of conflict,* its twin term *operational art* and the more recent *unified land operations* are very large; a detailed analysis of these terms is beyond the scope of this book. As mentioned earlier, the operational level has been studied by many military scholars and historians, and the literature in that area is quite extensive. In addition to the aforementioned US Army

© Springer International Publishing Switzerland 2016   33
M. Kress, *Operational Logistics*, Management for Professionals,
DOI 10.1007/978-3-319-22674-3_3

publications, there are other sources for the interested reader such as the books of Simpkin [4] and Schneider [5]. However, to better understand operational logistics, and as a backdrop for its in-context analysis, we need a richer definition for the term *operational level* than the one offered in the US Army publications. The revised definition adopted here is a combination of three main aspects that have appeared in the literature: *cognitive, functional,* and *practical.*

3.1.1   Cognitive Aspect

The operational level of conflict is a cognitive middle stratum in the three-level hierarchy comprising strategy, operations, and tactics. It is a medium between the general and mostly intangible goals of the strategic level above, and the tangible activities at the tactical level below [6]. There is usually no direct and continuous link between the macroscopic picture drawn at the strategic level and the microscopic and detailed view typical to the tactical level. The perceptual transition between strategy and tactics must pass through a middle stage – the operational level.

3.1.2   Functional Aspect

Of the three aspects, the functional one is the most visible. It is widely addressed in doctrinal publications and field manuals. The functional aspect is concerned with the objectives of the operational level and the means by which these objectives are to be attained. Specifically, the functions at the operational level are to deploy military forces and employ them in order to conduct major operations for the purpose of attaining strategic and operational objectives in the theater of operations [7].

3.1.3   Practical Aspect

While the cognitive aspect is concerned with the question "What does *Operational Level* mean?" and the functional aspect addresses the question "What does *Operational Level* do?" the practical aspect deals with the question "How does the *Operational Level* operate?"

The practical aspect describes the physical characteristics of warfare at that level. Schneider [8] defines this level of warfare as the one that comprises planning, execution, and sustainment of temporally and spatially distributed maneuvers and battles. According to this definition, the practical aspect can be viewed as a two-dimensional mesh in which military operations are generated, managed, and controlled. The two dimensions are *space* and *time,* and the practical objective of operational warfare is to "optimally" execute maneuvers and battles in this two-dimensional setting.

3.2   Defining Operational Logistics

As a provider of combat resources, logistics is an important and inseparable part of the operational level. The three aspects described above for the operational level are reflected in the definition of operational logistics. There are cognitive, functional, and practical aspects to this term.

3.2.1   Cognitive Aspect

Operational logistics is a cognitive medium between the economic and industrial base of a nation and the executors of the act of war – the combat units. This medium translates the macroscopic, and somewhat abstract, national potential imbedded in the strategic level into the microscopic and tangible logistic needs that characterize the tactical level.

The transitions between strategic logistics, operational logistics, and tactical logistics can be depicted by the logistic network introduced in Chap. 2. The set of intermediate logistic nodes, and the lines of communications (LOCs) that lead to these nodes, is a physical representation of this cognitive medium.

3.2.2   Functional Aspect

Recall that the function of the operational level is to attain the strategic goals by executing campaigns and large military operations. This function heavily depends on logistics in the sense that it can be implemented only if adequate support is provided for its sustainment. Thus, from the functional point of view, operational logistics comprises the tasks and missions that must be executed to sustain campaigns and large-scale operations. These tasks and missions can be collectively viewed as an "operator" that transforms the logistic capabilities at the strategic level to the demands for logistic resources generated at the tactical level.

3.2.3   Practical Aspect

According to the practical definition of the operational level a campaign is an ordered set of operations distributed in time and space. In order to effectively support these operations, *OpLog* must also be phased appropriately over time and space in the theater of operations. In other words, the practical aspect of *OpLog* is manifested in the resources, facilities, and logistic organizations at the theater of operations. The implementation of these entities must be in accordance with the time and space parameters of the operation.

Example 3.1

A typical example of an *OpLog* operation is the force accumulation (mobilization) process at the initial phase of a campaign (see Chap. 11). Combat forces and support units must be transported from their home bases and depots to the staging area in the theater of operations. One of the *cognitive* aspects of this process is manifested in the geographical medium that separates between the home bases and the staging area. That is, the cognitive aspect of *OpLog* is presented here by *space*. The *functional* aspect is represented by its objective – *transportation* – to move the force in a secure and timely manner from its origin to its destination. The *practical* aspect is embodied in *means of transportation* – airplanes, ships, trains, transporters and trucks – command, control and communication systems and transportation-related planning processes such as scheduling and routing.

3.2.4   Operational Logistics – A Definition

Following the discussion above, a suggested formal definition for *OpLog* is:

> A collection of means, resources, organizations, and processes that share the common goal of sustaining campaigns and large-scale military operations. This collection, which is derived from strategic logistics, is utilized as input for the tactical logistics. OpLog is designated to sustain battles that are distributed in time and space.

3.2.5   The Thrust and Language of OpLog

Operational logistics is aimed at supporting theater-level activities and operational moves, and not directly combat units per se – as at the tactical logistics level. Consequently, the objectives of *OpLog* are specified by the operational goals rather than by military units. Since the operational goals are determined in terms of time and space, operational logistics capabilities must also be specified by these parameters.

Example 3.2

At the tactical logistics level it is important to correctly assess the expected fuel consumption of tank battalion X in the next couple of days. At the theater level the operational logistician may be more concerned about finding out what is the minimal inflow rate of fuel to the theater of operations such that an operational maneuver scheduled to take Y days can be sustained.

The terminology used for *OpLog* is not as clear and unambiguous as the one used at the strategic or tactical logistic levels. The relatively quantitative determinism that characterizes those levels is augmented, at the operational level, with fuzzy and qualitative terms such as *flexibility, synergy,* and *foresight.*

3.3 Characterization and General Features

We have seen before that *OpLog* is a middle stratum in a three-level hierarchy – between the strategic and tactical logistic levels. However, the clear conceptual division of logistics among the three levels does not necessarily induce a clear-cut functional separation by formal military echelons. There may be overlaps between two adjacent levels. Specifically, a command post at a certain echelon (e.g., Headquarters, Corps, Division) may have to deal with issues linked to more than one logistic level. The following two examples demonstrate this point.

Example 3.3: (*strategic-operational overlap*)
The logistics headquarter of a military organization is in charge of establishing an adequate logistic infrastructure and stockpiles for the military forces – a task typical to the strategic level of logistics. However, in time of war, and when resources are limited, this headquarters may also be involved in determining support priorities among theater of operations and among zones within a certain theater. Prioritizing resources within a theater of operation is an operational logistics mission.

Example 3.4: (*operational-tactical overlap*)
The logistician at the division headquarters manages the transportation assets of the division and allocates its resources to the division's brigades and battalions. These activities are typically tactical. However, this officer is also required to forecast future demands for logistic resources, and to submit requests for these resources to a higher echelon. These tasks are closely related to the more general operational context.

The above two examples also demonstrate the current trend towards *seamless logistics*, namely, a "smooth" system where the three levels merge into a single well-coordinated process of logistic support. Advanced command, control, communication, and computer systems may indeed increase the in-transit visibility of logistic assets and therefore may shorten the strategic-tactic logistics span. However, as we have already seen before, there are cognitive, functional, and physical factors that hinder the quest for total elimination of "seams" among the three levels.

3.3.1   Effectiveness and Efficiency

In addition to the cognitive and functional bridge that *OpLog* creates between strategic logistics and tactical logistics, it is a conceptual bridge too.

Strategic logistics, which generates the logistic infrastructure and constitutes the national resources needed for defense, is brought to bear mostly during peacetime. It is planned and implemented, way in advance of any military contingency, through a systematic and methodical process where multiple criteria and considerations are examined. Many of these criteria are economic, which examine cost-effectiveness relations. In particular, expected operational needs are evaluated with respect to their corresponding short-term and long-term costs. Thus, an important factor in planning strategic logistics is *efficiency* – the ratio between the inputs invested in logistic capabilities and the estimated outputs in the battlefield. This issue was discussed in Chap. 2.

Tactical logistics, on the other hand, is evaluated by its *effectiveness*. The considerations are focused at successful execution of the mission and attaining the operational objectives.

Example 3.5
A battalion commander who is about to lead an attack on a fortified infantry position is concerned about capturing the position as fast as possible while incurring minimum casualties. During combat he is generally not concerned with questions like: "What is the cost-effectiveness ratio of the fifth round of fire?" or "Will approaching the target using route A consume less fuel than approaching it by route B?"

The dominant factor at the tactical level is the *effect* of the action and not so much its *cost*.

The two factors – *efficiency* and *effectiveness* – are merged in *OpLog*. The scale and scope of logistic activities at the operational level are such that efficiency must be considered too besides effectiveness. In the presence of limited resources, economies of scale, tradeoffs, and marginal utilities (e.g. the Pareto principle) play a major role in decisions concerning allocation of resources among military units, zones, missions, and actions. The term *optimization model* emerges as a standard decision support tool – in particular for optimizing logistic operations such as resource allocation and transportation. The effectiveness component of *OpLog* is imbedded in the term *Envelop of Operational Effectiveness*.

3.3.2   Envelope of Operational Effectiveness

This term, also called sometimes *Operational Reach*, [9] defines a boundary of the campaign that is operationally feasible from the logistic point of view. As a term associated with the practical aspect of *OpLog*, the *Envelope of Operational*

Effectiveness is measured in two dimensions: *time* and *space*. The bundle of logistic resources – materiel and services – that is available in the theater of operations determines the geographical boundaries and the time frame at which the campaign is logistically sustainable and hence operationally feasible. For example, the availability of fuel affects the distance that can be traveled, while the amount of ammunition determines the length of time during which combat forces can produce effective fire. This term is discussed and expanded furthermore in Chap. 4.

3.4 Operational Logistics and Operational Art

Schneider [8] defines *operational art* as "the creative use of distributed operations for the purpose of strategy," where a distributed operation is "a coherent system of spatially and temporally extended relational movements and distributed battles, whether actual or threatened, that seek to seize, retain, or deny freedom of action." The coherence of this system is derived from the operational objectives and it can be attained only if conditions such as *cognitive consonance, endurance,* and *mental agility* are satisfied. Cognitive consonance means common understanding of the situation and the objectives of the operation among all parts of the force. Endurance is manifested by the reaction of the combat units and their commanders to battle-field attrition. Mental agility – the ability to be "perceptually fast" [10] – makes it possible to react to incoming battlefield information faster that the rate of its arrival. These conditions are *necessary* for an effective execution of a military operation. But, as we shall see in Sect. 3.4.1, these conditions are not *sufficient*.

Operational art, as any form of art, is a creative discipline. The building blocks of operational art are movements, maneuvers, deployments, and battles, and the resulting "work of art" is the operational design, which is an ordered set of events generated by the aforementioned building blocks. Thus, operational art is *event-driven*. It comprises *sequencing* the events, *scheduling* them and *assigning* them to the various components of the force in the theater of operations. These three activities – sequencing, scheduling, and assigning – must be implemented in a coherent way that is consistent with the operational objectives.

3.4.1 The Constraints of an Operation

Consider for a moment an ideal situation in which the cognitive transition from the general strategic goals to the operational objectives in the theater of operations is clear, immediate, and unambiguous. In other words, based on the directives of the strategic level, the campaign commander can unequivocally determine the force composition, its deployment, and the order and time table of the distributed operations in the campaign. Is this ability sufficient for planning and executing optimally the campaign? The answer is obviously *no* since the commander does not operate in an ideal, benevolent, and cooperating world but in an environment full of constraints, hurdles, friction, and limitations.

Thus, the problem that the operational commander has to deal with is essentially a *constrained optimization* problem. Typical constraints are insufficient forces and weapons, incomplete intelligence information, and limited command and control capabilities. However, one of the most significant constraints that may hinder the execution of the operation is logistics. Absence of combat physical resources will clearly hamper the execution of a military operation.

The *OpLog* capabilities are therefore an important part in the decision process that determines the force composition and its deployment in the theater of operations. Moreover, the logistic capabilities also affect the sequence and the timetable of the distributed operations that comprise the campaign, and thus they play a major role in determining the *feasible* boundaries of the campaign within the *potential* (unconstrained) boundaries that are derived from the operational objectives. This feasible region has already been defined as the *Envelope of Operational Effectiveness*.

Example 3.6
During the first few days of the Lebanon war in 1982 the envelope of operational effectiveness of the Israeli forces was very tight – mostly because of shortage in artillery ammunition. Divisional supply units that were supposed to replenish the empty guns were stuck in huge traffic jams in the narrow and winding roads of Southern Lebanon. As a result, the advance of the Israeli divisions to the North was much slower than planned.

3.4.2   The Time Variables

Two important logistic decisions at the operational level are:

- *Timing* the request for logistic resources from higher echelons.
- *Scheduling* the distribution of these resources to the combat units at the tactical level.

These decisions embody tradeoffs between *tactical attainability* and *operational flexibility* – two properties discussed in detail later on. The values of the time variables associated with these two decisions are affected by three parameters: *lead-time, consumption rate,* and *attrition rate*.

Lead-time (also called sometimes *order-to-ship* time) expresses the time that elapses from the moment a request for a certain resource is submitted to a higher echelon, to the time when this resource is delivered to its destination at a certain combat unit. The length of the logistic support chain (See Sect. 2.4 in Chap. 2) is a typical representation of this parameter.

While lead-time represents the "supply side" of *OpLog*, the consumption and attrition rates represent the "demand side." These rates transform *time* into logistic demands and requirements that must be met by locally available resources and by the logistic support chain.

The three parameters – lead time, consumption rate, and attrition rate – embody a considerable level of uncertainty that affects the ability to properly determine the *timing* of the requests and the *scheduling* of the distribution process. Adequate estimates for the three parameters are essential for the operational logistician since the combination of the three determines the effectiveness of the logistic response to battlefield requirements. Chaps. 9 and 12 present models that deal with lead-time and its effect on logistic responsiveness. In Chap. 6 we discuss methods for forecasting logistic requirements based on consumption and attrition rates.

3.4.3   *The Logistic Clock*

As mentioned earlier, *time* is a principal dimension in *OpLog*. While some logistic activities, such as rearming, may be triggered by certain combat events, the majority of the *OpLog* processes are *time-driven*, as opposed to the *event-driven* processes that dominate combat. For example, the inter-echelon logistic support chain within the theater of operations usually operates in 12 or 24 h cycles. It follows that *OpLog* induces a timescale that affects the pace of the campaign and regulates it logistically. The discrepancy between the two modes of progression – *time* for logistics and *events* for combat – creates a serious dilemma that campaign leaders are not always aware of. For example, exploiting success and charging forwards is an event driven situation that may be hampered by delays caused by the time-constrained logistic support chain. Thus, a major campaign challenge is synchronizing the time-driven logistics with the event-driven operations [11].

> **Example 3.7**
> Following a successful assault, the attacking force intends to embark on a swift pursuit. The pursuit is prompted by two *events*: *penetration* of the defender's front line by the attacking force and *withdrawal* of the defending force. However, the feasibility of this pursuit is affected by the availability of fuel that is determined by the *timing* of the logistic support chain.

The components of the *OpLog* system – facilities, means, processes, and resources – are the springs, gearwheels, and levers of the clockwork. Their quality and the way they are aligned and tuned determine the accuracy and reliability of the logistic clock.

3.5   The Content of *OpLog*

Evidently, the *OpLog* picture drawn thus far is quite abstract. It is focused on general, qualitative, and "artistic" aspects of *OpLog*. Obviously, *OpLog* has also a practical and mundane side, which is reflected in the activities typical to this level of logistics.

The *OpLog* actions and processes are divided into three main phases:

- Creating the infrastructure in the theater of operations
- Deployment
- Employment

The first phase of *OpLog* implementation comprises preliminary actions aimed at establishing the in-theater logistic *infrastructure*. The main task at this phase is determining the structure and the basic operational procedures of the logistic network (see Sect. 2.4 in Chap. 2). Specifically, the objectives are to select the locations of the logistic nodes (units and facilities), and to determine the edges and paths (LOCs) that connect them to each other (internal LOCs) and to the strategic nodes at the rear area (external LOCs).

At the *deployment* phase military resources are accumulated and positioned in the theater of operations. The logistic network established at the first phase is utilized to direct and schedule the deployment. Typically, the first two phases are executed concurrently. Sometimes, because of operational constraints, a partial deployment may even precede the first phase of creating the infrastructure – as was the case during the early stages of the Gulf War in 1991. The third phase – *employment* – is concerned with the actual implementation of *OpLog* in order to sustain the operation. This phase is manifested by the execution of the *logistic support chain*.

OpLog comprises six major functions or processes:

1. Force accumulation.
2. Deployment of resources.
3. Management and control of the logistic flow.
4. Medical treatment and evacuation.
5. Prioritization.
6. Logistic forecasting.

3.5.1   Force Accumulation

Mobilizing and building up the military force in the theater of operations is the most critical activity during the early stages of a campaign. This activity comprises three tasks: *routing, prioritization,* and *scheduling*.

Routing

The accumulation of combat units and supplies in the theater of operations is done by moving these military assets from their home bases and peacetime storage facilities to the theater of operations. The first destinations of these assets are the gateways to the theater of operations: ports of debarkation (in a power-projection scenario) or dismounting areas (in a forward deployment scenario). From these gateways, military forces move to assembly and staging areas. In terms of the logistic network, the force accumulation process generates a flow of military assets on the external LOCs that connect the source nodes at the strategic level with the intermediate nodes at the operational level.

A typical problem in this process is to select the most appropriate LOCs for moving the force, namely, to find the best *routing*. Geographical, topographical, political, and most of all, operational constraints, affect the selection of these LOCs.

> **Example 3.8**
> During the early stages of operation Desert Shield, the US military faced the dilemma of whether to send a small part of the force to Saudi Arabia fast using air lift, or to ship a larger portion of the force, but slower, by sea lift.

In forward deployment scenarios typical to the Israel Defense Forces (IDF) the considerations according which ground routes are selected for moving military units to the front are throughput of roads, their length, and their survivability to enemy's hostile actions.

Dispatch Prioritization

The second issue is the order at which units are sent to the theater of operations. The main factor in determining this order is operational. It is derived from the military posture, the objectives of the campaign, and the operational plans. In particular, the induced priority order in the force accumulation process determines the rate at which the ratio between combat forces and support units – the "tooth to tail" ratio – changes over time and space.

> **Example 3.9**
> A prioritization dilemma was demonstrated during the earlier stages of operation Desert Shield. Without any substantive knowledge regarding the Iraqis intentions and capabilities, and in the face of limited transportation capabilities, the question was how to balance between combat units and logistic assets. The dilemma was whether to first send out a large combat force, at the expense of very small logistic support, or to improve the balance of shipments between the "tooth" and the "tail." Due to operational uncertainties, and the US perception of the Iraqi threat, the decision was to choose the first option. Namely, to increase the size of the combat force at the expenses of shrinking the initial envelop of operational effectiveness (see Sect. 3.3.2).

Despite the clear dominance of operational considerations, in some situations logistic constraints may affect dispatch priorities.

Example 3.10
Consider the following fictional situation. The first stage of the operation has just been completed and the 1st armored brigade is scheduled to move from its current position at point A to its new staging area at point B. The 2nd mechanized brigade is currently located at point C while its new staging area is at point D. The 1st brigade has a higher priority than the 2nd brigade. The two brigades are to be transported on-board wheeled transporters. The number of transporters is sufficient to carry only one brigade at a time. The transporters are currently located close to point C and the travel time from C to D is about 2 h. The travel time of the transporters from its current position to point A is 2 h and from point D 1 h. The travel time from A to B is 6 h. In this situation it may be reasonable to consider transporting the lower priority 2nd brigade (2 h operation) before the 1st brigade (8 h operation).

Scheduling

The third issue is timing the dispatch of ships and aircraft (in a power-projection scenario) and trains or convoys of vehicles (in a forward deployment scenario). The schedule is determined by the priority assigned to each shipment, by the availability of means of transportation and LOCs, and, most of all, by operational considerations. For example, when scheduling the dispatch of convoys of vehicles, the objective is usually to minimize the accumulation time in the theater of operations such that the combat force is ready for battle as early as possible. It is however also important to minimize the time spent en route and thus minimizing the exposure of the force to enemy's hostile activities. These two objectives are attained if the interaction among convoys is minimal so that one convoy (e.g., a slow moving convoy or a convoy that crosses an intersection and therefore occupies it) does not hinder the movement of another (see also Example 3.10 and Chap. 11).

The Operational Perspective

All three issues – routing, prioritizing, and scheduling – are incorporated in the planning and execution of the force accumulation process. The primary factor in this process is *time*. Time is crucial in particular when a defender is facing a surprise attack. Routing, prioritizing, and scheduling in such scenarios may be different than those that apply to a deliberate attack, where time constraints may not be so acute. In some situations force accumulation may be an operation by itself.

Example 3.11

A missile attack during force accumulation may severely hinder the preparation efforts of the combat units in their home bases, and their movement towards the front. Such a situation may necessitate a proper military response, which may evolve into a full-scale operation.

Example 3.12

A typical dilemma in ground transportation is whether to transport armored fighting vehicles (AFVs) on-board transporters or to let them travel on their own tracks. The first mode of transportation is usually faster, it causes little physical wear to the AFVs and it saves fuel that otherwise is consumed by the AFVs. Although there are possible shortcomings to this mode of transportation – it may be vulnerable to enemy's hostilities and less efficient in situations where roads are damaged or blocked – commanders prefer it over letting the AFVs travel on their own tracks. However transporters may be a scarce resource and therefore balancing between the two modes of transportation is a fundamental problem in force accumulation planning. This dilemma is elaborated furthermore in Chap. 11.

In a power projection postures, long-range sealift may constitute a separate operation when, for example, naval convoys are confronted by enemy's threats.

Example 3.13

During WWII Convoys of merchant ships crossed the Atlantic from the US to UK with supplies for the Allies. While en route, these convoys had been attacked by German U-boats. Considerable effort was invested by the US Navy to find operational solutions that minimized the losses caused by these attacks. Following a quantitative analysis it was concluded that it would be better to send fewer but longer convoys.

Because of the criticality, complexity, and vulnerability of sealift and airlift operations, they are considered sometimes as *strategic* missions [12]. However, these missions are closely related to a specific military operation and therefore they are treated here within the operational logistics context. An analysis of the force accumulation process is given in Chap. 11.

3.5.2   *Logistic Deployment*

The logistic rationalization of an operation is embodied in the logistic deployment in the theater of operations. It comprises setting up the logistic nodes such as ports of debarkation, supply points, ammunition dumps, maintenance areas, transfer points, combat service support (CSS) units and facilities, and selecting the corresponding LOCs – roads, railways, air routes, and sea-lanes. In terms of the logistic network, logistic deployment amounts to determining the size, shape, composition, and location of *intermediate* and *destination* nodes, and selecting the *internal* LOCs. Determining the logistic deployment is one of the most crucial decisions taken at the operational level.

Intermediate Nodes

The intermediate logistic nodes, also called *theater logistic nodes*, are usually divided into two sets: *rear* nodes and *forward* nodes. The rear nodes represent the gateways to the theater of operations. In a power projection scenario the rear theater nodes are the ports of debarkations - harbors and airports. In a forward deployment scenario these nodes are railheads and destination points for convoys sent from the rear of the communications zone. The forward nodes are Corps, and sometimes Division, logistic units. These units operate as buffers and intermediate service facilities between the rear nodes and the destination nodes, which are the CSS units attached to the combat battalions or brigades.

The intermediate nodes – in particular the rear nodes – are typically large, abundant with means and supplies, and quite lumpish. Some of these nodes, like ports, are inherently static. Others may have limited mobility at best. Therefore, at least some of these nodes, such as large maintenance centers, must be deployed prior to initiating combat activities. During the campaign it may be difficult, if not impossible, to build these nodes in the theater of operations or to move them around effectively.

The decisions regarding these nodes involve location, size, mix of resources, and mode of operation.

Example 3.14
The dilemma where to allocate the ports of debarkation in Saudi Arabia during operation Desert Shield was an important deployment decision. The port of Jubail and the nearby King Abdoul-Aziz airport were assigned to the US Marines, while the port of Dammam was allocated to the US Army.

Destination Nodes

The destination nodes, also called *tactical logistic nodes*, are the combat service support (CSS) elements of the combat units. Typically, these nodes represent brigade or battalion CSS units. Although these nodes are managed and controlled during the campaign by tactical combat units, their design is an operational-level problem. The size, mix of resources, and organizational structure of the CSS units are determined well in advance – before the beginning of an operation. Determining these factors is an integral part of the planning phase of the campaign (see Chap. 4) and therefore it is an operational task. The structure and content of these units may change over time according to the changes in the operational situation.

Example 3.15
A typical problem in the design of CSS units is determining the number and types of trucks allocated to each such unit. The optimal mix of trucks is affected by conflicting considerations such as maximizing logistic independence, minimizing the logistic tail and maintaining adequate logistic flexibility.

Internal LOCs

The intermediate and destination nodes are connected by internal LOCs, which are typically ground ways of various types – from four-lane highways to dirt roads and mountain trails. An assignment of a LOC to a pair of nodes must take into account the quality of the road, its capacity, and its vulnerability to hostile actions. It must also take into consideration the type and volume of the projected logistic flow between the nodes. Topography, geography, and severe enemy's threat in contested areas may necessitate aerial resupply and evacuation, in which case internal LOCs are aerial routes.

3.5.3   Managing the Logistic Flow

Sustaining an operation depends on a well-coordinated and effective logistic support chain that carries the logistic flow of materiel and services and distributes it (see Sect. 2.4 in Chap. 2). In order for this chain to operate effectively, adequate number of means of transportation and storage facilities must be assigned to the various distribution missions. Since the number of means of transportation and their capacities are usually limited, it is necessary to optimize their operation according to the logistic deployment (see Sect. 3.5.2) and the operational plan. The management of the logistic flow is manifested in a distribution plan that specifies what *mix* of resources is to be carried, from which *source* to which *destination,* by *whom, when,* and on which *route.*

Optimization

Some aspects of the distribution plan could be formulated as optimization problems. Typically, the objective is to minimize some measure of effectiveness such as completion time or cost. The constraints reflect limitations on resources, storage capacity, means of transportation, and travel time. Such optimization problems are rather complex and in many cases involve combinatorial aspects. A simple example of an optimization problem formulated by a distribution-type model is given in Example 3.16.

Example 3.16

A forward theater depot (*forward intermediate node*) supplies ammunition to three divisions: 1, 2, and 3. The travel time of the trucks between the depot and each one of the divisions is one time-period and therefore the demand at time period 1 must be satisfied by the divisions' on-board supplies. A round trip takes two time periods. Denote the demand for ammunition at division k, $k = 1,2,3$, at time period t by d_{kt} truckloads.

Q: *Assuming that the supply of ammunition at the depot is practically unlimited, what is the minimum number of trucks y that must be staged initially at the depot such that the demands are satisfied in a scenario that comprises T time periods?*

Let x_{kt}, $k = 1,2,3$, denote the number of trucks sent to division k at time period t, and let x_{0t} denote the number of trucks that stay at the depot at time period t. The problem of determining the minimum fleet size of trucks that satisfies demands is the following linear-programming (network) model:

(1) $Min \ y$

st

$$y - \sum_{k=0}^{3} x_{k1} = 0 \quad \text{(Balance of trucks at } t = 1\text{)}$$

(2) $$x_{01} - \sum_{k=0}^{3} x_{k2} = 0 \quad \text{(Balance of trucks at } t = 2\text{)}$$

$$\underbrace{x_{0,t-1}}_{\substack{\text{Trucks that stayed} \\ \text{at the depot from} \\ \text{time period } t-1}} + \sum_{k=1}^{3} \underbrace{x_{k,t-2}}_{\substack{\text{Trucks returning} \\ \text{from trips initiated} \\ \text{at time period } t-2}} - \sum_{k=0}^{3} \underbrace{x_{k,t}}_{\substack{\text{Trucks available} \\ \text{at time period } t}} = 0$$

(3) $x_{kt} \geq d_{k,t+1} \qquad t = 1,...,T-1, \quad k = 1,2,3.$

The objective function (1) minimizes the number of trucks staged at the depot at the first time period. The first set of constraints (2) represents the availability of trucks in subsequent time periods. Namely, the total number of trucks available at a certain time period (t) is equal to the number of trucks that arrive at the depot after a two-period trip (if there are any) plus the number of trucks that stayed at the depot from the previous time period. The second set of constraints (3) represents the supply requirements. This type of models is discussed in Chap. 12.

An important parameter that directly influences the distribution process is *velocity* – the throughput of the flow on the edges of the logistic network. A careful estimate of this parameter is necessary in order to obtain realistic and robust distribution plans.

Operating the Logistic Network

The logistic deployment (see Sect. 3.5.2), and the distribution plan form together the logistic network. The deployment determines the *graph* of the network while the transportation plan generates the *flow* on this graph. Thus, the logistic network is a reasonable and useful representation of the *OpLog* system in the theater of operations.

Three intermingled problems are associated with the logistic network. The first problem is *routing*: optimally selecting the internal LOCs. These lines of communication connect the rear theater nodes, through the forward theater nodes, to the destination nodes – the CSS elements of the tactical combat units. In selecting the LOCs, one must take into account the availability of means of transportation, the terrain, and the potential threat by the enemy. The technical characteristics of the means of transportation determine the set of feasible LOCs. For example, a mountainous dirt road may be a suitable LOC for a tracked vehicle or even a 4X4 truck, but not for a regular truck. An air route is obviously feasible only for airplanes and helicopters.

The parameters that characterize a certain pair – (*Means of Transportation, LOC*) – are the length of the LOC, its nominal throughput (e.g., how many vehicles can occupy the LOC concurrently), the average velocity on that LOC, its safety and its survivability with respect to enemy's hostile actions. The presence of a malevolent opponent may sometimes necessitate fighting for these LOCs and securing them. In such cases the logistic network may become an operational objective in the campaign – not just logistical.

The second problem is to determine the right mix of resources in the logistic flow. This problem occurs because logistic resources generate a *multicommodity* flow [13] on the network. Ammunition, fuel, spare parts, food, water, and other supplies compete for space on limited transportation and storage capacities.

The third problem is to schedule the flow and to estimate its velocity in the network in view of the expected congestion on the LOCs and the risks associated with moving along them. The flow rate is the principal parameter that affects the *Logistic Clock* described earlier (see Sect. 3.4.3) and therefore it has an influence on the pace of the entire campaign.

The logistic deployment and the management of the logistic flow create the conditions in which the logistic support chain is operating.

3.5.4   Medical Treatment and Evacuation

Medical treatment in the theater of operations and medical evacuation are two missions that are directly and immediately associated with human life. This association makes them special *OpLog* functions since their impact on the battlefield is more of a moral and psychological nature than operational. Time is of utmost importance in providing medical help at the battlefield, and it is more critical, in that respect, than any other aspect of the operation. Therefore, despite its relatively small scale, as compared e.g., to moving huge masses of combat supplies, medical support is considered an operational logistic mission. For example, a small field hospital, with no more than a few dozens of medical personnel, is usually an operational (theater) level facility despite its size.

A detailed description of the medical support function in the theater of operations is presented in Chap. 11.

3.5.5 Prioritization

Prioritization is a process that applies to all the operational issues listed above. It is discussed however separately because of its central and well-defined role in *OpLog* decisions. Priority considerations affect the composition of the accumulated force in the theater of operations and the rate at which it is accumulated. Prioritization affects the mix of materiel deployed in the theater facilities, and the inflow of resources from the strategic level and its allocation within the theater of operations. In particular, the priorities determine the content of the logistic nodes and the order at which the resources are moved among them. This order is important in particular when the various supplies "compete" for limited transportation capacities. In such cases, poor prioritization may result in situations where flow of unneeded supplies will block the flow of needed ones.

> **Example 3.17**
> Ammunition has usually a higher priority than fuel in static postures. This priority may be reversed in a dynamic posture were moving the force fast becomes a top priority.

A major prioritization issue is balancing between the "tooth" of the force and its "tail" – especially during the force accumulation stage (see **Dispatch Prioritization** in Sect. 3.5.1). Medical prioritization – commonly known as *triage*—may become a difficult ethical problem when the number of casualties exceeds the medical capabilities.

The priorities are set through a continuous dialogue between commanders and the logisticians, in particular during the planning phase (see Chap. 4).

> **Example 3.18**
> In 1941, George C. Marshal decided that the US would concentrate first on Europe and then on the campaign in the Pacific and Japan. For that end, the UK was designated as the logistic base for the European theater and was given a higher priority than Australia— the designated pacific logistic base.

3.5.6   Logistic Forecasting

As time passes, the force size, its mix in the theater of operations and the boundaries of that theater may change. As more forces are deployed and the boundaries of the theater expand, *OpLog* must be adjusted too. Because of the long lead-times imbedded in the logistic support chain, it is necessary to respond to these changes as early as possible. A proper and timely logistic response depends on an effective logistic forecasting. Logistic forecasting at the theater of operations is an on-going process in which potential scenarios are analyzed and evaluated with regards to their logistic derivatives. This process is the subject of Chap. 7.

3.6   The Principles of *OpLog*

One possible way to define *principle* is as an assertion concerning *cause and effect*. The assertion reveals a basic truth about the connection between a phenomenon and its consequences. A principle evolves through accumulated experience and by logical deduction from observations on processes and events. For example, the principle of force concentration represents the assertion that a commander who can concentrate his forces in the right place and the right time ("cause") will have a better chance to defeat the enemy ("effect") than if his force is dispersed. In this case the principle is in fact a property – *concentration* – that the force deployment should satisfy.

Similarly, we may also treat logistic principles as basic properties that any *OpLog* system must satisfy. Thus, the term *principle* is replaced from now on by the term *property*.

There are several lists of properties that have appeared in the literature [14, 15] and which may be divided into two types. The first type is associated with the way logistics is perceived in the operational level context. Properties of the second type apply to the way logistics is actually implemented in the theater of operations. The first type includes *cognitive properties* while the second type represents *structural* and *operational properties*.

3.6.1   Cognitive Properties

Cognitive properties of logistics describe the way operational aspects are perceived logistically. These intangible properties, which reflect the intrinsic relations between logistics and operations, are *synchronization, foresight,* and *improvisation*.

Synchronization

We have already seen before (in Sect. 3.4.3) that combat operations and logistics evolve according to two different scales. The distributed operations in the theater of operations are usually *event-driven,* while a relatively rigid *clock*, regulated by the pulses of the logistic support chain, determines the pace of logistics. Consequently, the tempo of the two processes may not coincide. Reconciling this physical discrepancy in the theater of operations is an essential and crucial objective in conducting military operations. The continuous attempt to attain this objective is what makes *synchronization* the top cognitive property.

The operations-logistics synchronization is embodied in the coordination between the operational event-driven clock, according which combat events are created, and the logistic clock that regulates the logistic flow in the theater of operations. Arguably, the mechanisms of these two clocks are different and therefore synchronizing them during a campaign is essential for creating "operational harmony." The operational harmony facilitates consistency among operational objectives, plans of combat missions, and actual execution of those missions.

Another metaphor that may be used in this context is a *wave*. Synchronization is attained if the amplitude and length of the logistic "wave," which is created by the logistic support chain, is consistent with the corresponding parameters in the operational "wave," which depicts combat intensities.

Foresight

The second cognitive property is *foresight*. Logistic foresight has nothing to do with prophetic talents or supernatural visions. It is about recognizing the need to continuously and systematically assess the possible future directions of the operation, and subsequently project their logistic consequences. Since quite often combat events occur at a higher pace than their associated logistic events (see *Synchronization* above), foresight is a necessary property for an operational plan to be logistically sustainable.

Foresight requires good communication between the commander and the logistician. It is based on three types of input:

- Assessments of the enemy's moves and actions (Intelligence input).
- Projections of possible battlefield initiatives (Operations input).
- Evaluations of logistic capabilities (Logistic input).

Foresight does not necessarily mean specific logistic forecasting, as described in Sect. 3.5.6. This property is measured by the ability to detect early enough "logistic predicaments" and by suggesting appropriate measures to overcome them. Foresight empowers the logistician to be proactive and anticipate the warfighter's requirements, as opposed to only reacting to them.

Example 3.19
Despite the cuts in the Israeli defense budget that occurred in the early 70s, the logistics branch of the Israeli Defense Forces managed to find the funding for relocating the forward logistic facilities at the Eastern Galilee closer to the Syrian border. This move turned out to be crucial few years later when the proximity of these bases to the Golan Heights facilitated an effective logistic support chain during the 1973 Yom Kippur War.

Improvisation

Operations are very seldom executed exactly as planned. The German theoretician Von Clausewitz attributed this statement to the effect of *friction* [16]. Friction at the battlefield exists even when there is no enemy around. It is created by fatigue, fear, misunderstandings among commanding officers, misinterpretations of commands, shortfalls in C^3 systems, technical failures of weapons, and the effect of the elements. Therefore, commanders must be capable to alter, sometimes at a very short notice, existing operational plans. In particular, the operational logistician may have to find fast and effective solutions to emerging unpredicted logistic requirements. In many cases he must *improvise*.

Generally speaking, *improvisation* is prevalent more at the tactical logistics level than at the operational level. Improvisation is typically manifested as a local initiative to solve an ad hoc problem. However, despite its tactical and local nature, the effect of an improvised solution may extend beyond the tactical level and have an impact on the entire operation. For example, changing quickly and effectively the original designation of certain means of transportation may facilitate supply of a critical resource that otherwise could not have reached the destination where it is needed.

The potential capability for improvisation depends on a flexible logistic structure (see Chap. 10) and reliable and updated information (see Chap. 5) regarding the availability of resources. The ability to improvise also depends on the mental creativity of the campaign commanders and logisticians, and on the command and control capabilities. It should be pointed out that *improvisation* does not replace *foresight;* it complements it when things do not happen as anticipated.

Example 3.20
The Allies invasion in northwestern Europe during WWII required that large amounts of supplies be transported onto the continent. The Germans, aware of the need for deep-water ports by the Allies, fortified every major port on the French and Belgian shores. To facilitate the mass transportation of supplies, the Allies created artificial harbors from sunken ships, concrete boxes (caissons), and pontoons. This improvisation effort at getting supplies across the Normandy beaches was crucial for Allies' success.

Cognitive Properties and the *OpLog* Plan

Notwithstanding the evident importance of the cognitive properties, their practical use for evaluating a certain *OpLog* plan is rather limited because they are abstract and associated with ad hoc situations. It is very difficult, if not impossible, to look at a certain *OpLog* plan and determine a priori if it contains an adequate level of *synchronization*. It is even less likely to be able to evaluate the intrinsic amount of *foresight* that is embedded in the plan. Moreover, the evaluation of *improvisation* is only possible *post-bellum* – after the campaign is over.

Thus, except for their educational and declarative contributions, cognitive properties are not very useful as criteria for evaluating a given *OpLog* plan. It is pertinent to synchronize, anticipate, and improvise, and therefore these properties must be assimilated by logisticians, but a logistic plan can hardly manifest explicitly these properties. The extent of these properties may be judged – mostly subjectively – after the operation is over.

Since some cognitive properties are associated with structural and operational properties, the latter may sometime be used as proxies for the cognitive properties. For example, *improvisation* is related to *flexibility*, which is a structural property that could be measured in a logistic plan in advance (see Sect. 3.6.2 and Chap. 10).

3.6.2   Structural and Operational Properties

Structural and operational properties portray the design and operational procedures of an *OpLog* system. These properties may be treated as *criteria* for evaluating *OpLog* schemes. The relative importance of the criteria depends on the specific operational posture.

Unlike the cognitive properties, the structural and operational properties are concrete and may be evaluated systematically before the logistic plan is actually implemented in the battlefield. Thus, these properties are useful parameters for measuring the quality of a certain *OpLog* plan.

There are several lists of *OpLog* properties that have appeared in the literature. These lists generally agree on the following set of structural and operational properties:

- Flexibility
- Attainability
- Continuity
- Tempo
- Simplicity
- Survivability
- Efficiency

Flexibility

Flexibility is a property associated with systems [17]. In general, flexibility expresses the ability to effectively handle changes in a system. Recall that a system is defined as a collection of entities and processes that are united by common objectives. A system is said to be *flexible* if its entities and processes can quickly respond to new constraints, demands, and environmental changes in such a way that its objectives can still be achieved effectively.

In the *OpLog* context, flexibility is measured by the capabilities of the logistic system to adjust and respond effectively to changes in the operational conditions and combat missions. Logistic flexibility enables to quickly update the allocation of resources in the *OpLog* system, and to efficiently alter the logistic flow according to the new emerging requirements. It follows that a logistic plan is flexible if at any given stage of the operation it can potentially support many possible future contingencies. There are two types of logistic flexibility:

- Intrinsic (technical) flexibility
- Structural (operational) flexibility

Intrinsic flexibility is embodied in the deployed logistic assets and the methods and procedures used in operating the *OpLog* system. Intrinsic flexibility is enhanced when the logistic assets are more versatile and the operating procedures are more general and less mission specific. A mean of transportation that can carry personnel, ammunition, ration, and fuel is more versatile, and hence more flexible, than a specially designated vehicle that can carry only one type of load.

Example 3.21
The *Palletized Load System* (PLS) [18] is a truck with a trailer that is capable of loading and unloading itself within a few minutes by pulling on or pushing off its entire load. The basic idea underlying this system is the physical and conceptual disengagement between the truck and its payload. Each truck can carry an assortment of supplies that are loaded onto a container that is mounted on a standard frame. The truck can independently load and unload this payload by its own equipment. This versatility in carrying various types of supplies translates into intrinsic (technical) flexibility.

OpLog structural and operational flexibility is imbedded in its design and procedures. A certain logistic deployment is structurally flexible if the corresponding logistic network is capable to shift the logistic flow from one edge (LOC) to another quickly and effectively.

Flexibility is a key attribute of *OpLog*. It facilitates *improvisation* when such a capability is needed. Chap. 10 rigorously defines the terms described above and presents metrics for measuring it.

Attainability

Attainability is quite related to tactical logistics. This property indicates the logistic independence at the end-points of the logistic network – the tactical combat unit. The higher the attainability, the longer is the time period in which the tactical combat unit is logistically self-sufficient. Attainability is achieved if enough resources are allocated to the combat units before the beginning of the operation and therefore it determines the size of the tactical logistic tail. Since the "length" of this tail is limited due to operational constraints and efficiency considerations, it follows that the duration of this logistic independence is limited too. The importance of this property in the overall evaluation of an *OpLog* plan depends on the required response time (*order-to-ship time*) for logistic demands.

> **Example 3.22**
> Medical services must be capable to respond within minutes of injury and therefore medical supplies and services must satisfy a high level of attainability. On the other hand, acceptable response times for maintenance services are measured in hours (or even days or weeks) and therefore replacement parts usually satisfy a lower level of attainability.

Continuity

Continuity is a property that represents the stability of the logistic flow between the logistic nodes at the rear area and the combat units at the front. The stability of the flow is maintained as long as there are no blockings in the LOCs, and no disruptions in the logistic flow. Obviously, continuity is a necessary condition for an effective execution of the logistic support chain.

A blocking can occur because of high congestion on low capacity LOCs or bad scheduling and routing. Failures in command and control systems can result in uncontrollable movements on the network that may generate chaotic effects that lead to blocking too. A disruption of the flow may occur when LOCs are exceptionally long and are subject to hostile activity.

> **Example 3.23**
> During the 1982 Lebanon War, the Israeli logistic support chain was cut off due to extremely high congestion on the narrow and winding roads of Southern Lebanon. As a result, in one occasion, a single supply battalion operated as the main theater supply source for three divisions – a situation that ultimately led to severe shortages in ammunition and other supplies.

Tempo

We have already seen before that logistics is time-driven. It contains an inner clock that dictates the time scale of logistic processes. This time scale determines the logistic tempo and represents, in general, the velocity of an "average" component of flow in the logistic network. The tempo of the logistic flow is affected by two properties – continuity and flexibility. Continuity is a necessary condition for the existence of a positive (nonzero) steady tempo of flow, and flexibility determines, to large extent, its rate.

Recall also that an operation is defined as an ordered collection of temporally and spatially distributed maneuvers and battles. The logistic tempo affects the order of these combat events and their schedule.

Example 3.24
The timing of the ground operation (Operation Desert Sabre) during the Gulf War was dictated by the logistic clock. The air campaign (operation Desert Storm) was extended for one week beyond the operational needs because of logistic constraints. The theater forward logistic facilities in the western part of the theater – Log-bases Bravo, Charlie and Echo – were not ready yet for the operation.

A related parameter is the *logistic momentum*. Similarly to the physical term, the logistic momentum is the product of tempo – the average velocity (V) – and the logistic mass (M) that is sent out to the theater of operations. Clearly, the logistic momentum VM increases as V and M increase. Moreover, this parameter exhibits the tradeoff between mass and velocity.

Example 3.25
Suppose M_{net} and V_{net} denote the average mass and velocity of the flow in a logistic network. The logistic momentum is maintained if cutting M_{net} by one half is complemented by doubling the velocity V_{net}.

The logistic momentum and the consumption rate affect the inventory level of supplies in the theater of operations. The utility or "value" of the logistic momentum does not necessarily increase with its size. Larger momentum does not always mean better logistics. A massive and uncontrollable push of supplies may not be absorbable in the theater of operations and therefore may cause congestion and leakage beyond the capacity of the available in-theater logistic facilities. In addition to the waste that this may create, the congestion and leakage may generate chaotic effects that may negatively affect the entire operation.

Simplicity

Simplicity is almost always a desired property; it is better to simplify things than to complicate them. This principle is true in particular when dealing with very large and complex systems such as *OpLog*. The imbedded friction in the battlefield – noise, confusion, uncertainty, miscommunication, exhaustion, and fear – make only simple plans, with as little interdependencies as possible, logistically, and operationally feasible.

The principle of simplicity relates to the "tooth-to-tail" ratio – the ratio between the size of the combat force and its attached support (CSS) units. When this ratio is small, which means that the logistic portion of the force is relatively large, the command and control range of the commander is expanded, sometimes beyond its C^3 capabilities. A commander who during battle has to divide his attention between conducting combat operations at the front and managing substantial logistic operations at the rear may find this task overwhelming. Thus, the smaller the portion of the *OpLog* system attached to the tactical combat units, the simpler, and thus more easily manageable, are the tactical logistics operations. Arguably, this aspect of simplicity is in contrast to the principle of attainability.

Survivability

Many of the logistic properties discussed thus far may apply to any logistic system – not necessarily a military one. For example, a retail company must be *flexible* to respond to market trends, maintain an acceptable response time (*tempo*) and stock an adequate amount of its products at its retail stores (*attainability*). A property that clearly distinguishes military logistics from a civilian one is *survivability*.

During campaigns and major operations, *OpLog* is typically implemented in an unfriendly environment, which is vulnerable to enemy's hostile actions. Threats have become more significant with the introduction of long-range and accurate weapons. For example, a well-coordinated and robust transportation schedule that could work perfectly in a neutral (peacetime or commercial) environment may be disrupted when it is executed in the malevolent battlefield environment where military convoys are subject to enemy's interdiction. Therefore, a considerable effort must be invested to secure the LOCs and their surroundings and protect the logistic assets in the theater of operations.

Conversely, the vulnerability of the *OpLog* system marks the enemy's logistics as a prime target for engagement. In some situations, when the enemy's logistics constitutes a center of gravity for its operations, *counter-logistics* – cutting the enemy's logistic support chain and causing it severe logistic discontinuities – may become the focus of the operational plan.

Efficiency

Unlike tactical logistics that is concerned with "here and now" effectiveness, operational logistics takes a wider view on the entire operational plan and therefore must also take into consideration efficiency and even optimization. In general, logistic efficiency at the operational level is manifested primarily in allocating resources among competing demands. Sometimes it is justified to withhold support to a certain unit in lieu of a more efficient (and subsequently – more effective) utilization of that resource. Terms like *utility* and *relative efficiency* are considered in particular when the resources bundle is limited and there is a need to prioritize the urgency of the logistic needs. Efficiency considerations range from determining support priorities to setting the most economical transportation schedule such that operational requirements are satisfied.

Efficiency is attained through a multidimensional optimization process that takes into account (a) physical constraints on the availability of logistic resources, (b) operational requirements and (c) preferences.

3.7 Summary

The *OpLog* system is a major part of military logistics characterized by tangible and intangible features. It is a cognitive, functional, and organizational stratum between the large-scale national-level strategic logistics and the localized combat service support (CSS) actions at the tactical level. The functions of *OpLog* range from force accumulation in the theater of operations, through management of the logistic support chain, to medical treatment and evacuation. The in-context quality and suitability of an *OpLog* system may be evaluated by several operational and structural properties such as flexibility, attainability, and survivability. These properties are important measures of effectiveness for *OpLog* planning, as discussed in the next chapter.

References

1. Meehan JF. III, The operational trilogy. Parameters, September 1986, pp. 9–18.
2. US Department of the Army, *Operations*, FM 100-5, 1996.
3. US Department of the Army, *Unified Land Operations,* ADRP 3-0, 2012.
4. Simpkin RE. Race to the swift: thoughts on twenty-first century warfare. London: Brassey's; 1985.
5. Schneider JJ. The structure of strategic revolution. Novato, CA: Presidio; 1994.
6. Luttwak EN. Strategy and the logic of war and peace. Cambridge, MA: Harvard University Press; 1987. p. 91.
7. US Department of the Army, *Operations*, Field Manual 100-5, 1986.
8. Schneider, p-51.
9. US Department of the Army, *Operations*, Field Manual 100-5, 1996, pp: 8-9.
10. Laffey TL. The Real-Time Expert. *Byte*, January 1991, p. 260.
11. US Marine Corps, *Campaigning,* FMFM 1-1, 1990, p. 45.
12. Baker SF, Morton DP, Rosenthal RE, Williams LM. Optimizing strategic airlift, NPS-OR-99-004. Monterey. CA: Naval Postgraduate School; 1999.
13. Lawler EL. Combinatorial optimization: networks and Matroids. Rinehart and Winston: Holt; 1976.
14. Thompson J. The lifeblood of war. Brassey's UK, 1991, p. 7.
15. Huston JA. The Sinews of War: Army Logistics 1775-1953, Office of the Chief of Military History, US Army, Washington, 1966.
16. Von Clausewitz C. On war. Princeton: Princeton University Press; 1976.
17. Mandelbaum M, Buzacott J. Flexibility and decision making. Eur J Oper Res. 1990;44(5): 17–27.
18. Haas PM. Palletized loading system: not just another truck. Army Logistician, September-October 1996, p. 14.

Chapter 4
Planning

The quality of an operational plan is determined by three main criteria: *compatibility, feasibility,* and *operational cost.* The compatibility criterion examines if the proposed plan properly addresses the campaign objectives, that is, if the expected *end state* of a successful execution of the plan is consistent with the operational objectives. The feasibility criterion estimates the chances that the operation will be carried out as planned, given operational and environmental constraints, and battlefield uncertainty. Through the third criterion – operational cost – the campaign planners assess the specific risks, and associated costs in personnel and equipment involved in carrying out the plan. Of particular importance is the cost of failure to attain the campaign objectives.

Operational Logistics (*OpLog*) is directly connected to the last two criteria – *feasibility* and *operational cost.* As a major factor in warfare, logistics imposes constraints on the way operations are executed. The logistic capabilities set the *feasible* boundaries of the campaign (See the term *Envelop of Operational Effectiveness* in Chap. 3, Sect. 3.3.2) and affect its *operational cost.* Therefore, *OpLog* planning is an essential part in the overall operational planning. Without it, operations may be either infeasible or prohibitively costly in terms of attrition, casualties, and unattainable objectives.

OpLog is also related, indirectly, to the first criterion – *compatibility.* Operational analysis of the situation may lead to the conclusion that the most effective way to achieve the campaign objectives is by identifying the *OpLog* system of the enemy as a center of gravity and thus a prime target. In this case, *counter-logistic* actions become the main thrust of the operational plan.

4.1 The Goal of *OpLog* Planning

OpLog planning is a complex multidisciplinary process that comprises qualitative "artistic" aspects as well as quantitative "scientific" ones. The qualitative aspects are based on principles of war and the theory of operational art, represented by the

© Springer International Publishing Switzerland 2016
M. Kress, *Operational Logistics*, Management for Professionals,
DOI 10.1007/978-3-319-22674-3_4

OpLog's cognitive and structural properties introduced in Chap. 3. Although an attempt is made later on in the book to visualize the structural properties (in Chap. 9), and even to quantify one of them (*flexibility*, in Chap. 10), these properties are essentially qualitative.

The quantitative aspects of *OpLog* planning are forecasting demand, resource allocation, routing, scheduling, and inventory control.

4.1.1 *The Two Gaps*

The main goal of *OpLog* planning is to obtain logistic responsiveness. This goal may be formalized as a two-dimensional optimization problem where the objective is to minimize two gaps: the *quantity gap* and the *time gap*. The quantity gap is created between the *true demand* generated by a certain military unit (e.g., a brigade) for a certain resource, and the *actual allocation* of that resource to that unit. One obvious cause for this gap is shortage in resources at the strategic level. Another reason is the combined effect of long lead-times of shipments and large variances in demand. Since it takes time to fulfill a request for resupply, supplies may be sent out before the actual demand is known. Because the demand may be subject to high variance, the supply sent may not be adequate. The two factors – demand uncertainty and lead-time – could cause severe discrepancies in the demand–supply matches, and therefore hinder precise allocation of resources.

The time gap is the difference between the time when a resource is needed and ready to be received by the combat unit, and the time when it is actually delivered. The time gap is created by operational constraints and the effect of, what Von Clausewitz calls, [1] the *friction* of war. The results of this friction are bad scheduling of logistic flow and unexpected breaks in the logistic support chain.

Example 4.1
Based on the fuel consumption so far and on the operational plans for the next 48 h, the logistician of the first Division sends out to the Corps Supply Center a request for 100,000 L of fuel at 17:00. A convoy of five bowsers, each loaded with 20,000 L of fuel, is ready to leave the Corps Supply Center at 08:00 the next day. It is scheduled to arrive at the first Division Supply Center at 18:00 that day. However, the operational plans for the division have changed and it is ordered, to move 50 km to the north. As a result, the fuel consumption is twice than expected and the updated demand is now 150,000 L. Also, the supply convoy has to change its route and as a result arrives at the division area 6 h later – at midnight. The *quantity gap* here is 50,000 L of fuel, and the *time gap* is 6 h.

The two gaps are not independent. Large quantity gaps tend to occur when large time gaps happen, and small quantity gaps are usually results of small time gaps. Thus, reducing the time gap may also decrease the quantity gap.

4.1.2 Interrelation Between the Two Gaps

To demonstrate the interrelation between the two gaps, consider the following hypothetical example of logistic flow management.

Example 4.2
Tactical maintenance units are deployed in a forward position in the theater of operations to provide immediate maintenance support for combat units in their respective zones. The maintenance units are connected, through efficient and reliable communication channels, to a central depot that stores repair-parts and equipment that may be needed by a maintenance unit. Moreover, numerous squadrons of transport helicopters are standing by at the depot to respond to any request for parts or equipment. The flying time between the depot and the front is negligible compared with typical activity times of these maintenance units. Thus, besides determining the inventory mix and capacity at the depot, there is no need for any logistic planning. When there is demand for a certain repair-part, a request is sent out to the depot where it is immediately processed and delivered. In this utopian situation the time gap is practically eliminated. Furthermore, because there is no need to consider demands in advance, there is also no quantity gap.

Obviously, the situation described above is unreal. In reality the communication times are not negligible, the reliability of communication channels is not perfect, the processing time at the depot is not negligible, and helicopters are usually committed to other missions. Thus, the supply process has to be initiated before the resource is actually consumed or built-in delays in the supply chain must be accounted for. The ultimate goal in logistic planning is to reduce these two gaps.

4.2 Planning at the Strategic and Tactical Levels

Planning at each one of the three levels of logistics – strategic, operational, and tactical – comprises several processes grouped into three main areas:

- *Structuring*: built-up and deployment of logistic assets and infrastructure.
- *Allocation*: distribution of supplies, equipment, and services.
- *Moving*: mobilizing and transporting military and logistic assets.

All three planning areas rely on estimating requirements for supplies, services, and equipment. The scope of each area depends on the level of logistics.

4.2.1   Planning at the Strategic Level

Logistic planning at the strategic level is mainly concerned with infrastructure needed for (1) building-up and maintaining the military force in peacetime, (2) deploying it during wartime, and (3) employing it in the theater of operations during a campaign. Therefore, the focus at the strategic level is on the first planning area: *structuring* the logistic system at the national level.

Planning the logistic infrastructure is a large-scale effort that includes a wide spectrum of logistic resources and capabilities. Because of their scale, the issues considered at that level have long-range economic and operational implications. Major considerations are efficiency, tradeoff relations, and national priorities. These considerations are affected by operational needs and estimated logistic requirements derived from threats and potential conflict scenarios.

The strategic logistic planning is concerned with:

- Technology
- Industry
- Inventory
- Facilities
- Transportation
- Medical services
- C4I (Command, Control, Communication, Computers, and Intelligence)

Technology

Building-up advanced technological capabilities and maintaining them at the cutting edge require large investments in facilities, equipment, and most of all – qualified personnel. The technological infrastructure of a nation includes universities, research institutes, labs, and high-tech corporations. This infrastructure facilitates the development of advanced weapons and their proper maintenance. Defense technology is usually unique. In many cases it is specially developed for the sole purpose of enhancing certain operational capabilities of the military force. Hence, defense technology is typically considered as classified national asset.

Throughout history there have been instances where defense technologies were modified for commercial uses. However in recent years there are opposite examples too, where military technologies are derived from off-the-shelf commercial technologies like software engineering.

Plans for developing defense and defense-related technologies are made at the national level in agencies such as the Office of Naval Research (ONR) and the Defense Advanced Research Projects Agency (DARPA) in the US.

Industry

The defense-oriented industry is divided into two groups: defense industry and commercial industry that provides supplies and services to the defense establishment. The first group comprises manufacturers and services providers that operate solely for military clients. Industries of this type apply technologies developed by the scientific and technological establishments and therefore are usually closely connected to R&D centers, and engineering labs. The size, structure, and mode of operation of this type of industries are affected (in some cases even dictated) by strategic decisions made at the national defense establishment.

The second group comprises commercial companies that dedicate a major part of their production lines or operations to defense-related products or services. For example, small-arms ammunitions (e.g., 9 mm bullets) are mainly supplied to the military but are also sold commercially. Food suppliers are another example. While the commercial nondefense-oriented part of these companies' operation provides some economic basis for their independent business existence, the government may affect their wherewithal by incorporating economic and social considerations in contracting their services.

> **Example 4.3**
> The government may contract a local supplier to provide products or services, even if it is not the most cost-effective option, to support the local economy or to sustain national production or service capabilities in case the alternative is to rely on a foreign provider that may not be available in times of need.

Inventory and Facilities

The national inventory of logistic resources includes stockpiles of ammunition, fuel, repair-parts, medical supplies, and other military supplies. A careful planning of the size and mix of these inventories must reflect projected requirements derived from potential threats and wartime scenarios. The size and mix of inventory bundles determine the type, intensity, and length of military operations that can be adequately sustained. There are essentially two dilemmas that govern the planning process of national stockpiles. One dilemma is *how much is enough*? The other dilemma is *stock or produce?*

Resolving the first dilemma must take into account factors such as potential threats, doctrine, acceptable risk levels, and budget. The cost of error may be high and therefore large safety margins are usually taken by the government. The second dilemma is a tradeoff between investments in military-related industries and inventories.

National logistic facilities (e.g., depots, arsenals, warehouses) are needed for keeping and maintaining the inventories in an adequate condition. Plans for constructions of such facilities include their designations, designs, capacities, and locations.

Example 4.4
An adequate production capacity for producing artillery projectiles in a relatively short notice can facilitate a reduction in the inventory of these munitions. Such an inventory may require routine maintenance, and may be subject to limited shelf life. Economic and operational (e.g., feasible production rates) considerations determine the balance between "stock" and "produce."

Transportation

One of the most critical logistic capabilities is to move forces and resources to and within the theater of operations. The whole rationale of *OpLog* is manifested in a stream of resources that flow through the logistic network (see Sect. 2.4). Thus, transportation is a crucial part in logistic planning. Large-scale transportation planning is crucial in power-projection scenarios where effective overseas mobility is essential for conducting campaigns. Transportation planning comprises static infrastructure – roads, railways, ports, airstrips – and dynamic entities – vehicles, ships, and aircraft.

The static components of a transportation infrastructure are mostly "civilian"; they are used routinely during peacetime, not necessarily only for military purposes. All roads and railways are utilized for daily transportation and, except for relatively few military installations, most seaports and airports are serving regularly civilian passengers and commercial cargo. However, when designing these entities, military-strategic aspects are taken into consideration too.

Example 4.5
Many military air bases share the runways and other facilities with adjacent major civilian airports. The design of such airports must take into account the special needs of the neighboring military installations.

Unlike the static components, the dynamic components are predominantly military. There are specially designated military cargo planes, supply ships, trucks, transporters, and containers. While the logistic fleet may be augmented in wartime by civilian means of transportation, the core of this dynamic part of the transportation system is clearly painted in military colors.

Medical Services

The medical care at time of war is a government responsibility. Medical services are designated both for combat forces at the front and civilian casualties at the rear. While the emergency medical-care system may have special military components that only operate at time of war, it generally relies on the existing national health-care system. Planning the infrastructure of hospitals and other medical facilities – their location and medical capabilities – must take into account also military needs at times of emergency.

> **Example 4.6**
> In a forward-deployment posture, planning the location of hospitals and their capacities takes into account, in addition to demographic data, military factors such as proximity to potential theaters of operations, vulnerability of the area to hostile actions, and estimated number of casualties.

C^4I

The advent of communication, computation capabilities, and computer networking in the past few decades has affected the way logistics is managed and controlled. Logistics is abundant with quantitative data that must be gathered, processed, analyzed, and distributed. Automated computation, communication, command, and control systems are appropriate in particular for these tasks. The design and development of such systems, which are typically done at the strategic level, are challenging and involves a thorough analysis of data factors such as relevance, accuracy, speed, and capacity. Crucially, the logistic and operational C^4I systems must be coordinated and compatible with each other. Doctrine and available communication and information technologies determine the design of logistic C^4I systems.

Other Planning Tasks at the Strategic Level

Manpower Planning. Operating a logistic system requires skilled and well-trained personnel. They constitute the "human capital" of the logistic system at all levels. Recruiting, training, and retaining military logistics specialists are important tasks that are handled at the strategic level.

Logistic Doctrine. Managing and controlling the logistic mammoth require clear and coherent rules and procedures that appear in doctrinal publications such as field manuals. Because of the broad spectrum of logistic doctrinal issues, their wide-range operational implications, and the need for uniformity across military units, doctrine for all logistic levels is developed at the top military hierarchy – the strategic level [2]. Matching doctrinal concepts and operational procedures with available C^4I capabilities is one of the most challenging issues in developing a logistic doctrine.

Structure of the OpLog System. Although deploying and employing the *OpLog* system in the theater of operations is clearly an operational-level issue, its overall planning is done at the strategic level for two reasons. First, except for special cases, the fundamental organizational structure of the deployed logistic units is uniform across similar combat units and scenarios. This uniformity is desired because it facilitates a modular structure that can effectively respond to the uncertainty associated with future scenarios. Determining the command level (e.g., battalion, brigade) to which a tactical logistic unit is attached as direct support is an example of such a fundamental decision issue. Planning the organizational structure of the *OpLog* network must take into account the possibility of several potential conflict scenarios, and this can only be done at the strategic level that has the required broad view.

Second, the design of the *OpLog* system has significant operational and economic implications on the force structure as a whole. A force built for power-projection scenarios will have different logistic design than a force built for forward-deployment scenarios. Tradeoffs among alternative *OpLog* structures have large-scale and force-wide implications and therefore they are considered at the highest military level.

Example 4.7
There are two basic options for designing the combat service support (CSS) at the tactical (combat) level:

1. Attaching a CSS battalion to each brigade.
2. Attaching a CSS company to each battalion.

   The choice between these two generic options may affect the tactical C^{4}I requirements on the one hand, and may have significant effect on the cost of building up the force, on the other hand.

Seamless Logistics

Advances in transportation capabilities, materiel handling methods, and command and control systems, together with logistic insights from recent campaigns and major operations, have resulted in the concept of *seamless logistics* [3]. There are two types of logistic "seams": *longitudinal* and *lateral*.

Longitudinal seams are formed when the logistic systems at the three levels – strategic, operational, and tactical – are physically and managerially separated. The seams are essentially brokers that transfer logistic resources from one level to the next.

Example 4.8
Ports of debarkation are seams between the logistic flow in the strategic medium and its split to sub-flows in the operational medium. These seams are demonstrated in actions such as unloading, storing, distributing, and reloading of resources at these ports.

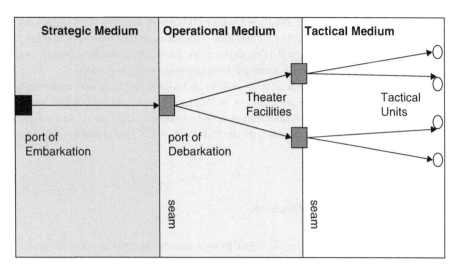

Fig. 4.1 Longitudinal seams

Figure 4.1 depicts longitudinal seams.

By minimizing the number of seams and their rigidity, the logistic support chain may become more flexible and more efficient. However, because lead-times and limited transportation capacities are still significant factors to reckon in operating the logistic support chain, seams – in the shape of inter-level buffers – are inevitable.

Lateral seams separate logistic "stove-pipes," which may be branches of the force or (more likely) the various types of logistic resources. Ammunition, fuel, maintenance, and medical services usually generate separate logistic support chains that result in operational and economic inefficiencies revealed in wasteful utilization of resources such as means of transportation. Some seams are inherent; they are consequences of the different processes and activities typical to a certain resource. For example maintenance resources cannot provide medical services. However, better and more versatile means of transportation, advanced C⁴I systems, and most of all – a cognitive leap by logisticians who must think "combined logistics," may enable partial ripping of these seams. Fewer and weaker seams mean a more integrative and efficient *OpLog* system that can benefit from economies of scale.

4.2.2   Planning at the Tactical Level

Planning logistics at the tactical level is relatively simple because it is relatively short-term and focuses on limited combat areas. Tactical logistic planning is concerned with immediate and short-range needs of the combat units directly derived from the combat missions. The myopic nature of tactical logistics means that planning is technical and prescriptive – it is more an accounting process than an elaborate resource allocation decision problem. Using an analogy from the restaurant business, plans at the strategic level deal with the design of the kitchen, pantry, and dining hall, the operational plan determines the monthly work schedule and menu, and the tactical level is concerned with planning today's dinner.

Logistic planning at the tactical level also includes scheduling and controlling movements within the tactical zone. In particular, the tactical logistician has to determine the deployment of his combat service support (CSS) units, and coordinate schedules and meeting points between subordinate CSS units and logistic convoys from higher echelons.

4.3 Logistic Responsiveness

The single most important requirement from a logistic system is *responsiveness*. Responsiveness is a complex and rather fuzzy concept that refers to all the logistic factors that generate combat power and retain the vitality and fitness of the military force over time. An *OpLog* system is responsive with respect to a certain scenario if it can provide the right mix of resources, at the right place and at the right time. The goal during the time before an operation and while it is in progress is to maximize responsiveness. Figure 4.2 depicts, schematically, the concept of responsiveness.

Each "box" in the three-dimensional graph in Fig. 4.2 depicts a bundle of resources that is available at a certain location and time. The box at the center – box 1 – indicates the actual demand, the place where it is required (for simplicity we assume a one-dimensional space) and the desired time of arrival. Boxes 2 and 3 depict the situation where the right bundle arrives at the right place but at the wrong

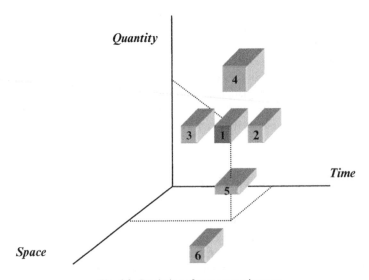

Fig. 4.2 Deviations from responsiveness

time. Boxes 4 and 5 represent punctual delivery but wrong quantity, and box 6 represents the situation where a logistic bundle went astray.

Thus, boxes 2–6 represent different types of *unresponsiveness*. The impact of these deviations from the goal at box 1 is not uniform across the three dimensions. Arguably, getting too much supplies, but at the right place and time (box 4), is much less serious than not getting it at all (box 6).

4.3.1   Logistically Feasible Region

The uncertainty in the theater of operations and the prevailing friction in the battle-field affect the extent at which responsiveness can be attained. There will always be delays, misunderstandings, and blunders that will cause deviations from the desired (*bundle, place, time*) triplet. Therefore, it is unrealistic to expect that responsiveness can be fully attained. A more realistic representation of the responsiveness goal is a (three-dimensional) region around the optimal reference point (Box 1). This logistically feasible region represents the acceptable deviation from the optimal reference point. The size of this region on a certain dimension reflects the in-context criticality of that dimension – quantity, location, or time. The boundaries of this region correspond to scenario-dependent acceptable ranges of deviations from the responsiveness goal.

Example 4.9
Typical scales for the three dimensions of logistically feasible regions are shown below for two types of logistic nodes:

	Port of debarkation	Battalion CSS unit
Quantity	Hundreds of Tons	Few Tons
Location	0 km[a]	3 km[b]
Time	Few Days[c]	Few Hours[d]

[a]A ship cannot dock and get unloaded outside the port.
[b]This is a typical average diameter of a battalion footprint.
[c]A delay of a few days in the arrival of a certain ship may have an operationally tolerable impact on the campaign.
[d]The typical time scale of tactical battles is hours.

Clearly, the "cost of failure" is not uniform across the three dimensions. Deviations on the *quantity* and *time* dimensions are more tolerable than deviations with respect to *space*. A partial quantity that arrives at its accurate destination late is preferred to a shipment that reached the wrong destination on time.

4.3.2   Over-Responsiveness

Box 4 in Fig. 4.2 represents a situation where too much supply reached the right destination on time. This deviation may seem at first look negligible (or even desirable) since the logistic requirement has been satisfied to the full. But, contrary to many situations in life, "more" here does not necessarily imply "better." Unlike a traditional assumption in economics, there is no "free disposal" in the battlefield. When there is a surplus of logistic resources in a certain zone of the battlefield, consumers of these resources may experience difficulties to absorb it. As a result, convoys may be stranded while waiting to be unloaded, a situation that may lead to blocking in the logistic network. Moreover, when resources are limited, logistic redundancy in one part of the theater may mean shortage in another part.

Over-responsiveness also occurs when resources arrive at their destination earlier than required (Box 3 in Fig. 4.2). In such cases, convoys may have to wait until the consumers of these resources – the combat units – are ready to receive the shipment. Similarly to the case of over-supplying, early arrival may cause disruptions in the operation of the logistic support chain since means of transportation, which may be needed elsewhere, are needlessly stuck.

Over-responsiveness in power-projection situations is particularly onerous because, on top of the huge effort that is invested in shipping the redundant resources to the theater of operations, excess supplies must be backhauled from the theater of operation at the end of the campaign at extra operational and economic cost.

Example 4.10
The Gulf War provided a good example for the consequences of over-responsiveness. The decision to stock 60 days of supplies in the theater of war resulted in the need to ship back over 90 % of the supplies at the end of the war [4].

4.3.3   Under-Responsiveness

The more serious indication of unresponsiveness is under-responsiveness, which occurs when the logistic response is either too little (Box 5 in Fig. 4.2) or too late (Box 2). The accumulated shortfalls generate a gap between the available and the required logistic resources, a gap that increases over time if under-responsiveness persists, up to the point where combat operations cannot be executed as planned. The point in time at which this gap is created is the logistic *culmination point* (or *break point*) of the campaign. From that point on, the effectiveness of combat operations decreases. Figure 4.3 presents graphically the effect of under-responsiveness. The *resources* curve represents the availability of resources in the theater of operations. The *demand* curve indicates the requirements for these resources as they evolve over time. The intersection between these two curves marks the logistic *culmination point*, which indicates the point in time when the gap between supply and demand is created.

The logistic gap is an outcome of three possible phenomena:

- The force accumulation rate in the theater of operations is greater than the rate at which logistic resources are accumulated.
- The boundaries of the theater of operations expand faster than the logistically feasible boundaries (see *Envelop of Operational Effectiveness* in Chap. 3).
- The consumption rate by the combat forces exceeds the throughput of the logistic network.

Notice that the gap is proportional to the *area* between the curves and, therefore, it increases over time at a rate higher than linear. To demonstrate these concepts, consider the following example.

Example 4.11
The fire-plan of an artillery brigade is specified in terms of expected daily expenditure of ammunition. The expected demand on day t, denoted as $d(t)$, forms the *demand curve* of the graph in Fig. 4.3. Let $D(t)$ denote the total accumulated demand by day t.

$$D(t) = \sum_{s=1}^{t} d(s).$$

$D(t)$ is the sum of the expected number of fired shells from the beginning of the operation up until day t. Denote by X the initial supply of ammunition, which is carried with the brigade at the beginning of the operation, and let $Y(t)$ be the cumulative amount of ammunition that has been pushed to the brigade from higher echelons till time t. The amount of ammunition attainable to the brigade at day t is

$$Z(t) = X + Y(t) - D(t-1).$$

The $Z(t)$ values (for each time period t) form the *resources curve* in Fig. 4.3. Suppose now that following an analysis it is concluded that $Z(t)$ becomes smaller than $d(t)$ for the first time when $t=3$. This means that on the third day the demand for ammunition, according to the fire plan, exceeds for the first time the expected available supply. It follows that the two curves – the demand curve and the resources curve – intersect on the third day, which marks the logistic *culmination point*. Consequently, the *Envelop of Operational Effectiveness* spans only 2 days.

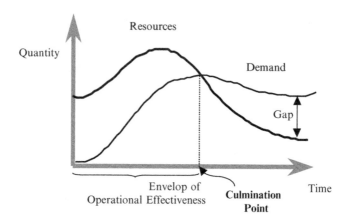

Fig. 4.3 The logistic gap

4.3.4   *Operational Culmination Point*

While the logistic culmination point is well defined in terms of resources and demand curves (see Fig. 4.3), the operational culmination point is a more elusive concept. It is more of a conceptual parameter than a well-determined point in time. The operational culmination point is best explained by using the physical concept *momentum*.

The *operational momentum* of a combat force (see also *logistic momentum* in Sect. 3.6.2, Chap. 3) is the "product" mv of its mass m (size and mix of the force) and its combat intensity v (maneuver and firepower). The operational culmination point of this mass can be viewed as the point in time at which "acceleration" in combat intensity turns into "deceleration." The logistic gap, which creates the logistic culmination point, combined with combat attrition (both physical and mental) degrades the strength of the combat force and its vigor, and thus creates the *operational culmination point*. The (nonlinear) rate at which the logistic gap increases beyond the logistic culmination point affects the time until the operational momentum is halted altogether, that is, when $v=0$.

The main objective of an *OpLog* system is to help combat forces to avoid reaching the logistic culmination point, or at least to postpone it as long as possible. This will also help to avoid or delay the operational culmination point. One way to attain this objective is by skillfully phasing the campaign and scheduling *operational pauses* for replenishment, refit, and retrograde. Despite the temptation to exploit success and charge forward with the operation, it is sometimes necessary to deliberately pause in order to synchronize the operational clock with the logistic clock or equivalently, to align the demand curve with the resource curve (see Fig. 4.3).

4.4   Logistic Planning in an Operation

A key to a successful operation is an effective and well-balanced combination of operational and logistic planning.

Logistic planning comprises two stages that partially overlap. The first stage is general and macroscopic; it gives a logistics-oriented view of the operational plan as a whole. It is the logistic angle of the commander's "estimate of the situation." At the second stage, a detailed and technical plan of the logistic support is sketched based on the insights gained from the first stage. Admiral Eccles [5] labeled the first stage *logistic planning* and the second stage *planning for logistic support*. We how-ever adopt here different names that, we believe, capture more accurately the essence of each stage. The first stage is called *macro-logistic planning,* and the second stage – *micro-logistic planning*.

4.4.1   Macro-Logistic Planning

The *operational concept* and the *estimate of the situation* characterize the percep-tion of the combat situation by the commander and his staff. These terms represent the operational objectives and their interpretations in terms of time, space, forces, and combat intensity. The operational concept also embodies a logistic concept, and the estimate of the situation includes a macroscopic view of the logistic require-ments. Thus, macro-logistics considerations play a major role during the early stages of operational planning; they shape and formulate the initial operational plan.

Example 4.12
The operational mission is to restore order and capture terrorists among hos-tile population. The theater of operations is a large desert area. The general operational idea is to sparsely deploy small elite infantry units over a large area. From the macro-logistics point of view it is estimated that the critical resources will be small-arms ammunition, water, food, and medical support. The large spread of the deployed combat units affects the parameters of the desired *OpLog* system. In particular, the distribution of water and medical services from theater facilities to the combat units is identified as a critical link in the logistic support chain.

Interrelations Between Operations and Logistics

Planning of military operations is a complex process in which operational objec-tives are analyzed with respect to factors such as the adversary's force and its deployment, size, and composition of friendly forces, terrain, and the environment. Some aspects of this analysis are tangible, such as firepower, rate-of-advance, and consumption rates, while other are abstract concepts such as *center of gravity* and *culmination point*. The first outcome of this analysis is a set of *operational concepts* (*ideas*).

The logistic part within the operational planning process has two roles – a *screener* and a *provider*. As a screener, the operational logistician has to identify, during the initial planning stages, operational concepts that are evidently unsupportable logistically. The logistician has to run the gamut of ideas that are generated by the commander and his staff through the logistic filter, to discard infeasible ideas and to point out the logistic ramifications of the other ideas.

Example 4.13
- The operational feasibility of large maneuvers is affected by the supply of fuel and the available maintenance resources.
- Intensive fire engagements are constrained by the supply of ammunition.
- Power-projection operations depend on sealift and airlift capacities.
- Combat operations in heavily populated urban area may require extensive deployment of medical resources.

The result of the screening process is a set of initial operational plans that *are not evidently infeasible* from the logistic point of view. Some of these plans may turn out, however, to be logistically infeasible later on during the more detailed micro-logistic planning phase.

As a provider, the logistician translates the objectives and the set of operational concepts not evidently infeasible into an initial *logistic design*. This design applies to the logistic deployment in the theater of operations and the principles of its employment during combat.

Macro-logistic planning is characterized by close interrelationship between the operational planner and the logistician. On the one hand the logistician reviews the commander's ideas and evaluates their initial logistic feasibility. On the other hand, he has to generate an initial logistic design that is potentially responsive to the requirements implied from the operational concepts. Once such a logistic design is generated, a tentative *operational design* emerges from the set of *operational concepts*. This interrelationship is manifested by a continuous dialogue between the commander and his logistician. Figure 4.4 presents graphically this process as a cyclic sequence of iterated ideas and evaluations.

In the first iteration (step 1 in Fig. 4.4) the operational planner specifies an initial *operational concept*. This concept is then given a crude and preliminary evaluation by the logistician for logistic feasibility (step 2). Through several cycles of synthesis and analysis (steps 1–4) the process finally converges into a *potentially* sustainable *operational concept* that becomes a tentative *operational design* (step 5). The driver for this iterative process, its focus and its final objective, is the abstract term *operational design*. This term is discussed and given a visual interpretation in the next subsection.

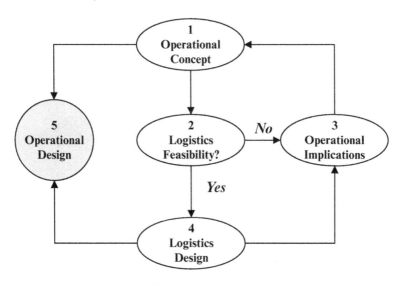

Fig. 4.4 Macro-logistic planning cycle

Operational Design

A simple, albeit abstract, way to visually interpret the term *operational design* is by a series of three-dimensional plots. Each plot, as shown in Fig. 4.5, represents a certain facet of the operation such as fire or maneuver. The three dimensions of the plot are *time* (X), *distance* from the initial FLOT (Y)[1] and *intensity* (Z). The interpretation of the Z-dimension depends on the specific facet under consideration. For example, for the fire facet the Z-value represents the projected fire intensity at time X and distance Y. For the maneuver facet, Z corresponds to the total number of, say, armored vehicles that reach distance Y at time X.

Peaks in the plot (e.g., point A in Fig. 4.5) represent times and places in which high-intensity activities (e.g., fire or movement) are expected. Low areas (e.g., point B) indicate low intensity. The edges of the plot on the XY plane correspond to the boundaries of the operations with respect to time (X) and distance (Y). The slopes represent transitions from high (low)-intensity regions to low (high)-intensity ones. Each such plot in the series implies a certain distribution of logistic requirements over time and space.

One of the main factors that affect the ability to maintain the desired shape of the operational design is logistics. Metaphorically speaking, and notwithstanding other factors such as adversary's actions and the environment, the operational design

---

[1] A more realistic variable for the Y-axis is *location,* which is obviously two-dimensional. However, such a representation leads to a four-dimensional model. To facilitate a simple visual model we use the one-dimensional variable *distance* as a proxy for *location.*

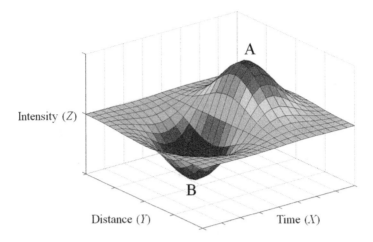

Fig. 4.5 3-D interpretation of an operational design

surface is kept in its shape by air pressure that is generated by logistics. Low air pressure (under-responsiveness) will result in the collapse of the surface. A pressure that is too high (over-responsiveness) may alter the shape of the surface to an undesirable shape (e.g., when logistic flow hinders operational movement on limited-capacity routes). The logistic support flow must be regulated according to the peaks and pits of the surface.

The source node of the logistic network is the compressor that generates the air pressure. The intermediate and destination nodes are the valves that regulate the air pressure according to the desired shape of the surface. However, unlike the crisp metaphor of the physical air-pressure system, combat operations are fuzzy and uncertain. Therefore, safety margins must be added to the nominal flow to avoid possible incidences of under-pressure. Consequently, the operational design surface must be also flexible enough to absorb the extra flow that is pre-positioned, as buffers, in the theater of operations.

The Thrust of Macro-Logistic planning

Macro-logistic planning has very little to do with quantities, allocations or specific timetables. It is essentially qualitative, nontechnical and somewhat abstract. Its main purpose is to gain insights about *OpLog* possible impacts and to produce initial operational and logistic designs. The logistic design includes a conceptual layout of resources in the theater of operations and principles for their employment.

For example, if the operational design calls for fast advances in open areas with little expected resistance from the enemy, then the logistic design must manifest a stable, high-capacity logistic flow over relatively long lines of communication. In this case, the focus of the operations-logistics dialogue is the balance between desired rate of advance and feasible throughput of the logistic network. If, on the other hand, the main operational issue is vertical envelopment, then the logistic design is concerned with airlift capabilities and the continuity of the logistic support chain.

4.4.2 Micro-Logistic Planning

The logistic design produced at the macro-logistic planning stage constitutes a framework for a detailed analysis at the micro-logistics stage. Specific issues such as forecasting attrition and consumption rates, allocations of resources, lead (order-and-ship) times, location of units and facilities, and selection of lines of communication are looked at closely in order to verify and validate the existing logistic design and to implement it in a concrete plan. This stage adds another loop to the planning process depicted in Fig. 4.4. The complete Macro/Micro-Logistic planning process is shown in Fig. 4.6 as two interconnected stages that eventually converge into two coordinated plans – an operational plan and a logistic plan.

The micro-logistic planning stage commences as soon as an initial logistic design is generated at the macro-logistics stage. The robustness of the design (step 4) is examined through a detailed analysis of all logistic factors (step 6). Once a robust logistic design is obtained, it is declared as a *logistic plan* (step 7). Consequently, this plan facilitates the convergence of the operational design into an *operational plan* (step 8).

It should be noted that although the two stages – macro- and micro- logistic planning – appear to be executed sequentially, it is not necessarily the case. The logistician is the pivot around whom the two planning cycles are executed almost concurrently. On the one hand the logistician actively participates in the operational design process within the macro-logistic planning phase, and on the other hand he coordinates the technical-computational effort of micro-logistic planning performed by the logistic staff.

Inputs

Micro-logistic planning is technical and mostly quantitative. The inputs for this process are logistic demands, attrition, lead-times, capacities, and probabilities of principal events. The operational design obtained at the macro-logistics phase is the basis from which time-dependent demand rates for logistic resources, and their spatial distribution across the theater of operations, are estimated. Conceptually, at the background of this planning process, there is a (*time x place*) "demand table" that indicates the required mix of resources at a certain time and place. Given such a table of demand entries, the main objective of the

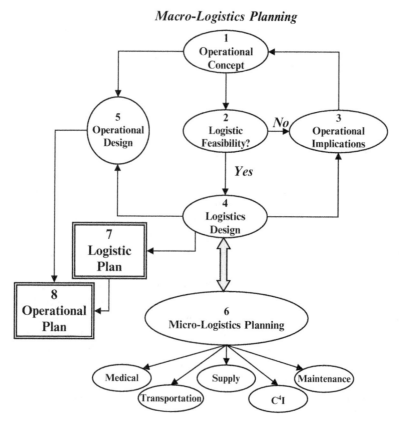

Fig. 4.6 Macro/micro-logistic planning cycle

micro-logistics process is to generate a logistic response that minimizes the deviations from the entries of that table.

Attaining this objective is hampered by the fact that such a deterministic table does not really exist in reality due to uncertain future events and situations. Specifically, consumption and attrition rates are not known in advance, and therefore the entries of the demand table cannot be determined with confidence beforehand. However, the estimated demand table is one of the main inputs for micro-logistic planning. Without it, the planning process is not anchored to any real context of the operation and the danger is that well-balanced and consistent forecasts are replaced by subjective estimates that may be skewed by personal views and biased experiences. Thus, an effort must be made to utilize systematic forecasting methods to produce as good as possible *estimates* for the entries of the demand table (see Chap. 6).

Other inputs, such as time and survivability parameters, also embody a considerable level of uncertainty that must be treated by appropriate probability and statistical methods.

Logistic Properties

Micro-logistic planning is essentially a translation of the estimated demand table, which is continuously updated during the operation, into logistic activities such as positioning logistic units, determining inventory levels, scheduling supplies, and selecting transportation routes. The actual effectiveness of such a translation can only be evaluated and judged after its execution, when the operation is over. While such a *posterior* evaluation may play an important role in *lesson-learned* analysis and *after-action-reviews*, it is practically useless for assessing the quality of a logistic plan *a-priori*. For this end, the operational logistician may need criteria for evaluating the various aspects of the emerging plan. These criteria are the structural and operational properties introduced in Chap. 3 (Sect. 3.6.2): *Flexibility, Attainability, Continuity, Tempo, Simplicity, Survivability,* and *Efficiency*.

The characteristics of the operational design, and its logistic derivatives, dictate the relative importance of the various properties.

Example 4.14
The commander estimates that the operational design is volatile and that the emerging situation is subject to a high level of uncertainty due to partial and unreliable intelligence. It follows that *flexibility* is a dominant property since plans may be subject to significant changes in a short notice. If the outlook is for a static and relatively stable scenario, where intensive firefights are expected, then *attainability* is important. If there is a considerable threat by the enemy on the communication zone, then *survivability* becomes a significant factor to consider.

Once the high-priority properties are determined, the logistic plan is evaluated with respect to them. For example, if *flexibility* is a high-priority property then the logistic plan should be designed such that it may give a *reasonable* (i.e., not necessarily complete) response to as many as possible contingencies, as opposed to *complete* response to fewer situations. This tradeoff is further discussed in Chap. 10.

Prioritization

An important task of the operational logistician is to *prioritize* among possible assignments of resources (see Sect. 3.5.5 in Chap. 3)). Historical experience indicates that during operations the probability for under-responsiveness is considerably higher than complete or over responsiveness. When resources are scarce, it is imperative to set priorities among the various consumers of logistics in the theater. While, arguably, prioritization is done during the operation – as the situation unfolds – the policy that directs it must be determined during the planning phase. In particular, decision rules for contingent resource allocations and prioritization must be specified well in advance, in the macro-logistic planning stage.

Example 4.15
- A combat unit that is tasked to maneuver will get high priority regarding fuel,
- If the mission of an infantry force is to attack a fortified area then it will get the highest medical attention.

The prioritization principles are guidelines for the logistic planners at the micro-logistics stage. At this stage the general planning principles are broken down to specific resource allocations that are examined with respect to the estimated demand table. Possible inconsistencies in the specified priorities should be detected at this stage.

4.4.3 An Animated Example

The implementation of the two planning stages – macro and micro – is demonstrated in the following simple animated example of an imaginary scenario.

Example 4.16
Background: According to the operational objectives, the adversary's posture, and the conditions in the theater of operations, the operational concept is a wide and deep flanking maneuver.

Macro-logistics Cycle: The commander, who is in the midst of planning the maneuver operation, consults with his logistician about the plan's logistic implications.

Commander: The operational concept is a deep flanking maneuver in the desert, by three corps, to a distance of 200 km. We expect little to medium resistance from the enemy.

Logistician: To facilitate this operational maneuver, we need a logistic base for each one of the three corps. Each such base must be stocked with 1 M liters of fuel, 0.5 M liters of water 30,000 tank rounds, 80,000 artillery shells, three maintenance units and five medical units. Currently there are only two such bases in the theater – one for first Corps and the other for second Corps. The third base – for 3rd Corps – is still being built up. It is expected to be operational in 5 days.

Commander: (deliberating between two options: (1) immediately employing only two corps in the flanking maneuver, and (2) delaying the three-corps operation, as originally planned, by 5 days. Obviously, other operational considerations heavily affect this decision). **Decision:** *Option (1), immediate employment of first and second Corps.*

Logistician: In principle, this maneuver operation is logistically feasible.

Operational Design: Flanking maneuver by two corps.

Logistic design: Two theater rear area logistic bases, one for each corps. Corps and division transportation battalions that push/pull resources from the corps logistic bases to the division logistic units execute the logistic support chain. The chain operates in 2-day pulses (round trip).

Micro-logistics Cycle: A deeper and more detailed logistic analysis of the operational and the logistic designs is performed at the logistic center of the Command.

Logistic center (to Logistician): Following in-depth analysis of the terrain and time parameters associated with the maneuver operation (an analysis that is supported by a computerized decision support system) it seems that first Corps may need about 50 % more fuel than second Corps. While the fuel inventory at the logistic base of first Corps is adequate, there are insufficient fuel tankers to carry it forward towards the divisions. It is necessary to transfer 50 tankers from second Corps to first Corps. This operation is expected to take 7 h.

Logistician (to Commander): There is a problem concerning the availability of fuel tankers at first Corps. We need to transfer tankers from second Corps to first. As a result, we need to delay the departure time by 7 h or to execute the maneuver stepwise – second Corps may start its movement right away while first Corps will wait for 7 h until the tankers arrive.

Commander: The distance first Corps has to travel is considerably longer than that of second Corps. There is no point in letting second Corps move first. We shall wait for 7 h and start the operation only after the tankers arrive at the logistic base of first Corps.

4.5 Summary

Logistic planning at the operational level is an inseparable of operational planning. Its purpose is to logistically validate proposed operational moves and suggest ways to sustain and support them. The objective of logistic planning is to avoid a logistic gap between the demand for logistic resources and their supply, or at least control this gap. The gap results in *under-responsiveness*, which may create a culmination point. The goal is to reduce the probability of reaching that undesired culmination point. *Over-responsiveness*, a situation when supplies exceed demands, is also undesirable and should be controlled.

Logistic planning has two stages. At the first stage – *macro-logistic planning* – the attention is focused on the "big operational picture." The operational and logistic "colors" of this picture are observed, and the balance between the two sets of colors is considered. The objective at this stage is to reach a generally harmonious "composition" of operational and logistic colors and shades. This harmony is manifested in the operational and logistic designs.

At the second stage – *micro-logistic planning* – The different colors and shades are examined more carefully and local "disharmonies" are located and treated. At the end of these two stages, a complete, balanced, and harmonious picture is produced. The resulting picture is transferable to logistic and operational plans.

Because of the uncertain operational environment, there is little chance that an operational plan will be executed exactly as planned. Even the best plan is not sufficient to guarantee a successful operation. It is, however, a necessary condition for a successful execution. A carefully analyzed and robust plan may reduce unavoidable "disharmonies" to a minimum level, and thus enhance the probability of a successful operation.

References

1. Von Clausewitz C. On war. Princeton: Princeton University Press; 1976.
2. Joint Publication 4-0, *Joint Logistics,* 16 October 2013.
3. Williams N. The revolution in military logistics. Military Technol. 1997;21(11):50–7.
4. Foss JW. Challenge for operations research in the coming decade. Phalanx (Newsletter of the Military Operations Research Society), March 1994.
5. Eccles HE. Logistics in the national defense. Westport, CT: Greenwood Press; 1981.

Chapter 5
Information

Designing an *OpLog* system, implementing it, and adjusting it according to changing conditions in the theater of operations depend on updated, relevant, and reliable information. Logistic information is derived from quantitative and qualitative data that must be filtered, processed, and routed in accordance to the logistician's needs. The quantitative data include inventory levels, transportation capabilities such as the load capacity of a convoy, time parameters such as force accumulation time, service rates of maintenance and medical units, and consumption rates. Qualitative data regarding the identity, condition, and location of logistic assets is typically contained in situation reports.

Logistic information is required for creating a logistic picture of the battlefield, predicting readiness and sustainability, and evaluating alternative courses of action [1]. Specifically, this information is needed for:

- Proper allocation of resources among military units in the theater of operations.
- Determining the feasibility of certain operational moves.
- Controlling and operating the logistic support chain.

The ability to effectively respond to demands at the right place, on time, and with the right mix of resources relies on logistic and operational information. Logistic information concerns inventories at logistic nodes, in-transit supplies, availability and status of means of transportation, and capabilities of combat service support units. Operational information complements logistic information in the logistics decision-making process. Operational information concerns current and projected status of lines of communication and logistic units, the situation of friendly and enemy's forces, and data regarding the environment. The operational information is usually fuzzy, uncertain, incomplete, and noisy. These predicaments apply, albeit to a lesser extent, to the logistic information too.

© Springer International Publishing Switzerland 2016
M. Kress, *Operational Logistics*, Management for Professionals,
DOI 10.1007/978-3-319-22674-3_5

In this chapter we examine the role of information in planning and executing operational logistics. The issues we examine are:

- Information needs by the operational logistician.
- Structure of the logistic information network.
- Information flow.
- Standard vs. ad hoc information.
- Total vs. efficient information.
- Data, information, and decision-making.

5.1 Information Needs by the Operational Logistician

Logistic information is the primary input for logistic planning, execution, and command and control. This information is utilized for three main tasks of the operational logistician:

- **Advising** the commander about logistic aspects of the operation.
- **Planning** logistics in the theater of operations.
- **Managing** and **controlling** the force accumulation process at the beginning of an operation, and the logistic support chain during its execution.

5.1.1 Advising

The operational logistician needs two types of information to effectively advise the commander:

- *Logistic information* regarding existing and projected capabilities in the theater of operations.
- *Operational information* on current and future combat situations.

The logistic information is general, aggregated, and not necessarily quantitative. It relates to the deployment of logistic units in the theater of operations and the expected inflow of resources through the logistic support chain. This information is used primarily for preliminary assessment of operational concepts (see Sect. 4.4.1 in Chap. 4).

The operational information is imbedded in the *assessment of the situation*. It includes information regarding the deployment and condition of combat units, operational plans, and intelligence information. Combining the two types of information – logistic and operational – enables the logistician to systematically examine the feasibility of operational concepts and plans, and identify potential limitations or bottlenecks due to logistics. Observation and insights obtained by the logistician must be passed on to the commanding officer.

5.1.2 Planning

The second task of the operational logistician – planning – is more elaborate than the first. It is also more technical and detailed and thus it requires richer, more detailed, and updated information than the information needed for the advising task. This information applies to:

- Supply of logistic resources.
- Demand.

Logistic Supply

The availability of logistic resources is one of the main factors determining the *envelop of operational effectiveness* (See Sect. 3.3.2 in Chap. 3). Therefore, information regarding logistic availability is one of the main inputs for operational planning.

The information regarding logistic availability of resources is expressed by two sets of parameters:

- Logistic parameters.
- Operational parameters.

The *logistic parameters* apply to both supply and demand. On the one hand they measure inventory levels in supply units and service capabilities among maintenance and medical units, and on the other hand they provide information regarding inventory levels and medical and maintenance needs in combat units. The *operational parameters* describe the functionality of the logistic network, which is embodied in the operational status of the *logistic nodes* (e.g., the location of a certain supply battalion, the congestion in a port of debarkation) and the physical condition of the *edges* (i.e., traffic congestion, accessibility, navigability, and survivability of lines of communication). The logistic parameters describe the content of the *OpLog* system in the theater, while the operational parameters indicate its operational status.

Logistic Demand

While "supply-side" information – inventories and service capabilities – relates to both logistic and combat units, the "demand-side" information applies primarily to combat units – the *consumers* of the *OpLog* system. Current and future demands for logistic resources are derived from expected consumption and attrition (logistic parameters) as well as details regarding combat scenarios and future missions (operational parameters). Figure 5.1 summarizes the different facets of information for logistic planning.

	Logistics Units and LOCs	Combat Units
Logistic Parameters	- Inventory Levels - Service Capabilities	- *Inventory Levels* - *Expected Consumption*
Operational Parameters	- *Location of Log. Units* - Operational Status of Log. Units - Condition of LOCs	- Operational Situation - Missions

Fig. 5.1 Logistic information for planning

The shaded and clear areas in Fig. 5.1 correspond to supply and demand information, respectively.

Example 5.1

An armored division is ordered to move from its current position to a location 100 km away. The necessary information regarding this mission for the logistician at the corps headquarters includes:

- Operational plan (i.e., 300 tanks travel 100 km).
- Threats by the enemy and their potential effect on combat attrition.
- The terrain and its potential effect on technical attrition.
- Average fuel availability.
- Amount of fuel supply in divisional CSS units.
- Number and capabilities of divisional maintenance units.

5.1.3 Management and Control

The third task of the operational logistician is to manage and control logistic assets. The focus is on managing means of transportation and coordinating the distribution of the logistic flow that enters the theater from the communications zone.

The information required for this task is detailed account of the current status of means of transportation. Because time constraints during the execution of an operation are usually tighter than during the planning phase, this information must be timely – almost real-time. Specifically, the logistician must know the current location of means of transportation, their activities, and their condition. This information is crucial in particular when he needs to promptly respond to emerging contingencies that diverge from the existing plan.

Another type of managerial information concerns "outliers" – unexpected events that have severe and immediate impact on the logistic plan. Exceptionally high consumption or unexpected attrition of logistic (e.g., supply) units may necessitate quick improvised solutions. In such situations, timely information regarding these events is of utmost importance.

5.2 Logistic Information Network

Similarly to the term *logistic network* defined in Chap. 2, the *logistic information network* is a graphical representation of entities and their interrelations. The *nodes* of this network are information sources, relays and destinations, and the *edges* are information channels that connect the nodes. Notice that the terms *information network* and *(military) communication network* do not necessarily coincide. Information network is a virtual model that depicts possible transfer of information among individuals in the theater, while communication network is a physical construct that utilizes wired or wireless channels to facilitated communication among a set of users. A communication network is an information network but the reverse is not necessarily true. Certain nodes of an information network may not belong to the same communication network.

> **Example 5.2**
> The tactical operations center and the logistic center in a division headquarters belong to the same information network but they may not belong to the same communication network. Transfer of information between the two centers may be done by other means such as direct, face-to-face communication.

Information-node in a logistic information network may be an intersection of several (physical) networks such as wireless communication, telephone, satellite communication, and computer network.

5.2.1 Components of a Logistic Information Network

The logistic information network is one of the largest and most elaborate networks in the theater of operations. The nodes of this network represent various logistic and logistics-related functions. The information flow is rich and diversified. It includes logistic data (e.g., consumption data, inventory levels, resources in-transit) and operational data (e.g., location and state of logistic units, operational and physical conditions of lines of communication).

Each logistic information node is connected with other nodes through lateral and longitudinal channels. The lateral channels connect information-nodes within an echelon (e.g., between the commander of the combat service support regiment of a division and the logistician at the division headquarters), while the longitudinal channels connect nodes between echelons (e.g., between the brigade and the division logisticians). Thus, the information network is a hierarchical grid. It is composed of interconnected levels of information-nodes that correspond to the various echelons – battalion, brigade, etc.

The set of logistic information-nodes is divided into three groups, not necessarily disjoint, according to the general role that they take in the *OpLog* system:

- Managers.
- Operators.
- Customers.

Each group may contain more than one level (echelon).

Managers

Logistics *managers* are decision-makers. Their role is to design the *OpLog* system, to plan its deployment and to coordinate and control its employment. The *managers'* nodes usually represent command posts at high echelons in the theater of operations. The senior operational logistician in the theater heads this group of logistics decision-makers, which includes staff officers at the various areas of logistics responsibility – supply, maintenance, transportation, medical – and logisticians who coordinate and integrate those activities into a unified and coherent system.

Typically there are two main levels (echelons) of *managers* – *theater (wide) level* and *sectional level*. The theater level corresponds to the highest echelon (e.g., Command or Corps) in the theater of operations. The decision-makers at this level are in-charge of the entire operation. The sectional level corresponds to a lower echelon (e.g., Division) that is responsible for a certain section or zone in the theater.

The need for the two levels of *managers* is prevalent in particular when the theater of operations is wide and deep, and therefore separated into several zones. In such situations, planning, coordinating, and controlling the entire logistic flow by a single headquarters may become prohibitively difficult and therefore some responsibilities must be delegated to the sectional headquarters. The theater-level headquarter is usually the single interface between the strategic level and the *OpLog* system in the theater. The resulting single information channel enables more effective and efficient coordination than multiple channels that must exist if the sectional logistic headquarters are directly connected with the strategic level.

While the functions of the two levels are similar, the resolution of the information that they utilize is different. The information at the theater level node is more general and aggregate than the information that is needed at the sectional level, where logistic processes are watched more closely and in much more detail.

Operators

The *operators* are logistic units that implement the logistic plan. These units, such as transportation companies, maintenance battalions and field hospitals, supply materiel and provide services to the troops. The information-nodes that correspond

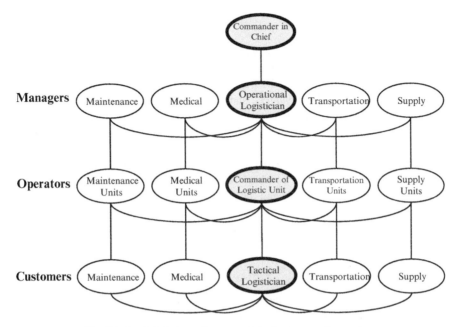

Fig. 5.2 Logistic information network in the theater of operations

to the *operators* are generally located in the network between *managers* and *customers* (see Fig. 5.2). The *operators* receive instructions and information regarding potential resources from *managers*, and provide *managers* with information about the logistic and operational situation in their units.

The group of *operators* may intersect with the group of *managers*. That is, a logistician at an operational headquarter (theater-level or sectional) may also be a commander of a logistic unit.

Example 5.3
The commander of the Corps Support Command (COSCOM) in the US Army is responsible to develop detailed plans, policies, and directives for combat service support units at the corps level. Hence, he is a *manager.* However, as a direct commander of logistic units, COSCOM headquarter is also an *operator.*

Note that the group of *operators* may also be divided among several echelons. For example, corps combat service support units and divisional logistic units may provide two levels of logistic support in the theater of operations.

Customers

The *customers* (or *consumers*) in an *OpLog* information network are the logisticians of the combat units. As suppliers of resources, these logisticians are responsible to provide the direct logistic support to the warfighters. As customers, they submit demands for logistic resources to the *managers*, and coordinate the delivery of these resources with the *operators* (e.g., scheduling time-tables and setting up meeting points).

The information nodes that correspond to the *customers* are located at the lower part of the logistic information network (see Fig. 5.2). The information gathered at these information nodes is of two types. On the one hand the *customers* obtain demand information from the combat units, and on the other hand they assimilate information from the *operators* and the *managers* on in-transit and future support. The *customers* transmit to the *managers* and *operators* information regarding demands for logistic support, their logistic situation (inventory, maintenance, etc.) and their operational situation (location, attrition, etc.).

> **Example 5.4**
> In the Israeli Army, the commander of a divisional logistic unit is an *operator*. He receives instructions and directions from the logistician (G4) at the division headquarters (*manager*) and coordinates supply and service activities with the brigade or battalion logistician (*customer*).

5.2.2   The Combined Network

The graph in Fig. 5.2 depicts the logistic information network. The vertical path shown in boldface lines in the center of the graph is the backbone of the logistic information network. It connects the principal *managers, operators,* and *customers.* The other vertical paths represent professional information links within each logistic class – supply, transportation, maintenance, and medical. The horizontal links represent information channels between each class of logistics and the logistic coordinator at that group. This type of information links play an important role in reducing the "stove-pipes" effect, where each logistic class operates independently and thus inefficiently. Stronger horizontal links are necessary to achieve seamless logistics.

> **Example 5.5**
> Typical information that passes through the (vertical) channels of the maintenance class includes:
>
> - Location of maintenance units.
> - Location and condition of damaged weapons and equipment.
> - Workloads and backlogs at maintenance units.
> - Requests for spare-parts, tools, and equipment.
> - Technical instructions and advice.

In addition to the information nodes shown in Fig. 5.2, there are additional peripheral nodes that are connected to the logistic information network. These nodes belong to the following information networks:

- Operations
- Personnel
- Military Police

Operations

Commanders and staff officers at each echelon must be aware of logistic events that may affect current or future operations. The information concerning these events, which is generated in the logistic information network, is passed on to the operations officer. Conversely, information concerning situation assessments is generated in the operations network and delivered to the logistician. Thus, at each echelon, there must be a direct information channel between a central node in the operations information network (e.g., the G3 in a US division) and the corresponding logistic information node (e.g., the G4).

Personnel

Although manpower planning and personnel are not considered logistic functions, there is a considerable volume of information – in particular medical and transportation – that must be shared between logisticians (G4) and personnel support officers (G1). The G1 must be updated about casualties, evacuation efforts, and in-transit reinforcement. It follows that there must be an information channel between the *medical* and *transportation* nodes of the logistic information network and appropriate nodes in the personnel information network.

Military Police

Military police (MP) is in charge of controlling the traffic in the communications zone and in the rear area of the theater of operations. The MP activities, which are directed by operational and logistic considerations, affect the velocity of the logistic support chain. Specifically, MP traffic-control officers implement transportation priorities and objectives set by transportation managers, while taking into consideration actual road-conditions and traffic constraints. The coordination between the two functions – transportation and traffic control – is through an information channel that connects *transportation* nodes in the logistic information network with the traffic-control information nodes in the military police network.

5.3 Information Flow

The logistic information that flows through the network during a military operation is rich and diverse. It includes data concerning inventory levels, consumption and attrition, transportation and transhipment, service capabilities, and more. Following the discussion in Sects. 5.1.2 and 5.1.3, this information is divided into two main classes:

- Logistic parameters.
- Operational parameters.

Recall that the logistic parameters indicate *what* and *how much* while operational parameters imply *where* and *when*.

5.3.1 Logistic Parameters

The set of logistic parameters is further divided into three groups:

- Potential resources.
- Actual resources.
- Demand.

Potential Resources

Potential resources are supplies and services that have been committed to the operation but have not yet arrived in the theater. They are in the pipeline between the strategic level and the theater of operations. These in-transit resources are either still positioned at the strategic level (e.g., stockpiles in the port of debarkation waiting for shipping) or are en route to the theater of operations. Upon arrival in the theater, the potential resources become *actual resources.*

The capacity of the strategic-theater pipeline is relatively high, and therefore the accumulated amount of potential resources inside this pipeline constitutes a significant portion of the logistic mass. Thus, information regarding potential resources is critical both for immediate decisions and for future planning. The two most important pieces of information regarding potential resources are their mix and the expected time when they will become *actual resources* in the theater of operations. Visibility of these resources is necessary for obtaining this desired information.

The trend of moving from *mass-oriented* logistics to *velocity-oriented* logistics also affects the characteristics of the required information. When large masses of supplies and elaborate service centers are replaced by rapid and accurate "just-in-time" deployment, the importance of information on potential resources becomes more critical. The term that has emerged in recent years in this context is *In-Transit Visibility* (ITV) [2]. ITV is an important ingredient in modern logistic information systems.

Actual Resources

The *actual resources* in the theater of operations are divided between the *operators* – logistic facilities and combat service support units – and the *customers* – the combat units. The resources carried by the combat units facilitate a certain level of logistic self-sufficiency (attainability). The logistic parameters associated with an *operator* describe the resources stored in or carried by that unit.

> **Examples 5.6**
> The logistic parameters of an ammunition supply unit indicate the number and mix of rounds that are carried by the unit.

> **Example 5.7**
> The logistic parameters of a medical company indicate the medical capabilities and treatment capacities of that unit. These parameters depend on the size and expertise of the medical staff, and on the equipment and medical supplies that are available.

The logistic parameters of a *customer* such as an infantry battalion describe the resources carried by the unit itself or are readily available.

> **Example 5.8**
> The logistic parameters of a tank battalion refer to resources of two types:
>
> 1. Supplies – ammunition, fuel, water, and food - carried inside each tank.
> 2. Supplies, medical capabilities and maintenance capabilities available at the attached combat service support company.

Demand

The demand parameters depend on operational factors such as type of battle, combat intensity, terrain, and environmental factors.

The main source for demand information is the *customers* who generate it due to attrition and consumption. This information may be delayed or distorted because of difficulties in collecting and transmitting it. These difficulties are typically a result of the "fog of war" and combat friction. The information distortions created by these battlefield phenomena are not symmetrical. Demands from combat units may be inflated by the "panic factor." Thus, in many situations demand rates must be *projected* by the *managers* and not relied entirely on *customers* input. Automated sensors that measure attrition and consumption, and transmit it directly to *operators* and *managers*, may reduce the time delays and distortions in the information.

5.3.2   Operational Parameters

The *operational parameters* in a logistic information network relate to the state of logistic units, transportation capabilities, and combat units.

Logistic Units

The operational parameters of a logistic unit record its functionality, operability, location, and level of readiness.

> **Example 5.9**
> A maintenance company is functional only when it is fully and properly deployed, and all its equipment is ready for use. While the logistic parameters of this maintenance unit may indicate high supportability (i.e., the unit is well equipped, well stocked with spare parts and staffed with skilled personnel), its operational parameters tell the logistician if this support is currently available in practice.

Transportation Capabilities

OpLog Management is about controlling the logistic flow to and in the theater of operations. This flow affects the course of an operation, and means of transportation are one of the main instruments logisticians use for controlling the logistic flow. The control is executed by the way trucks, transporters, tankers, trains, helicopters, and airplanes and ships are assigned, routed, and scheduled. Effective management of these assets depends on updated and accurate information regarding their operational status that includes current location of assets, their load, activity (e.g., parking, loading, moving), and mission (origin, destination, time of completion).

Effective employment of means of transportation depends also on the condition of the lines of communication. Thus, another set of operational parameters includes information on road physical conditions, traffic congestion, accessibility, navigability, and vulnerability to hostile activity. In particular, weather conditions and enemy's anti-air threats are important operational parameters for air transportation.

> **Example 5.10**
> A divisional convoy carrying artillery ammunition is about to leave the rear theater logistic base to a forward logistic unit in one of the divisional zones. There is only one main road that leads from the base to the forward unit. The enemy has bombed the main road during the last hour – damaging it severely. The convoy cannot travel on that road and therefore must be either rerouted (through back roads) or delayed. The presumably *actual* supply of artillery shells on-board the trucks are practically unavailable to the division.

A typical example when joint information regarding potential resources, combat readiness, and transportation capabilities is needed is during the force accumulation (mobility) phase.

> **Example 5.11**
> Information concerning the force accumulation process is critical in particular at the initial stages of an operation. While combat units are not considered *logistic resources* but rather *means of combat* (see Sect. 1.3.2 in Chap. 1), mobilization and force-accumulation are perceived as logistic operations. Therefore, the operational logistician must be updated about the identities of the force units in-transit, the readiness level of the units, their location in the pipeline and their expected arrival time.

Combat Units in the theater of Operations

The entire *OpLog* system is designated to satisfy the demand for *logistic resources* by the *customers* – the combat units. The logistic flow must reach these units at their most convenient time, and therefore the meeting points must be properly coordinated to minimize disruption to combat plans. For this end, the *managers* and *operators*, who control, regulate, and execute the logistic flow, should be aware of current and future activities in the combat zone. This information includes time-phased account of current and future missions of the supported friendly force, and intelligence information regarding possible threats.

The main role of the operational information regarding combat forces is for estimating attrition and consumption. These estimates constitute the basis for projecting demands, and subsequently composing adequate and robust logistic plans.

5.3.3   Managers, Operators, *and* Customers

Each one of the three groups of nodes in the logistic information network has distinct characteristics.

Managers' Nodes

The logistic *managers* are also planners and thus require information regarding all three types of logistic parameters: *potential resources, actual resources,* and *demand.* They also require information on operational parameters of logistic and combat units.

Information about *potential resources* is gathered from higher echelons. The theater logistician (at the Command or Corps levels) obtains this information from the strategic level, and the sectional logisticians (at the Corps or Division level) receive it from the theater logistician. Note that resources that are considered *actual* at the theater (e.g., supplies that have just left the port of debarkation en route to the corps logistic base) may still be considered *potential resources* by the sectional (e.g., divisional) logisticians.

Information regarding *actual resources* is obtained from other *managers* (e.g., theater logistician get it from sectional logisticians), from *customers*, and mostly from *operators*. *Demand* information is received from *customers*. The *operators* also provide information on *operational parameters* concerning the status of their respective logistic units.

Operators' Nodes

The information nodes of the *operators* are the main source of information on *actual resources*. The *operators*, who are in-charge of handling, storing, transporting, and supplying logistic resources, have the most updated and accurate information on logistic and operational parameters regarding in-transit resources. The logistic information coming in to the *operators'* information nodes is *potential resources* from the *managers* and *demand* information from the *customers*. The *operators* need also operational information on routes' conditions, as well as location and state of designated *customers*.

Customers' Nodes

The *customers* are the principal demand-generating entities in the *OpLog* system. The tactical logisticians represent the *customers'* nodes in the information network. They generate demand information that is transmitted to higher echelons. The time cycle of these transmissions should coincide with the time cycle of the logistic support chain. If information is transmitted faster than the scale of the logistic clock, then the effect of the gap is relatively marginal. However, slower information flow than the physical flow rate in the logistic support chain may result in delays, under-responsiveness, and a widening logistic gap (see Sect. 4.3.3 in Chap. 4).

During each time-cycle, consumption data and requirements for logistic resources are gathered from the combat units and delivered to logistics *managers* at a higher echelon. The route that this information follows is typically: *combat unit (customer)* → *sectional logistician ("low-level manager")* → *theater logistician ("top-level manager")*. The demand information, combined with future consumption projections, constitute the basic input for planning the next "pulse" of the logistic support chain. The little information that the *customers* rely on is usually supplied by the *operators* who advice them about delivery time and location.

Thus, *customers* are more suppliers of logistic information than consumers. This observation has profound consequences on the availability and quality of logistic information. The stressful conditions at the battlefield negatively affect the quality of demand information sent out by *customers*. When the focus of attention is on

Fig. 5.3 Information interrelationships

combat activities and the perils of the battlefield, attention for logistics may be secondary up to a point when it is acutely needed. In such situations the "panic factor" may prevail. Instead of balanced and timely reckoning of consumption rates and supply levels, exaggerated and urgent requests may be sent out to higher echelons. This predicament may be mitigated when automated logistic sensors, gauges, and counters, networked in reliable computerized systems, are introduced into the battlefield. Such systems can alleviate the need to rely on human reports and thus reduce the noise, errors, and delays usually contained in human transmissions of *customers'* information.

Figure 5.3 summarizes the information interrelations among the logistic *managers*, *operators,* and *customers.*

5.4   Standard vs. Ad Hoc Information

Two categories of information pass through the logistic information network:

- Standard information.
- Ad Hoc information.

5.4.1   Standard Information

Standard information is displayed in formal reports that typically follow rigid formats. These reports are produced periodically and are updated either manually or automatically. The format of these reports is determined ahead of time in such a way that it is best suited for the needs of the various stakeholders (i.e., *managers, operators,* and *customers*) using logistic information. The standard information includes periodic reports of logistic and operational parameters.

Standard Information as a Data Base

Because of their standard format, periodic reports can be easily implemented in computerized information systems. The computer facilitates a convenient way to compose, deliver, and analyze such reports. The standard information, implemented in data bases, establishes the basis for planning before and during an operation.

5.4.2   Ad Hoc Information

Contrary to standard information that is typically *pushed* from the source of information regularly and in standard formats, ad hoc information is usually *pulled* by the information consumer. This information is needed when the standard information is insufficient or not clear enough for making decisions. Ad hoc information is usually verbal, not necessarily structured or formatted, and is in the form of a specific answer to a specific question. Ad hoc information is solicited by decision-makers when needed.

The need for ad hoc information is acute in particular when the standard information is insufficient at times when unexpected events occur, or sudden decisions with immediate and serious impact have to be made. Events like blown-up oil reservoir, sudden change in an operational plan, or unexpectedly high consumption of ammunition in a certain engagement must be treated urgently and effectively. In such situations a burst of requests for information is sent out from the *managers* to the *operators* and *customers,* asking for situation reports, logistic implication of the event and even a quick and brief update of existing standard information.

Ad hoc information is also used when there is a disruption in the flow of standard information in the network. In such cases alternate, sometimes improvised, information channels are established through which ad hoc information is transmitted.

5.4.3   More Standard Less Ad hoc

The process of requesting, producing, and transmitting ad hoc information can be elaborate, lengthy, and may divert attention and waste time at critical stages of the operation. Moreover, the larger the share of ad hoc information in the information flow, the less robust and efficient is the system since potential noise associated with ad hoc information may affect the accuracy and fidelity of the information. Thus, it is desired to minimize as much as possible the reliance on and use of ad hoc logistic information.

This objective can be attained only if the standard information is generated and transmitted effectively. This information must be focused, continuously updated (preferably, on-line), and mission oriented. It must be delivered by well-structured reports that cover all the relevant information in a resolution and focus that fits decision-makers' needs – not too aggregate and not too detailed.

Example 5.12
To monitor the location and state of a logistic convoy, information has been typically drawn from checkpoints positioned at junctions and other control points along the route. However, request for information sent out from logistic headquarters (*Managers*) to these checkpoints (*Operators*) may be ignored because of preoccupation with other, more urgent, matters at the checkpoint, or its transmission may be delayed due to technical issues. Even if delivered on time, the information may be subject to errors and misinterpretations. These predicaments could be avoided or at least mitigated by a system of sensors and reliable communication channels. See also *Example 5.13*.

5.5   Total vs. Efficient Information

In recent years the term *Total Asset Visibility* (TAV) has become prevalent in logistic publications [3, 4]. It is argued that TAV is a desired feature – even a goal – of logistic information systems. The TAV concept is based on a collection of C⁴I systems, processes, and rules that are supposed to generate the "ideal" situation where *anyone knows everything on anything*. That is, the logistic system is totally transparent to everyone at all times.

In principle, it seems that it would be worthwhile to aspire for such an ideal goal since a sound decision-making process depends on a reliable and updated picture of the *OpLog* system. The necessity for such complete logistic visibility is acute in particular when it is required to logistically analyze future actions or when immediate logistic response is needed for a new, unexpected combat situation. However, from the practical point of view, it is not at all clear that it would be efficient to invest the time, effort, and resources needed for producing such a complete, perfect, and total picture of *OpLog*. There are two reasons for that doubt, which stem from two well-known economic principles: The principle of *Diminishing Marginal Returns* and the principle of *Free Disposal*.

5.5.1   Diminishing Marginal Returns

Resolution, accuracy, reliability, timeliness, and range of information are features that incur economic and operational costs. The economic cost, measured in time, manpower, and money, increases with each one of these features. Moreover, the marginal cost of extra features may be increasing too. The operational cost is imbedded in the robustness and stability of the information system. As the system becomes more complex, both technically and operationally, it is less robust to the effects of friction during combat.

Thus, as it is the case in the developing any system, there is a point from which on additional features result in *diminishing marginal returns*. The enhanced capabilities do not justify the extra development and maintenance costs, and the potential decrease in the system's operational robustness. *Total* visibility may be attained at prohibitive economic and operational costs and therefore it would be wise to identify the *proper* visibility that satisfies logistic and operational requirements. The diminishing marginal informational returns call for a careful and well-balanced design of an *efficient,* rather than *total,* asset visibility.

5.5.2   Free Disposal

A situation of *Free Disposal* occurs when there is no cost associated with surplus or redundancy. For example, consider a thirsty person who asks for a glass of water and is given a whole bottle. She drinks as much as she desires and may dispose the rest of the water at no cost. Since the person can freely dispose excess supply, from her point of view, *more* is not worse than *less*. Consider now a contractor who orders a shipment of 5 tons of cement. He is told that as of last week, shipments are sent in batches of 10 tons and not five as before. Since the contractor did not know about this new arrangement, the supplier charges him the price of only 5 tons. The contractor however has no alternative use for this surplus and therefore he has to dispose it at an extra cost. Here disposal is not free; although the contractor gets 5 tons more than he needs at no extra purchasing cost, *more*, in this case, may be strictly worse than *less*.

Arguably, military information during combat, and logistic information in particular are assets that resemble cement more than water. Excess information at the battlefield may not only be useless but may even cause damage by wasting C^4 resources on handling redundant information. Logistic information must be focused on logistic decision-making. If visibility is total, considerable effort must be invested to filter down irrelevant data in order to extract the *relevant* picture from the *total* picture, which may be cluttered and even blurred. During a campaign, this filtering is time consuming and it imposes a cognitive burden on the logistician and technical burden on his staff. The filtering process must be incorporated at the design stage of the information system such that visibility will be focused and adjusted to the logistic decision-maker needs.

Another argument for favoring efficient (focused) visibility over total visibility is associated with the quality of the data. As more data is poured into an information system it is more difficult to control its quality – its reliability and accuracy. In such cases, the information system may be infected with the "garbage in, garbage out" syndrome. An information system that is trimmed according to the real logistic decision-making needs may be easier to control for quality than a system that aspires for total visibility.

5.5.3   Information Technology (IT)

Notwithstanding the reservations presented above, advances in communication and information technology have the potential to significantly impact the way logistic information is generated and transferred [5]. Inventory tracking systems, sensors, internet, intranet, and positioning systems could potentially enhance the accuracy and timeliness of logistic information. However, transforming this potential into reality may not be simple in the friction-infested environment of the battlefield. Processes and procedures that seem obvious in the business world during peacetime (e.g., FedEx, Amazon) may be difficult, if not impossible, to implement in the relatively chaotic and hostile conditions in the battlefield.

Obviously, the objective is to incorporate as many as possible new information technologies in a logistic information system. Effective IT systems may reduce the reliance on human interference that usually enters errors, noise, and delays in the flow of information. Moreover, because of the quantitative nature of logistic information, implementing IT in logistic systems may be relatively simpler compared to other information systems at the battlefield (e.g., operations and intelligence).

Example 5.13
Real time tracking of military convoys is an important task of an operational logistician (*manager*). New IT systems provide effective means to help the logistician accomplish this task. First, physical coding of supplies, e.g., radio frequency identification (RFID), create a match between the identity of the convoy and the identity (or content) of its load. Second, Global Positioning Satellite (GPS) systems installed in the vehicles give real time position of the convoy. The combined input of RFID tracking and the GPS localization generate a visual picture that is displayed on a computerized map. The desired information is shown as dynamic "snakes" on the map. Each such visual representation of a convoy also contains alphanumerical information on the location of its head, length, velocity, destination, and content of its freight.

5.6   Data, Information, and Decision-Making

The logistic information system is one of the most data intensive military information systems. It contains qualitative information and mostly quantitative data. There is no other information system in the theater of operations (e.g., Intelligence, Operations) that contains such a wide and diversified collection of quantitative parameters. Rich information system is of course useful but, as we have already seen in Sect. 5.5, this abundance of data may be also harmful. Data is not necessarily information, and without proper screening, processing, and analysis the benefit of this gamut of information may be limited. In order to utilize it efficiently, the raw information and data must be transformed into simple formats that are easily read and understood.

5.6.1 Decision Support Systems

Properly processed information may not be enough for effective decision-making. While in some cases a decision-maker can make a good decision, e.g., selecting the best alternative, simply by looking at basic logistic and operational parameters and using his experience, knowledge, and common-sense, in other cases this may not be enough. Some decisions require additional processing and analysis of the logistic information – beyond basic screening, classifying, and formatting. The additional processing and analysis may be done by mathematical models and algorithms usually labeled as *Decision Support Systems* (*DSS*) or *Decision Aids*. Mathematical models are capable of performing elaborate and complex computations that are difficult and time-consuming for a human brain. A brief review of such models was given in Chap. 2.

Example 5.14
There are several dilemmas associated with deploying medical units in the theater of operations:

- Number of deployed units, and their spatial distribution in the theater.
- Medical capabilities (e.g., first aid, trauma, surgical) in each unit.
- Treatment capacity (number of casualties that can be treated at any time).
- Number and type of means of transportation (e.g., armored vehicles, ambulances, helicopters) to be deployed at the various edges of the medical evacuation network.

These are complex decision issues that can be treated systematically and effectively by formal optimization techniques like queuing models, stochastic optimization, and simulations. Information regarding operational plans, availability of lines of communications, projected number of casualties (including type of injury and severity) and treatment capabilities generates the input for these models.

5.7 Summary

Like any other managerial discipline, managing and executing logistics effectively relies on relevant, updated, and accurate information. This information flows through the logistic information network whose nodes are divided into three groups: *managers* who plan the deployment of the *OpLog* system and manage its employment, *operators* who actually implement the plans and execute the tasks and the *customers* – the combat units – that consume the logistic supplies and services. Each one of the three groups is characterized differently as supplier and consumer of information.

Logistic information is abundant with data – mostly quantitative – that must be screened, processed, analyzed, and routed to the appropriate recipients. Information production is the backbone of *OpLog* management, it generates the main input to the planning process and it enables the operational logistician to effectively control and coordinate the logistics efforts in the theater of operations. Clear, focused, and accurate information is a necessary condition for effective logistics management but it may not be sufficient. In many cases, the information system must be augmented by decision support systems that take raw or processed information and produce sound, and sometimes even optimal, decisions.

References

1. Schrady D. Combatant logistics command and control for the joint force commander. Naval War College Rev. 1999;LII(3):49–75.
2. Johnson LD. User's Guide to ITV. Army Logistician, September-October 1996.
3. Hammons MJ, Chisholm G. Enabling total asset visibility. Defense Transport J. August 2006;12–14.
4. Ebert DE. Evolution of revolution: application of information technology in military logistics. Carlisle Barracks, PA: Army War College; 1997. p. 11.
5. Novak LA, Drazek GP, Stimatze GL. Logistics technology 2010, implications for DoD. McLean, VA: Logistics Management Inst; 2000.

Chapter 6
Forecasting Logistic Demands

Two battlefield phenomena affect the outcome of combat activities and generate demand for logistics resource: *attrition* and *consumption*. Fire engagements deplete the inventory of ammunition and increase the demand for medical supplies, maneuvers consume fuel and maintenance resources, and chemical-warfare events require exceptionally large amount of water. The consumption rates, and the logistic requirements derived from them, are the most important inputs for logistic planning. Quoting von Clausewitz, [1] *"A prince or general can best demonstrate his genius by managing a campaign exactly to suite his objectives and resources, doing neither too much nor too little."* A necessary condition for satisfying this maxim is to understand the relation between the *objectives* and the *resources* needed to fulfill them.

The matching of resources to objectives relies on proper forecasting of future logistic requirements in both *time* and *space*. The questions a logistics planner must answer are:

- *Who* will need logistic support?
- *What* is the composition of the needed bundle of resources?
- *Where* the bundle should be sent to?
- *When* will it be required?

In this chapter we discuss the requirements from a logistic forecasting system and sketch the framework of a methodology that can meet these requirements. In particular, we review the uncertainties that underlie attrition and consumption, and highlight the inherent limitations of such a forecasting system. With these limitations we describe a forecasting system that may produce reasonable logistic estimates.

The importance of such a forecasting system cannot be overstated. On the one hand, it can enhance the accuracy and credibility of logistic demands and allocations, and on the other hand, it may improve the flow velocity and allocation efficiency in the logistic network.

© Springer International Publishing Switzerland 2016
M. Kress, *Operational Logistics*, Management for Professionals,
DOI 10.1007/978-3-319-22674-3_6

6.1   Forecasting at the Three Levels of Logistics

The characteristics of logistic forecasting depend on its level – *strategic, operational* or *tactical*. Each level has different requirements regarding the forecast resolution of a certain resource and the level of aggregation of the forecast across resources and scenarios.

The forecast resolution determines the scale or the granularity of the units according which consumption of a certain resource is measured. For example, while at the tactical level consumption of tank ammunition is measured in tens or hundreds of rounds, at the strategic level the resolution may be ten thousands, and perhaps even hundred thousands, of rounds.

The level of aggregation of resources indicates the way similar resources are lumped together.

Example 6.1
At the strategic level it is usually sufficient to classify artillery ammunition into only two groups – *high explosive* and *cluster shells*. At the operational and tactical levels this crude classification may not be sufficient for planning purposes. A detailed reckoning of all types of shells may be required.

The reference scenario is the starting point and initial input for any logistic demand forecast. The level of aggregation of such scenario determines how detailed and specific its description is. Planners at different logistic levels may aggregate differently. Generic and general scenarios, which may be adequate for strategic planning, may be insufficient for operational and tactical forecasting. Such scenarios must be fleshed out with combat details such as terrain, environment, enemy, types of engagement in order to be meaningful for forecasting logistic demands at the operational and tactical levels.

Example 6.2
At the strategic level it may be sufficient to estimate consumption aggregately by referring to generic scenarios such as *deliberate attack* or *hasty defense*. Such a crude description may not be sufficient for estimating logistics demands at the operational or tactical levels.

We conclude this section with a brief description of forecasting at the strategic and tactical levels.

6.1.1   Strategic Level

The size and composition of logistic assets at the national level are determined according to perceived or projected future *reference scenarios*. The goal is to satisfy demands for logistic resources by all combat forces in all (or at least, most) possible reference scenarios. To obtain aggregate estimates for the demands, these scenarios are usually broken down to a collection of various low-resolution *brigade* (or *division*) *days of combat* (BDC) for which logistic requirements are estimated based on historical data, war games, simulations, and opinions of subject matter experts. The total requirements are computed by summing up the BDCs.

The time factor in a strategic forecasting process is secondary since strategic planning is usually done during peacetime when there is no significant sense of urgency. The imbedded low resolution of logistic estimates and the marginal effect of time constraints make logistic forecasting at the strategic level a relatively simple task compared to the forecasting effort at the operational level.

6.1.2 Tactical Level

At the tactical level there is hardly any systematic forecasting. The reason for that is the nature of tactical logistics, which is prescriptive and generally quite myopic. At the tactical level the logistician has direct his attention to mundane "here and now" activities that are essential for facilitating the combat readiness and the impetus of the combat units. The tactical logistician has neither the time nor the tools of analysis that are needed for systematic forecasting. Any forecasting effort made at the tactical level is short-termed and usually limited to selected resources (e.g., medical services) in special circumstances (e.g., chemical warfare).

6.2 Forecasts as Input to Logistic Planning

Logistic planning was described in Chap. 4 as a two-dimensional minimization problem, where two gaps are minimized: *quantity* gap and *time* gap. The quantity gap is created when there are discrepancies between the requirements for resources and their availability. The time gap happens when there is a difference between the time when a resource is needed and its actual delivery time. These gaps are created because of two main reasons:

- Considerable lead-time (order-to-ship time).
- High variability of consumption and attrition.

6.2.1 Logistic Lead-Time

A considerable length of time may elapse from the moment a request for a certain resource is sent out from a combat unit to the moment this resource reaches its destination at that combat unit. This time varies among the logistic levels. Typically, it is measured in hours within echelons at the tactical level. At the other end, a request for a certain resource that is sent out from an expeditionary force to the strategic level in the home country may take weeks to fulfill.

Example 6.3

Perhaps the most significant impact of lead-time is on medical aid during combat. Medical lead-time is the time between the moment of injury and the moment when basic trauma treatment is given to the casualty. Time is critical for casualties; immediate medical care is necessary to save life and to minimize long-term health effects and disabilities. Ideally, a well-equipped medical team, which has basic trauma capabilities, should follow each small combat unit and provide immediate medical help when needed. Obviously, such a close medical support is unrealistic if only because of limited number of available medical units. Clearly, lead-time is an unavoidable factor. However, well-based estimates on the distribution of casualties can guide the deployment of medical resources and thus abate the effect of this factor.

Despite significant advances in communication, information, and transportation technologies, and the emergence of logistic tenets such as *precision logistics* and *velocity management*, lead-time is still a significant factor in logistic management. While these technologies and initiatives may reduce, at the fringes, the length of lead-times, their impact on shortening the length of the logistic operational-level links is marginal at best.

Because of lead-times, the *OpLog* system must initiate the logistic response process *before* demands are specified by the *customers* (the combat units) and sometimes even before consumption has actually occurred. Therefore demands must be projected well before they are known. At the operational level the range of the forecasting horizon must be at least the typical lead-time of the logistic support chain. According to the US Army doctrine [2] the *predictive logistics* range is 72 h.

6.2.2 The Fallacy of the Mean

Forecasting demands at the battlefield is a difficult problem. A simple solution for that problem is to use "averages" of the type "A division on the attack consumes on a day of combat *x* rounds of ammunition per tank." Arguably, this sentence contains at least four hidden "averages": (1) average over time, (2) average over the various types of *attack* scenarios, (3) average over the subunits of the division, and (4) average over tanks in a subunit.

While such "grand averages" may be adequate for planning purposes at the strategic level (see Sect. 6.1.1), these estimates are insufficient for planning and managing logistics at the operational level. Allocation of resources to the various units in the theater of operations depends on the combat posture, on the mission, and on the environment. The consumption rate of a certain resource is not necessarily uniform across units, missions and environmental conditions – even within a certain battlefield scenario such as an *attack*. Therefore, a single average figure that represents consumption rate at all units, combat situations, and times is wrong and misleading.

Example 6.4
Unit X is a column of tracked artillery pieces climbing up a narrow and winding dirt road in the mountains. Unit Y is an armored brigade that moves on a flat highway. The tactical posture in both cases is the same – *advance*. However, it is quite clear that the fuel consumption of unit X is higher than the fuel consumption of unit Y.

Example 6.5
The consumption of high explosive shells by a divisional artillery unit on the first day of an offensive may be considerably different (higher) than the consumption of the same ammunition, by the same unit, on, say, the third day.

Adopting mean values as consumption estimates for resupply may result in severe shortcomings. Because consumption is subject to high variance among combat units, applying an aggregated and uniform measure across units and missions will certainly lead to situations where some units are oversupplied, and therefore wasting resources, while other units may experience shortages. At the strategic level, such discrepancies may be canceled out when looking at the aggregate logistic picture, but at the operational and tactical levels these discrepancies may severely constrain combat capabilities.

6.2.3   The Need to Forecast Demands

The operational logistician is typically concerned with three main issues:

- Mix and quantity of resources to be requested from a higher (strategic) echelon.
- Operational constraints imposed by logistics.
- Allocating resources to subordinate echelons.

Dealing with each one of these three issues requires a clear account of the logistic situation at the theater of operations. This account is composed of three types of logistic information, as described in Chap. 5:

- Actual resources in the theater of operations
- Potential resources in the pipeline
- Demands

The Uncertainties

All three types of information contain various levels of uncertainty and noise, which hinder the logistician from obtaining a complete, reliable, and clear account of the logistic situation. There are however two different categories of uncertainty.

The first category relates to *current information* regarding the past – events that have already occurred. The second category applies to *future information* concerning projected events and actions. While the first category of uncertainty is typical to the first two types of information – *actual* and *potential resources*, the second category is typical to the third type of information – *demand* information.

Uncertainty Regarding *Current Information*

In principle, uncertainty regarding current information should not really exist since it concerns events that have already occurred. Some nodes in the information network know the logistic outcome of these events but the problem is that the information has not yet been shared with other nodes in the logistic network. This uncertainty exists as a result of cuts, overflows, and noise created in the information network because of limited C^3 capabilities and the effect of battlefield friction. Thus, data concerning current information exist in the system – it is known with certainty to someone – but not necessarily to the decision-maker who needs it.

> **Example 6.6**
> The commander of an ammunition supply company knows for sure the size of the load on the trucks of his company and its destination. Most likely he also knows the precise location of the company. This information may not be available, at the same time, to the logistic headquarter of the division to which this company belongs. In such situations, the divisional logistician, who needs to make decisions based on this information, may have to postpone his decision, or to make it based on partial information.

Current information concerning supplies is usually known to the *operators* (see Chap. 5) but it is not always available to the *managers* and *customers*. Similarly, information concerning recent consumption may be known to the *customers* but it may take time, and accumulate considerable noise, until it reaches the *managers*. Advanced logistic C^3 initiatives, such as *In-Transit Visibility* [3] and tactical logistics data channels, may reduce the uncertainty imbedded in current information.

Uncertainty in *Future Information*

Contrary to current information, where uncertainty is only due to insufficient situational awareness, uncertainty concerning future information is inherent; it follows from the trivial fact that this information relates to events and actions that have not yet occurred. This type of uncertainty cannot be reduced by better C^3 systems but rather by effective forecasting. Obviously, longer planning horizon implies higher uncertainty with respect to future information.

Uncertainties and Information Gaps

The diagram in Fig. 6.1 presents schematically the issues discussed so far. It describes the state of logistic knowledge at the transition between two time-steps: t and $t+1$.

The first time-step (t) has just ended, while the second time-step ($t+1$) is just about to begin. The consumption and supply at time-step t have already materialized and therefore the "state-of-the-world" has been revealed regarding attrition and consumption data in time-step t. However, the logistic picture may not be completely and accurately visible to the logistician.

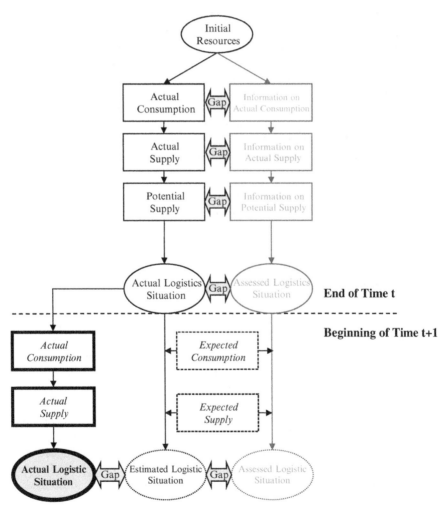

Fig. 6.1 States of logistic knowledge

   The top left branch of the diagram represents the true logistic state-of-the-world in the theater of operations – the *actual logistic picture*. The top right branch, which is marked by a lighter color, represents the logistician's state of knowledge concerning these data – the *perceived logistic picture*. As we can see, there are gaps between the two logistic pictures. The extent of these gaps may vary among the three logistic factors – *consumption, actual supply, and potential supply*. These gaps are created because of battlefield friction and limitations of command, control, and communication capabilities. Advanced and more effective C^3 systems may reduce the size of these gaps.

   At time-step $t+1$ a new major factor amplifies uncertainty: the *future*. Consequently, there are three possible "states of knowledge":

1. The **right-hand branch** in Fig. 6.1 represents the *assessed picture*, which is based on the *perceived* knowledge at time t compounded with forecasts of consumption and supply at time $t+1$. This branch, which embodies the highest level of uncertainty, represents the knowledge that is actually available to the logistician. This is the realistic scenario for the logistician state of knowledge
2. The **center branch** represents the true situation at time t and the forecasts for time $t+1$. Thus, the only source for uncertainty at this branch is the unknown future. This is the best case scenario for the logistician.
3. The **left-hand branch,** which branches off from the center branch, symbolizes an ideal state of *total* knowledge. This state is obviously infeasible in reality.

   The knowledge gaps created between the branches can be reduced by effective and robust C^3 systems (see also Chap. 5) and by reliable forecasts that produce estimates for future (time $t+1$) consumption and attrition.

6.2.4   Features of Logistic Forecasting

Logistic forecasting has two dimensions: *operational* and *logistic*. The entities that affect the operational dimension are planned or projected *scenarios*. These scenarios induce in-context demand estimates, and therefore a set of representative scenarios forms a basis for any forecasting process. The number, scope, and level of detail of the representative scenarios depend on the level of aggregation required by the logistic plan.

   The second dimension includes logistic forecasting functions that fit consumption and attrition parameters to a given scenario. Formally, a forecasting function Φ transforms operational data into logistic data. This function is defined on a set of reference scenarios and produces an array of numbers representing estimates for attrition and consumption. Such a transformation is described in *Example 6.7*.

Example 6.7

For the sake of simplicity assume that there are only three possible reference scenarios in a certain operational plan:

S_1 – *Maneuver towards contact with the enemy.*
S_2 – *Fire engagement between two tank brigades.*
S_3 – *Hasty defense by a mechanized infantry brigade.*

   The logistic parameters are:

1. Number of casualties, classified to *killed* (L_1), *seriously injured* (L_2), and *injured* (L_3).
2. Attrition of weapons, classified to *destroyed* (L_4) and *damaged* (L_5).
3. Average consumption of ammunition per weapon (L_6).
4. Average fuel consumption (L_7).

   The transformation is of the form:

$$\Phi\left(S_i\right) \rightarrow \left(L_1\left(i\right), L_2\left(i\right), \ldots L_7\left(i\right)\right), i = 1, 2, 3.$$

Here we can assume that, $L_6(1) \le L_6(3)$, $L_4(1) \le L_4(2)$, and $L_7(3) \le L_7(1)$.

The conceptual validity of such a transformation is based on the premise that combat situations are distinguishable in terms of attrition and consumption. While the exact form of Φ is usually unknown, effort must be invested to find the best possible estimate for it. Such approximate *cause-and-effect* relations are the building blocks of a logistic forecasting system.

Dependence on the Type of Resource

The requirements from a forecasting process, and its robustness, depend on the type of the logistic resource under consideration. They are affected by the variability of the demand for that resource, its criticality, and its interchangeability with other resources.

Example 6.8

The consumption of food is, to a large extent, invariant to combat situations; each soldier needs about 2000 calories a day. While this requirement may vary between two extreme climates (e.g., arctic and desert) it is practically independent of the type of warfare in a given theater of operations. Thus, forecasting ration consumption in an operation is a relatively easy task. Its consumption rate is proportional to the size of the sustained force. Also, different types of food (e.g., warm meals, meals ready-to-eat) are interchangeable.

Example 6.9
Similar arguments as in *Example 6.8* apply to water, however with one exception. Chemical warfare may require large amount of water for decontamination. Thus, scenarios that include chemical-warfare components are given different consumption rate estimates for water than conventional counterparts.

Example 6.10
Medical supplies and equipment are critical resources during combat. Therefore, the inventory level of these items is usually very high to guarantee adequate medical responsiveness even in extreme situations. Thus, an "accurate" forecast of medical requirements is quite superfluous since the supply of this resource is tailored to the most extreme possible situation. However, classifying combat scenarios according to the projected types of injuries may have an effect on the mix of medical resources. Casualties during infantry operations mostly suffer wounds caused by small arms and shrapnel, while casualties in armor warfare mostly suffer burns. Chemical warfare affects the neural and respiratory systems.

Example 6.11
The consumption of fuel and ammunition is subject to variability with respect to three dimensions:

1. Among combat scenarios.
2. Among combat units.
3. Along time.

These resources are also critical, their supply is often limited, and they are usually not interchangeable (resources that may be interchangeable, such as *armor piercing* or *high explosive* antitank shells, may be grouped into one type of ammunition). Here an in-context (scenario-dependent) forecast of consumption is necessary for logistic planning.

Safety Threshold and Saturation Threshold

Two thresholds – *safety threshold* and *saturation threshold* – are set for supplies of high-priority, high-variance, scenario-dependent resources. The safety threshold indicates the minimum supply level that is necessary for a combat unit to carry out its mission. The size of this threshold increases with its priority and variance.

The saturation threshold indicates the maximum capacity of a combat unit. Any additional supply arriving to the unit, beyond this threshold, is redundant. This redundancy may result in waste that has two consequences. First, resources may be abandoned and lost. Second, in the presence of limited resources, unnecessary surplus in one zone of the theater may result in shortages in other zones.

The two thresholds can be viewed as confidence limits estimated by statistical tools. The safety threshold applies to consumables such as ammunition, fuel, and water, while the saturation threshold applies to logistic capacities manifested by available means of transportation and storage facilities. The two thresholds are important forecasting outputs.

6.3   Factors Affecting Uncertainty

The two main factors that create uncertainty in the theater of operations are:

1. Battlefield events.
2. Combat outcomes.

These two factors are not independent.

6.3.1   Battlefield Events

The starting point of any combat scenario is a definition of the mission and a description of the operational plan. The operational plan is usually presented in document called *task assignment program* that details the composition of the military force and its planned time-phased tasks. These descriptors however provide only a *tentative* narrative of the planned scenario. The *actual* progress of the scenario is determined by additional factors such as the size, composition, deployment, and course of action of the enemy, the environment, C^3I capabilities, and the readiness of the various combat units. First, we focus on the main source of battlefield uncertainty – the *enemy*.

The strength of the enemy, its deployment, operational plan, and tactics are not known to the friendly forces with certainty since intelligence information is neither complete nor clean of distortions. But, these factors have a significant impact on the way the combat scenario evolves and therefore they must be included in the operational decision-making process. Because the uncertainty associated with these factors does not rise from *random processes* that are dealt by probability theory – there are no empirical *probability distributions* that describe the randomness of these factors: statistical techniques will be useless for estimating them.

Example 6.12

Consider the question: *What are the chances that the enemy will use attack helicopters against our first armor brigade?* The answer to this question depends on the *capabilities* of the enemy (which are not always known with certainty) and on its *intention*, which cannot be estimated by formal statistical tools applied to empirical data. The above question is formalized below as a Bernoulli random variable:

$$X = \begin{cases} 1 \; if \; the \; enemy \; employs \; attack \; helicopters \\ 0 \hspace{5cm} Otherwise \end{cases}$$

$$Probability\left[X = 1\right] = p$$

Arguably, p can only be estimated subjectively.

Reasonable estimates for possible realizations of enemy's future actions must rely on judgmental inputs of subject matter experts such as intelligence analysts. These experts bring to bear their knowledge and experience to assess the likelihood of possible scenarios.

6.3.2   Combat Outcomes

Two tangible outcomes of an operation are *attrition* of people, weapons, and equipment, and *consumption* of logistic resources. Given a certain scenario concerning friendly forces, for which operational factors such as force size, deployment, and tactical plans are known, and enemy forces, for which these factors can only be assessed, the question a logistician would be interested in is: *what are going to be the logistic-related outcomes of that scenario?* The combat outcomes of a scenario are uncertain and may be subject to large statistical variance.

The two aspects of uncertainty – battlefield events and combat outcomes – are not independent. On the one hand, combat outcomes at intermediate stages of a campaign may affect subsequent battlefield events. For example, high attrition at the penetration phase of a campaign may severely hinder subsequent offensive plans. On the other hand, decisions concerning current operational plans may shape battlefield events that, in turn, will affect attrition and consumption rates.

However, unlike the qualitative nature of the uncertainty associated with *battlefield events*, *combat outcomes* may be viewed as more formal and quantitative random variables that could be statistically estimated. In principle, it is possible to find approximate functional relations between combat scenarios and the parameters of the resulting attrition and consumption statistical distributions. Consumption of artillery ammunition is directly affected by the fire support plan, attrition of fighting vehicles is derived from the length and intensity of fire engagements, and fuel consumption of trucks is determined mainly by the distance traveled. It is also possible, in principle, to estimate these parameters empirically from historical data. The problem is that this type of estimation is rarely practical since the samples of data are usually very small. Moreover, only part of the data is recorded, and even these partial data are typically infested with inaccuracies and even errors. Also, significant changes in weapons and doctrine from one war to another render even the little available data to be of limited use.

6.3.3   Is Logistics Forecasting Possible?

In view of the discussion above, one may ask if it is at all possible to forecast combat attrition and consumption, and if it is, is such forecast meaningful? These questions are equivalent, to some extent, to the question: *can we assume that combat scenarios are statistically indistinguishable with respect to attrition and consumption?* If the answer to that question is positive then it is clear that there is no point to project logistic demands – the same way it is pointless to project the winning number in the next week's lottery drawing. If, however, the statistical distributions of these parameters – attrition and consumption – are significantly different, then the association between a combat scenario and its corresponding statistical distributions of logistic parameters may be utilized for forecasting. Recall the function Φ in Sect. 6.2.4.

According to accumulated evidence from past wars, and inputs from subject matter experts, the demand distributions *are* significantly different. Thus, operational details of a certain combat scenario also contain relevant data for logistic forecasting. Transforming the operational details into logistic demand metrics is an important issue in logistic research. Several attempts to formalize this transformation are recorded in the literature [4, 5]. In the next section we present a general framework for logistic forecasting.

6.4   A Framework for Logistic Forecasting

The general methodology proposed here comprises four stages:

1. Designing a hierarchical structure of "generic" scenarios.
2. Constructing a representative library of scenarios.
3. Developing scenario-to-consumption/attrition transformations.
4. Estimating in-context parameters.

6.4.1   The Hierarchical Structure

In his book *Attrition: Forecasting Battle Casualties and Equipment Losses in Modern War* [6] Dupuy describes a six-level hierarchy:

1. War
2. Campaign
3. Battle
4. Engagement
5. Action
6. Duel

However, for the purpose of constructing *OpLog*-oriented library of scenarios it may be sufficient to focus on only four levels: *Campaign* through *Action*. The level of *War* is relevant to the strategic level, which is beyond the *OpLog* framework considered here, and a *duel* is a fundamental tactical combat event that constitutes a building block of an *action*. Logistic implications of such an event are limited.

Similarly to Dupuy's classification, we adopt the following hierarchy of generic combat situations. This hierarchy generates a spanning tree that comprises four levels:

Level 1 – Operation: Large military force (say, 1–3 corps) engaged in high-intensity combat that spans over days, weeks, and perhaps even months.

Level 2 – Tactical Battle: One or two divisions involved in combat that extends 1–3 days.

Level 3 – Engagement: Brigade or a number of battalions engaged in battle for 8–24 h.

Level 4 – Action: A relatively short (1–8 h) combat event that involves small formations – up to a battalion.

Low intensity combat, such as counterinsurgency operations (see Chap. 7), or operations other than war, such as humanitarian relief operations (see Chap. 8) are classified differently. While such scenarios may be considered as *Operations* in terms of their time-space span, they are only at the level of *Tactical Battle*, or even *Engagements,* when deployed force size is considered.

Figure 6.2 demonstrates the four-level hierarchy.

To keep the library of combat scenarios within tractable limits it is important to distinguish between a *generic* combat situation and a *variant* of it.

Example 6.13
An armored battalion moving up a narrow and winding hill is an *action*. This action may be completed with or without interference by an anti-tank ambush of the enemy. Are the resulting two combat situations – secured movement with or without enemy's ambush – different actions or the latter is a variant of the former? The answer depends on factors such as the resolution of the operational plan and the logistic implications of the action.

Example

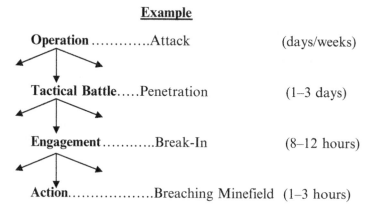

Operation ....Attack	(days/weeks)
Tactical Battle.....Penetration	(1–3 days)
Engagement............Break-In	(8–12 hours)
Action...................Breaching Minefield	(1–3 hours)

Fig. 6.2 Battlefield hierarchy

Engagements are composed of *actions* that occur sequentially or simultaneously during a time period of 8–24 h. Combining actions into engagements must be done carefully so that operational and logistic interdependencies are taken into account. For example, fuel consumption of a battalion at later stages of an engagement depends on its attrition at earlier stages. Similarly, the aggregation of *engagements* into *tactical battles*, and *tactical battles* into *operations* must be done cautiously, possibly with the aid of combat models and war-games. For example, the projected average consumption of ammunition in a *tactical battle* is not necessarily a simple algebraic mean of the respective projected consumption rates in the various *engagements*.

6.4.2   Forecasting Methods

One or more of the following three generic methods can project logistic demands: [7]

- Intuitive Approach.
- Extrapolative Methods.
- Causal Models.

Intuitive Approach

Intuitive forecasting relies on human judgment and personal experience. Subject matter experts (typically, experienced commanders and staff officers) are asked to give their opinions regarding likely rates of attrition and consumption in certain combat scenarios. While this informal method reflects in-context knowledge and experience of the military milieu – compelling features for decision-makers – the resulting subjective estimates could be biased. The judgment of a military expert may be affected by limited and biased experience or a singular nonrepresentative traumatic past event. Also, significant changes in combat capabilities and doctrine may render even rich experience irrelevant for projecting future combat scenarios.

However, despite its limitations, intuitive approaches are common in forecasting military logistic parameters. This approach facilitates a simple way for obtaining estimates when other, more formal and "scientific," methods are not available, or when relevant and reliable data are sparse. To improve the robustness of intuitive forecasts, and reduce its potential bias, the group of selected experts who provide the projection should be as large and as varied as possible. Structured *Group Decision-Making* processes (e.g., Delphi, Brainstorming) [8] or formal distance-based aggregation methods [9] may be applied to elicit robust consensus estimates.

Extrapolative Methods

An extrapolative method seeks a mathematical relation between a set of data regarding the past and projections of future events. In this method we extrapolate current and past data into the future. The data is obtained from records of past operations, and sometimes from simulated results of major military exercises, war-games and computerized simulations. The extrapolation takes into account trends that have evolved from past military conflicts as a result of new threats, emerging combat technologies, and updated doctrine. These methods analyze the data statistically, and based on an estimated trend, project the consumption and attrition data into the future.

Explorative methods are based on statistical techniques such as *time-series analysis*. These methods do not explore explicitly the direct impact of new weapons and revised doctrine on logistic outcomes, but rather define a general trend that is based on these parameters. An example of a forecasting model that combines extrapolative methods with judgmental (intuitive) inputs of experts is Dupuy's *Quantified Judgment Model* [4].

Causal Models

Causal models seek to harness cause-and-effect relations among variables. These models forecast the value of one set of variables (the "effects") based on known (or estimated) values of the other set of variables (the "causes"). For example, weather forecasts are based on meteorological data that are obtained from measurements elsewhere. The current local weather ("effect") depends on the meteorological measurements ("causes") in other geographical areas. *Linear multiple regression* in statistics is probably the most well known causal model. The value of a single dependent variable Y is estimated by a linear function of a set of n independent variables X_j, that is:

$$Y = b + a_1 X_1 + a_2 X_2 + \ldots + a_n X_n$$

Analytic combat models, simulations, and war-games are common causal models in military analysis. Given input parameters regarding size of forces, weapons, doctrine, environment, and the enemy, these models produce logistic metrics regarding attrition and consumption.

Example 6.14
Suppose that $D_1, \ldots, D_n$ are n numbers, each representing the simulated daily travel distance (in km) of a mechanized infantry battalion in days $1, \ldots, n$, respectively. The battalion comprises 3 types of vehicles, and the number of vehicles of type i is $N_i, i = 1, 2, 3$. The fuel consumption depends on the scenario (which may differ from one day to another) and suppose that the average fuel consumption of vehicle of type i in the simulated scenario of day j is C_{ij} liters/km (this is an exogenous input and probably the most robust and reliable parameter in this logistic projection). The battalion's estimated consumption of fuel during the n days of operation is:

$$Fuel\_Consumption(n) = \sum_{j=1}^{n} D_j \left(N_1 C_{1j} + N_2 C_{2j} + N_3 C_{3j} \right).$$

6.4.3 Choosing a Forecasting Method

Recall that the purpose of forecasting is to obtain reliable estimates for attrition and consumption in order to enhance the efficiency of the logistic support chain. In constructing a forecasting system the advantages and limitations of each of the aforementioned methods must be considered.

An intuitive approach is inherently subjective. As a result, forecasts may be biased. Moreover, the intuition of commanders, executive officers, and staff officers is derived from past battles, operations, and exercises. There is no guarantee that this intuition will be relevant to future battles, and therefore the risk exists that the *past* will be projected, rather than the *future*. Thus, a purely intuitive forecasting method should be used only as a last resort in the absence of any reliable data.

Extrapolative methods are data intensive. They rely on current and past data that are typically neither sufficient nor reliable for statistically robust warfare analyses. Moreover, even the relatively little data that are available, reflect past military operations which may not be relevant for forecasting future battles. However, in certain cases extrapolative methods may be useful if sufficient reliable data is available and operational trends at the battlefield can be clearly identified and quantified.

The most effective methods for forecasting logistic parameters are causal methods because they are based on direct deductions from current combat capabilities, scenarios, and doctrine. In other words, while intuitive approach and extrapolative methods are heavily based on the *past*, the focus in causal models is on the *present*. Thus, causal models have the potential for utilizing the most relevant and up-to-date information.

The recommended forecasting system is therefore based on causal models – war-games, combat analytic models, and battlefield simulations – which transform updated combat information into *in-context* logistic estimates.

> **Example 6.15**
> We wish to estimate the daily consumption of anti-tank (AT) missiles by a light division in a *hasty defense* situation. By analyzing a typical scenario, and taking into account parameters such as potential number and posture of enemy's targets, fire-rate of AT launchers, accuracy of AT missiles, topography, etc., two estimates are obtained. First, it is projected that on average two third of the division's 100 launchers will be engaged in battle on any given day. Second, it is estimated that each active launcher will deliver, on average, between 6 and 9 missiles. It follows that the estimated average daily consumption of AT missiles is between $67 \times 6 = 402$ and $67 \times 9 = 603$ missiles. A more rigorous statistical analysis may produce confidence intervals for these estimates.

It should be noted however that in order to successfully implement causal models it is necessary to support them with inputs that range from qualitative information, such as enemy's doctrine and description of the theater topography, to quantitative measures such as fire-rates, rates of advance, and kill probabilities. These inputs can be generated by experts – using intuitive approaches – or by processing historical data – using extrapolative methods.

In summary, the suggested forecasting system is based on causal models that are supplemented, when necessary, by intuitive approaches and extrapolative methods.

6.4.4   A General Paradigm for Forecasting Demands

A general paradigm for forecasting logistic demands comprises three stages:

- **Stage I:** Create a library of representative tactical and operational scenarios with the help of military experts.
- **Stage II:** Construct a set of combat models (e.g., simulations, stochastic combat models) that translate the (probabilistic) characteristics of the scenario into attrition and consumption rates.
- **Stage III:** Estimate quantitative parameters of the models in Stage II by

  - Systematic elicitation of expert opinions.
  - Evaluating technical data regarding new weapons and equipment (e.g., nominal fire rates, detection ranges).
  - Processing data from military field exercises (e.g., instrumented ranges).
  - Analyzing historical data.

A possible application of such a forecasting system is shown in Example 6.16.

Example 6.16

The *operation* (see Sect. 6.4.1) planned for the 13th Corps is *Offense*. The first Division will *penetrate* the barriers and obstacles of the enemy's front line and the second and third Divisions will pass through the lines of the first Division. The second Division will execute a *frontal attack* on the first echelon (mechanized brigade) of the enemy, while the third Division will execute a *flanking maneuver* from the South. Each one of the three *Divisional Battles* (see Fig. 6.2) is broken down into *engagements*. Further breakdown into *actions* is possible (and may even be necessary) depending on the resolution of the operational plan. When detailed battalion-level plans are part of the operational plan, *actions* must also be considered explicitly. In this example we stop at the *engagement* level. Also, the types of *engagement* that are used here are created just for illustrative purposes. The following table presents the first day *engagements* of the first Division. Divisions 2 and 3 may be analyzed similarly.

The fuel consumption parameters in Table 6.2 have been estimated following a combined effort of military experts and operations research analysts who applied analytic models and simulations.

Table 6.1 First division – penetration

Combat unit	Engagement
Division artillery	Preparation fire
11th brigade	Movement to contact
	Obstacle breaching
12th brigade	Movement to contact
	Obstacle breaching
13th brigade	Movement to contact
	Passage through a breaching brigade
	Close protection

Table 6.2 Metrics for fuel consumption

Type of engagement	Mean daily consumption rates (liters per vehicle)	Standard deviation
Preparation fire	200	50
Movement to contact	1000	200
Obstacle breaching	1500	300
Passage	1000	200
Close protection	500	100

A careful time phasing of the engagements shown in Table 6.1, and an appropriate scaling of the numbers in Table 6.2 result in estimates for the fuel consumption in the first day of operations for each of the brigades of the first Division.

6.5   Summary

The theater of operations is shrouded with many uncertainties and therefore predicting battlefield outcomes is difficult if not futile. Given an operational plan for a certain scenario in a given theater of operations, a field commander would like to know the operational end-state of the campaign. This desire is infeasible; no model – analytic or simulative – can give a clear and reliable picture of the correct end-state. There are no military Oracles.

The situation in logistic planning is somewhat different. The quantitative nature of logistic planning relies on real or projected data regarding attrition and consumption. The logistics-related forecasts are usually more robust than predictions regarding operational outcomes of the campaign, which incorporate also intangible factors such as leadership and morale. Logistic forecasting can be valuable for planning, and therefore the effort in developing forecasting systems is worthwhile.

Logistic forecasting is composed of models, judgmental input and data. A careful well-balanced blend of these components may produce reasonable estimates for logistic parameters.

The forecasting approach that has been advanced in this chapter is based on the premise that the best predictor of logistic derivatives is the battlefield scenario since the operational setting embodies most of the parameters that affect consumption and attrition. Consequently, it has been shown that there is a need to create a logistics-oriented operational "dictionary" that helps to translate a scenario into logistic metrics. The dictionary comprises terms that range from types of *operations* to types of *actions*. Each such term is in fact an entity that contains several types of data, and therefore the dictionary is practically a library of combat scenarios. This library must be continuously updated since potential battlefield situations change over time as a result of new threats, weapons, and doctrine. An updated library of combat scenarios and causal models is necessary for facilitating effective logistic forecasting.

References

1. von Clausewitz C. On war. Princeton: Princeton University Press; 1976. p. 177.
2. Center for Army Lessons Learned. Logistics – Supporting the Offense, CAC Newsletter No. 94-2, US Army Combined Arms Command, Fort Leavenworth, 1994.
3. Johnson LD. User's Guide to ITV. Army Logistician, September-October 1996.
4. Dupuy T. Attrition: forecasting battle casualties and equipment losses in modern war. Fairfax, VA: HERO Books; 1990.
5. Hartley III DS. Predicting combat effects, K/DSRD-412. Oak Ridge, TN: Martin Marietta Inc.; 1991.
6. Dupuy T. Attrition: forecasting battle casualties and equipment losses in modern war. Fairfax, VA: HERO Books; 1990. p. 10.
7. Gilchrist W. Statistical forecasting. London: John Wiley & Sons; 1976.
8. Hwang C-L, Lin M-J. Group decision making under multiple criteria – methods and applications. Lecture Notes in Economics and Mathematical Systems No. 281, Springer-Verlag, 1987.
9. Cook WD, Kress M. Ordinal information and preference structures – decision models and applications. New Jersey, NJ: Prentice Hall; 1992.

Chapter 7
Insurgency and Counterinsurgency Logistics

The main thrust of the logistic principles, activities, and theories discussed in Chaps. 1 through 6 was directed towards military campaigns and major operations, also called "regular warfare." This thrust was reflected in the various examples presented therein. However, most of the military conflicts since the beginning of the twenty-first century have been in the form of insurgencies, which have triggered counterinsurgency (COIN) operations. These "irregular" armed conflicts bear certain tactical and operational characteristics, which are different from those of regular warfare. These distinct characteristics affect the structure and implementation of logistics on both sides of the conflict – the insurgents and the regime forces who confront them. In this chapter we highlight and discuss the unique logistic aspects of insurgency and COIN operations.

7.1 Characteristics of Insurgencies

Force-on-force armed conflicts (e.g., WWII, the 1973 Yom Kippur war, the Gulf War, and the first stages of Operation Iraqi Freedom) involve masses of forces, have high intensity, and are symmetrical in terms of force structure and tactics adopted by the two sides. Insurgencies are different. They exhibit low intensity of combat and are inherently asymmetric.

Insurgency is typically a grassroots violent struggle aimed at subverting or displacing a constituted regime. It is triggered by political, economic, cultural, or social grievances. In one-on-one situations, insurgents are no match to the regime forces, who are significantly larger and better equipped and trained. To avoid eradication, the insurgents must reduce their signature as targets, and this elusiveness is attained by blending in with the civilian population among which the insurgents operate. The insurgents use relatively simple, yet lethal, weapons such as small arms, improvised explosive devices, and suicide bombs.

The asymmetry described above is one significant characteristic of insurgencies. The second characteristic is the active role played by the civilian population in such

© Springer International Publishing Switzerland 2016
M. Kress, *Operational Logistics*, Management for Professionals,
DOI 10.1007/978-3-319-22674-3_7

conflicts. Civilians provide the insurgents, either willingly or as a result of coercive actions by the insurgents, hiding places, shelters, logistic support, and most importantly – information and recruits. Civilians play other roles too: they may provide relevant information (intelligence) to the government forces regarding insurgents' activities, consume social and economic resources that are provided either by the insurgents or the government, and are possible targets to violent actions by both sides (see e.g., the conflict in Syria that started in 2012). All these characteristics make civilians a key component during insurgencies. This fact has also logistic implications.

Insurgencies typically follow four stages:

- Pre-insurgency.
- Incipient conflict.
- All-out insurgency.
- Resolution.

7.1.1 Stage I: Pre-insurgency

At this stage most of the insurgents' activity is underground and no signs of violence can be detected by the regime. Actions conducted in the open, such as demonstrations and rallies, may be easily dismissed by the regime as benign political activity. During this stage the insurgency is beginning to organize both politically and militarily, establishing identity and presence among the civilian population, and identifying potential sources of support.

7.1.2 Stage II: Incipient Conflict

At this stage insurgents begin to use violence in sporadic incidents to demonstrate viability, publicize their cause, rally supporters, and provoke regime overreaction that may generate collateral casualties. The violence may be directed against regime forces and civilians, but may be dismissed by the regime as criminal acts of bandits. This is a volatile stage for the insurgents. Their presence as a source of violence is revealed and their signature as targets becomes noticeable to regime forces. Yet they are still weak, not fully organized and may be fatally hit by an alert and forceful regime.

7.1.3 Stage III: All-Out Insurgency

This is the main stage of the insurgency where the insurgents are overtly challenging the regime and actively seeking control over people and territory. The frequency and severity of attacks substantially increase and may result in some significant political and social gains. Support to the insurgency will increase either through the "bandwagon" effect where people join a winning party, or through aggressive coercion. This stage is marked with high violence, on both sides, and possible intervention of foreign political and/or military elements.

7.1.4   Stage IV: Resolution

Insurgencies are protracted conflicts. Because of their low intensity and the elusiveness of the insurgents, these conflicts may linger on, in various levels of intensities, for many years. Insurgencies are resolved either when the insurgents defeat the regime and take over or when hostilities subside and the conflict transitions into a stalemate that is eventually resolved by negotiations and agreements.

7.2   Insurgents' Logistics

As in any organization involved in physical actions, insurgents rely on logistics. They need weapons and ammunition to execute violent actions, means of transportation to move around, food and shelter for sustenance, some medical capabilities to treat their injured, and communication capabilities for passing on information and coordinating activities. Above all, they need money for obtaining all these resources. Ineffective logistics, by itself, could eradicate an insurgency.

Example 7.1 [1]
The Greek civil war (1946–1949) was fought between the Greek government and the Democratic Army of Greece – the military branch of the Greek Communist Party. The defeat of the Communist insurgents is mostly attributed to their failure to establish a solid logistic infrastructure in their transition from Stage II to III (see Sects. 7.1.3 and 7.1.4).

Example 7.2 [2]
One of the great accomplishments of the Farabundo Marti National Liberation Front (FMLN) – a coalition of five left-wing guerrilla organizations in El Salvador – was their sound logistics that enabled them to sustain the insurgency for 12 years of armed conflict. They later on became a legitimate party in El Salvador. During the insurgency the FMLN managed to obtain extensive external logistic support from Nicaragua and medical support from humanitarian groups.

Recall from Chap. 1 (Sect. 1.6) that the three logistic options are: *obtain*, *carry*, and *ship*. It was argued that while in ancient times logistics relied on the first two options – *obtain* in the battlefield (foraging, looting) and *carry* resources with the troops – modern operational logistics of regular warfare is dominated by the third option – *shipping* forward to the battlefield. Insurgency logistics is different; it mostly relies on the first option but also utilizes the third one – shipments of means and supplies from external supporters.

Unlike regular warfare, insurgency, at least at its early stages, is not linear in the sense that violent encounters are typically of small scale and scattered throughout a region without a clear line that divides between the insurgents and the regime forces. The terms Forward Edge of Battle Area (FEBA) and Forward Line of Own Troops (FLOT) used in regular warfare are seldom relevant in insurgencies. This "unordered" geometry, reflected for example in the map of controlled areas by various groups in Syria in 2015, affects the logistic deployment and capabilities of the insurgents. Insurgents' logistics depends on the stage of the insurgency.

7.2.1 Pre-insurgency

The logistic support required at the pre-insurgency stage is quite meager. This is a planning and organization stage and logistic needs are mostly venues for gatherings, some means of communication and perhaps some items to be used in mass demonstrations (e.g., banners). At this stage individual members of the insurgency are responsible for their own sustainment, transportation, etc.; no significant organized logistics.

7.2.2 Incipient Conflict

At this stage insurgents start to use weapons obtained by criminal activity, or acquired in the black market. Weapons may also be provided by a third interested party such as transnational terrorist group, or an enemy state of the regime. As becoming more structured and organized, the insurgents need shelter and sustainment that is mostly provided by civilians, either willingly or as a result of coercion.

7.2.3 All-Out Insurgency

When the armed conflict between the insurgents and the regime reaches full scale, the insurgents need continuous supply of weapons, ammunition, means of transportation, medical supplies, and economic resources to finance these needs. There are three logistic sources insurgents utilize to sustain their campaign: civilians, regime assets, and external sources.

As in Stage II, civilians provide shelter, money, and recruits. In addition, the civilian population provides conditions that facilitate the establishment of production capabilities, as well as storage facilities and caches, for ammunition and explosives. Insurgents take over buildings and seize homes, recruit explosive experts, and send out innocent civilians to obtain row materials for preparing explosives (e.g., fertilizers). Capturing military bases and troops of the regime provides abundance of materiel – weapons of various types and equipment – as well as supplies such as ammunition and fuel. These resources are of course denied from the regime forces. Moreover, capturing strategic economic assets of the regime such as oilfields or power plants provide much needed cash for the insurgents' operations. Finally, external entities such as a supportive diaspora or states that oppose the regime support the insurgents with money, arms, and shelter.

Example 7.3
Utilizing engineering and technical capabilities among local civilians in the Gaza Strip, the Hamas managed to develop and successfully deploy a simple steel artillery projectile – the Qassam rocket – in 2001. This rocket was used to attack villages and towns in south-west Israel.

Example 7.4 [3]
During WWII, caches and depots of weapons, ammunition, and materiel established before the war and during the retreat of the Red Army after the German attack, were used later on by partisans operating at the rear of the advancing German troops.

Example 7.5
Iraqi stockpiles of weapons and ammunition were captured by insurgents belonging to the Islamic State of Iraq and Syria (ISIS) terror organization during 2003–2011. Later on, Coalition materiel left behind after the withdrawal was also looted by ISIS people. During the Syrian civil war ISIS captured assets from the Assad's government and opposition (Free Syrian Army) forces.

7.3   Counterinsurgency Logistics

Counterinsurgency (COIN) operations are executed by the regime forces (sometimes with the aid of an external constituent) with the objective to eliminate or at least contain the insurgency. As an armed conflict, COIN operations obviously involve military and paramilitary actions. However, because the general population plays an important role in such conflicts, COIN operations must also include humanitarian assistance, reconstruction, economic development, and civic activities. The two types of operations – military and civilian – require different type of logistic capabilities.

7.3.1   COIN Military Logistics

COIN military operations are typically of low intensity, involving small and light infantry detachments dispersed over a relatively large geographical area. This dispersed and "thin" deployment requires a different, lighter, logistic structure then the traditional *OpLog* system discussed thus far in previous chapters. The masses of supplies and extensive capabilities necessary for campaigns and major regular operations are unnecessary and therefore inappropriate for a COIN setting. Not only that such an *Oplog* system would be costly and redundant, it may actually hinder the execution of COIN operations, which are "thin" and must be flexible and agile. Moreover, the sheer size and clear signature of a massive *OpLog* deployment would make it a prime target for insurgents' attacks.

Because the battlefield is dispersed, typically with no clear FEBA or FLOT, it is never clear which part of the region of interest is reasonably secured. As a result, lines of communication used for moving supplies and evacuating casualties may be vulnerable to insurgents' attacks.

Example 7.6
Improvised explosive devices (IED) used by insurgents in Southern Lebanon, Iraq, and Afghanistan affected the logistic capabilities of the COIN forces. Supply convoys were repeatedly hit by these devices and it took a herculean effort, with limited effectiveness, to mitigate the effect of such attacks.

The regime's most critical logistic challenge during COIN operations is the terrain. Typical insurgency battlefields are jungles (e.g., Colombia, Vietnam), densely populated urban areas (e.g., Aleppo and suburbs of Damascus in Syria), remote mountainous regions (Afghanistan, Peru) and vast desert areas (Iraq). The insurgents, who apply guerrilla warfare, seek to drag the regime's forces to battlefield located in these types of areas in which they can utilize their stealth and agility advantages.

The consequence of these observations regarding the operational settings – dispersed thinly covered battlefield, elusive yet effective opponent, and hostile terrain – is that self-sufficiency is essential for COIN combat units. Because such units are typically light infantry patrols or platoon-size strongholds that do not require heavy weapons and ammunition, self-sufficiency is more easily attainable than in legacy major operations. Thus, the second logistic option – *carry* – (see Sect. 1.6) becomes an effective option for the regime in COIN operations. Instances of resupply from the rear should be as sparsely spaced as possible.

Example 7.7
The Afghan National Army, fighting the Taliban, deployed companies in outposts located in remote mountainous areas, which were poorly accessible. These units had to rely, to a large extent, on their own resources, accepting the fact that resupply missions were scarce and unreliable.

Example 7.8 [4]
General Flynn: "The men of 1st Battalion, 5th Marines who fanned out across the district that hot July morning had to operate with no more supplies than they could carry on their backs. For weeks, they had no hardened bases, little electricity, and only radios for communication."

7.3.2 COIN Civilian Logistics

Alongside the military tasks in COIN operations, the regime also has civic missions that range from essential daily services, such as healthcare, education, and social support, to economic aid and reconstruction activities. Besides the obvious humanitarian aspects (see Chap. 8), these actions are also targeted at winning "the hearts and minds" of civilians who otherwise may support the insurgents. Providing medical help, executing public works and supplying food, water and other necessities require extensive logistic activities, which are not always compatible with regular operations of military logistics. In particular, social sensitivities that are usually absent in applying regular military logistics on the battlefield are crucial when dealing with civilians. The discord between the rough and rigid military environment during an armed conflict and the sensitive and subtle handling needed for treating civilian population under stress is hard to reconcile, as demonstrated in numerous events in Iraq and Afghanistan during the Coalition Forces presence in those countries.

Example 7.9
Building a well in a village in Afghanistan, where the women were accustomed to walking a long distance to draw water from a nearby river, turned out to be a mistake. The well was destroyed, not by insurgents, but by the women who loved the social opportunity presented by hiking to the river.

Example 7.10
Swedish troops found that building a well in one area in Afghanistan diminished the aquifer in an adjacent area, thereby creating conflict between neighboring tribes.

One way to mitigate the effect of this discord is to delegate some of the civilian logistic missions to civilian contractors and Non-Governmental Organizations (NGO). A significant benefit for the regime from contracting out civilian logistic tasks is the ability to ramp up logistic support capabilities and surge capacity without the cost of maintaining these capabilities during peacetime. Moreover, in power-projection scenarios, such as in Iraq and Afghanistan, mobilizing local contractors may have a positive effect on the civilian population by injecting money to the local economy and providing employment.

Example 7.11 [5]
During the U.S. war in Vietnam, the Civil Operations and Rural Development Support (CORDS) Program proved to be one of the most successful aspects of the war effort. Created in 1967 to coordinate support to the South Vietnamese government and people, the program's objective was to meet the population's needs in basic infrastructure, governance, and security. This program allowed US Agency for International Development (USAID) advisers to work with their Vietnamese counterparts at the province and village levels to improve local security and develop infrastructure.

Since the regime's military force is in charge during COIN operations, a major challenge for the regime is coordinating the nonmilitary missions, executed by civilians, with military operations. The two cultures – the rigid military and the business-oriented civilian – must reconcile.

Another challenge is security. The civilian logistic tasks are executed in a hostile environment that may be subject to insurgents' violent interference. Contractors and NGOs must rely on military forces to protect them; absent a sense of security, these civilian support organizations will simply leave their projects.

Example 7.12 [6]
USAID had succeeded in building a school in Khakriz, Afghanistan, but insurgents moved in while it was still under construction. In this case, the project failed due to lack of effective security.

> **Example 7.13 [6]**
> Geologic surveys identified extensive coal resources throughout Afghanistan, a potential boon for the economy. But it was mostly in remote locations that would require new roads. A military historian who spoke to the geologists in 2005 summed up the essential dilemma: "No security, no roads. No roads, no coal."

In addition to the aforementioned challenges, a serious concern is corruption. COIN civilian logistic operations – in particular construction and reconstruction projects – involve very large amounts of money. Lucrative projects, assigned in chaotic times typical to insurgencies, may lead to severe cases of corruption and embezzlement. Such phenomena are usually detected by the populace who may blame the regime for misuse of funds that could otherwise help the people directly. Such sentiment can damage the legitimacy of the COIN effort.

7.4 Summary

COIN logistics has three facets – insurgents' sustainment, regime's military support and civilian aid.

Insurgency is a collection of low-intensity violent engagements distributed over space and time, and often executed in the vicinity of civilians. Both insurgents' and the regime military logistics must be light, agile, and flexible. Insurgents' "lean" logistics is derived out of necessity – lack of a substantial, persistent, and reliable source of support. The insurgents start with very little resources and accumulate logistic capabilities over time as they mobilize popular support, capture regime's assets and obtain support from external sources. On the other hand, the regime controls a massive and well organized logistic infrastructure. However, that abundance of resources must be utilized, during combat COIN operations, in a way that fits the low intensity typical to COIN operations. It should reflect the relatively small demands and the thin and precarious lines of communication between rear logistic bases and forward deployed combat units.

The civilian aid requires a different kind of logistic support than the logistics needed for combat operations. This logistics must be tailored to population needs. The problem is that "population needs" may sometimes turn out to be an elusive objective, which is affected by tradition, culture, and local politics. These factors need to be studied and well understood by the regime before conducting civilian logistic operations.

References

1. Shrader CR. The withered vine: logistics and the communist insurgency in Greece 1945–1949. Westport, CT: Praeger; 1999.
2. Bracamonte JAM, Spencer DE. Strategy and tactics of the salvadoran FMLN Guerrillas: last battle of the Cold War, blueprint for future conflicts. Westport, CT: Praeger; 1995.
3. Turbiville Jr GH. Logistic support and insurgency. Hurlburt Field, FL: Joint Special Operations University; 2005.
4. Flynn MT, Pottinger M, Batchelor PD. Fixing Intel: a blueprint for making intelligence relevant in Afghanistan. Washington, DC: Center for a New American Security; 2010.
5. Cassidy RM. Back to the street without joy: counterinsurgency lessons from Vietnam and other small wars. Parameters. Summer 2004;73–83
6. Maloney SM. Confronting the chaos: a rogue military historian returns to Afghanistan. Annapolis, MD: Naval Institute Press; 2009.

Chapter 8
Humanitarian Logistics

Humanitarian crises evolve from either protracted situations such as civil wars and famine, or sudden-onset disasters such as major terror attacks, earthquakes, tsunamis, and floods [1]. Epidemics could either be considered protracted situations (e.g., Cholera in Africa) or a sudden outburst of a highly infectious and fatal disease (e.g., Ebola in West Africa in 2014). Crises could be localized (e.g., an earthquake affecting a single small region) or disperse, such as a wide-spread epidemic. Responding to humanitarian crises and handling their aftermath require a large and coordinated effort by government agencies, nongovernmental organizations (NGOs), donors, and industry. However, being typically one of the largest, best equipped, disciplined, and trained organizations, the military takes a major role in such events. Military forces are usually the first significant entity at the scene of a disaster and many on-going relief operations rely on the logistic capabilities of military forces. For example, many disasters occur in littoral regions and the US Navy, with its unique capabilities, is usually one of the first to respond. Thus, humanitarian logistics – from supplying food and equipment to providing medical help – is an important military *OpLog* mission.

Humanitarian logistics is a wide and complex area, involving economic, social, organizational, and political aspects. A significant body of research has been devoted to this area (see a good review in reference [1]). However, this chapter only focuses on the military logistic aspects of humanitarian relief operations. Specifically, in this chapter we focus on three topics:

- The role of an *OpLog* force as a facilitator of humanitarian relief actions during a disaster.
- The nature of *OpLog* operations during humanitarian disasters.
- Challenges an *OpLog* force faces while operating in a predominantly civilian environment.

© Springer International Publishing Switzerland 2016
M. Kress, *Operational Logistics*, Management for Professionals,
DOI 10.1007/978-3-319-22674-3_8

8.1   Handling Disasters

There are four classes of activities related to managing and handling disasters:

- Prevention and mitigation.
- Preparedness.
- Response.
- Recovery.

8.1.1   Prevention and Mitigation

Arguably, the best response to a disaster is avoiding it altogether. Taking actions that eliminate or reduce the likelihood of a crisis, or mitigate its effect is probably the most cost-effective policy. Reinforced buildings may prevent, or at least mitigate, the effect of earthquakes in urban areas, well-constructed dams and levees can prevent floods, and bio- or syndromic-surveillance sensors, together with an effective vaccination program, can help containing the effect of epidemics or bioterror attacks.

Despite the clear economic and social advantages of prevention and mitigation actions, authorities are not always eager to commit large budgets to such infrastructure projects whose benefits may never be realized and recognized. In any event, such large-scale disaster-mitigation projects require national resources and are mostly handled by civilian agencies. The military logistic force is seldom involved in such efforts because defense organizations are neither organized nor budgeted for regularly handle such missions.

Example 8.1

A well-known case where the military was involved in a disaster-mitigation project is the construction of levees in New Orleans. These levees were designed and constructed by the US Army Corps of Engineers, but were maintained by local levee boards.

8.1.2   Preparedness

Preparedness actions are executed to facilitate a fast and effective response to a disaster when the effect of the prevention or mitigation actions is insufficient and time-critical needs for recovery and supply must be met. Preparedness activities involve prepositioning of supplies and equipment in carefully planned locations, setting up infrastructure for aid facilities, establishing contracts with aid agencies, determining lines of communications for shipping goods and evacuating casualties, and allocating means of transportation.

There are some "usual suspects" for disasters. Earthquakes occur close to geological faults, wild fires happen in dry wooded areas such as Southern California, and hurricanes devastate the East Coast of the US during summer and fall. Yet, the location, time, characteristics, and scale of the next disaster are unknown, and subject to significant uncertainty. This uncertainty poses a big challenge for preparedness activities – in particular regarding the location of a disaster. Facilities and prepositioned supply depots must be situated in locations that optimize some measure of effectiveness such as the expected response time.

Example 8.2
The US Navy Maritime Prepositioning ships are forward deployed around the globe to provide, among other military missions, fast disaster response to affected areas. These prepositioned ships are currently stationed in the Mediterranean, the Indian Ocean at Diego Garcia and the Western Pacific Ocean (Guam)

8.1.3 Response

The highest impact action in a disaster is a swift and effective response. The first few hours after the onset of a disaster are crucial for saving lives, and the first few days are critical for the welfare, and perhaps even survival, of those who survived the disaster but lost access to water, food, and shelter. Timeliness of effective support actions is essential, but the effect of such actions may be hindered by the ensuing chaos and limited information that characterize the immediate aftermath of a disaster. Moreover, critical infrastructure such as roads, seaports, and electric grid may be destroyed or damaged – further accumulating the difficulties faced by a humanitarian rescue effort.

Main challenges at the response stage are effective distribution of supplies, management of on-site inventories, transportation control, and in some situations – coordinating evacuation. In many disaster situations such as earthquakes and chemical or biological terrorist attacks the first responders are medical crews who need to deploy health professionals and equipment, quickly identify critical tasks, perform triage, and treat the casualties.

Logistic and medical military units are best organized, trained, and equipped to effectively cope with such complex situations.

Example 8.3
One of the first medical groups to arrive in Haiti following the 7.0 earthquake on 12 January 2010 was an Israeli Defense Forces medical team. This team set up and operated a field hospital with specialized facilities for treating children, the elderly, and women in labor. This field hospital, which was sent from a location 5000 miles away from Haiti, was in full operations within 4 days from the disaster.

8.1.4   Recovery

The immediate response to a disaster, which is aimed at saving lives and providing essential subsistence requirements for the affected people, is insufficient for restoring normal living conditions. *Recovery* is the last phase in a disaster situation, and it is typically longer and less intensive than the preceding response phase.

Removing debris, cleaning the affected area, restoring the power grid and water distribution network, repairing buildings, and rebuilding roads are long-term projects that involve major management efforts and significant economic investments. Such projects are typically undertaken by qualified contractors and are funded by national or international agencies. The military logistic capabilities are hardly manifested in such efforts for the same reason they are seldom involved in prevention and mitigation efforts – they are not designed and built for this type of long-term civilian effort.

8.2   Intervention of Military Logistics

As mentioned above, there are two fundamental types of humanitarian crises: (1) situations that have evolved over time – draught, prolonged epidemics, protracted wars – resulting in severely distressed population mostly seeking food, shelter, and medical help, and (2) sudden events such as natural disasters – earthquakes, tsunamis, floods – and major terror attacks that generate abrupt surge in need for humanitarian help. While the first type of humanitarian crises – protracted situations that take many months or even years to evolve – poses great challenges for international relief organizations (e.g., United Nations World Food Program (WFP) and Doctors Without Borders), military forces per-se seldom intervene in such situations, which require long-term, continuous, and persistent operations by fully committed organizations.

Military establishments, dedicated to protecting the security and welfare of a state, can hardly commit their resources and capabilities to long-term persistent support operations. The impact of the military's vast logistic capabilities is mostly manifested in responding to sudden or short-term disasters such as the tsunami in the Indian Ocean in 2004, the earthquake in Haiti in 2010, and the outbreak of Ebola in West Africa in 2014. It may also respond to a humanitarian needs resulting from major war operations affecting civilian population, but in such situations the time-span of the operation is limited, as shown in Example 8.4 below.

Example 8.4
Following the end of the Gulf War in 1991, operation *Provide Comfort* deployed 13,000 American troops, as well as 10,000 soldiers from 12 other nations to deliver more than 25 million pounds of food, water, medical supplies clothing, and shelter to Kurds in northern Iraq.

According to the Federal Emergency Management Agency (FEMA) a disaster is defined as an event resulting in at least 100 casualties and damage worth at least US$1M [2]. Typical disasters in recent years, as the ones mentioned above, are of much larger scale. In a relatively short period of time there is a surge in the number of people who need immediate life-saving and life-supporting help, typically in hostile environments with no or very limited supporting infrastructure. Military forces are best equipped and trained to operate in such harsh circumstances and therefore effective responses to disasters heavily rely on intervention by military logistics forces.

The most important capability of a military force is its ability to relatively quickly amass qualified, disciplined, and well-trained people (soldiers), as well as critical equipment, at the site of the disaster. Command and control capabilities, which are the backbone of any military organization, become critical in particular during the first few hours or days of the disaster when the disarray is at its peak.

8.3 The Challenges

OpLog activities for humanitarian assistance and disaster relief face some unique circumstances and challenges that do not exist while supporting regular military operations. Logistics forces are trained and equipped to support combat operations, typically in harsh and contested environments. Such operations require specialized and well-protected equipment, such as armored vehicles and hardened packages, as well as security forces. Logistics forces are subject to combat attrition by adversaries – a fact that dictates the way supplies are moved and distributed throughout the area of operations. This type of "combat friction" is typically absent, or at least not dominant, during humanitarian relief operations. The heavy, hardened (often armored) transportation vehicles and handling equipment designated for ammunition and other heavy-duty military gear are usually redundant, and may even be obstructing, during relief operations.

On the other hand there are some unique challenges that *OpLog* forces must deal with during humanitarian relief operations, which are described below.

8.3.1 Response Time

Military operations are typically planned ahead of time or are anticipated based on intelligence assessments. In both cases the *OpLog* system has some time, which may range from a few days to weeks and months, to prepare and be ready for action when needed. This "readiness" lead-time is absent in disaster relief operations. Since an *OpLog* force cannot be put in a continuous and permanent stand-by position, and disasters usually occur with no warning, there will always be an inherent time gap between the occurrence of the disastrous event when immediate relief is needed and the time when first effective relief operations commence. This time gap is called "gap of pain." While medical support units are relatively agile and can arrive at the disaster scene within hours or a few days, supply operations, beyond the immediate airborne shipments, may take longer. Indeed, military logistics forces are best prepared to effectively handle disaster relief operations, but even they may not be able to respond fast enough due to existing protocols of request and response, set-up time, and transportation time.

Example 8.5
It took a full week after an earthquake pulverized Haiti before large shipments of emergency supplies of water, food, and medicine reached the affected area. It took over 10 days to accumulate about 10,000 US troops to assist with transporting and distributing supplies, providing security and clearing debris [3].

8.3.2 Last-Mile Operations

The *OpLog* system is designed and trained to operate in uncertain, friction-intensive environments. However, this uncertainty has some structure that is derived from existing operational plans, known deployment of friendly forces, and regularly scheduled demand reports received from combat units. This structure is usually absent in disaster situations. The time, location, and extent of the disaster are unknown in advance and demands for critical relief operations may be randomly scattered over a large geographical area. Advance plans of relief operations usually do not exist – in particular in third world countries – and demand requests may be sporadic and unreliable. Moreover, the nature of the disaster, e.g., an earthquake or a hurricane, may damage lines of communication thus limiting, or even denying, access to locations with the greatest need for help. In addition to possible broken physical infrastructure, relief operators may have to deal also with broken social infrastructure, which normally exists in resilient communities. Social orders may be broken in the face of life-threatening conditions.

Notwithstanding coordination with other agencies (see Sect. 8.3.3) the main part of the humanitarian supply chain – shipping goods and equipment to a central port of debarkation – may be a relatively simple task that is not much different from regular commercial transport. The "last-mile" movement of supplies and relief equipment may, however, impose extremely hard challenges.

Example 8.6
Following the 7.8 earthquake in Nepal in April 2015, there were villages in remote mountain areas that were still cut-off from any help 5 days after the earthquake. Roads were ruined and blocked, and aerial supply was limited because of lack of transport helicopters.

> **Example 8.7 [4]**
> Military aircraft delivered food to Sudan in 1985. However, rains that came in the middle of the operation rendered the land lines of communication to the rural villages useless. The capacity of the helicopter airlift delivery was insufficient and ineffective compared to the needs.

8.3.3   Military–Civilian Coordination

Humanitarian relief operations involve many entities – local government, foreign military, private organizations, nongovernmental organizations, and individuals. This plethora of entities typically lack coordination and sometimes will have different objectives, managerial styles, and mode of operations. While coordination could be improved by technology-enabled collaboration [5] the difference in the "operational culture" between military and civilian organizations is profound and may be expressed in serious frictions while operating side-by-side. The strict hierarchical chain of command and the culture of discipline and obedience to orders that characterize the military are not always present in civilian organizations. Moreover, the civilian environment of operation may necessitate the military dealing with issues of fairness, civilian grievances, and even corruption, which do not exist in regular military operations. Beyond the clash of cultures, there may be operational conflicts. Uncoordinated prioritization of relief support may result in unnecessary or unwanted donations from individuals or civilian charities that clog the supply chain and delay the delivery of more crucial supplies.

Another problem is perception. Civilians are hardly knowledgeable about military capabilities in relief operations and thus may harbor unrealistic expectations. To un-experienced civilian authorities huge transport planes, groups of uniformed well-equipped people, and an army colonel disembarking a helicopter followed by an entourage equipped with advanced communication gear may seem like heaven-sent. On the other hand, military relief forces may be greeted with suspicion and perhaps even hostility, in particular in countries with repressive regimes. People may associate uniformed soldiers – local or foreign – with internal security forces whose role is to control – not assist – the local civilian population. This potential mistrust and negative perception can hinder disaster relief operations.

8.3.4   Political Constraints

Humanitarian assistance by foreign organizations in general and foreign military forces in particular, is typically provided in a nonneutral political environment. Local politics that range from national pride, through strained relations with the country offering military logistic support, to blatant aversion to the population in need, affect the ability to provide effective humanitarian aid.

Example 8.8
Following a magnitude 7.2 earthquake in southeast Turkey in 2011, the Turkish authorities declined an offer of aid from Israel. The Turkish foreign ministry claimed that Turkey had received offers of help from dozens of countries but had declined assistance from all of them.

Example 8.9
In 1987 the Indian Air Force air-dropped relief supplies to Tamil minorities in the Jaffna peninsula who had been under siege by the Sri Lankan forces. While claimed by India to be a humanitarian relief operation, Sri Lanka viewed the operation as a prelude to potential military intervention for supporting the Tamil rebels.

8.4 Summary

Disaster and civilian crisis areas are not the typical "battlefields" in which military forces are regularly operating. The military primary mission is to defend national interests. Accordingly, combatants are trained and equipped to operate in contested areas, fighting opposing forces and not nature, which is the typical cause for humanitarian crises. However, military logistic forces are best organized and equipped to confront such crises and therefore quite often they are the first to appear at the disaster area and commence relief operations.

In this chapter we described the types of humanitarian crises, the stages of handling humanitarian aid, and the characteristics of military support operations in disaster areas. In particular, we highlighted the challenges that emerge in such situations from friction resulting from military–civilian relations.

References

1. Celik M, Ergun O, Johnson B, Keskinocak P, Alvaro L, Pekgun P, Swann J. "Humanitarian Logistics". Tutorials in operations research, INFORMS; 2012. http://dx.doi.org/10.1287/educ.1120.0100
2. Apte A. Humanitarian logistics: a new field of research and action. Found Trends Technol Inf OperManage. 2009;3(1):1–100.
3. The Wall Street Journal, 17 January 2010.
4. Cuny FC. The Lost American – use of the military in humanitarian relief. Frontline, PBS. 1989. http://www.pbs.org/wgbh/pages/frontline/shows/cuny/laptop/humanrelief
5. Ergun O, Gui L, Heier-Stamm JL, Keskinocak P, Swan J. Improving humanitarian operations through technology-enabled collaboration. Prod Oper Manag. 2014;23(6):1002–14.

Chapter 9
The Visual Network Model

In Chap. 2 we defined the term *logistic network* (Sect. 2.4) as an ordered set of logistic nodes (bases, facilities, plants, logistic units) and lines of communication (LOCs). The logistic network embodies the physical components and attributes of an operational logistics (*OpLog*) system. In particular, it represents the *logistic deployment* in the theater of operations and the *logistic support chain* (see definitions of these terms in Chap. 2, Sect. 2.4). The logistic nodes and the LOCs constitute the *OpLog* deployment, while the logistic flow in this network is generated by the logistic support chain. Thus, the logistic network is a tangible, observable, and measurable entity. It is the physical representation of the *OpLog* system.

In order to evaluate the components of an *OpLog* system, and to optimize its performance during an operation, it is useful to model the logistic network by a class of models called *network flow models*, or in short – *network models*. A network model is a formal construct that provides an abstract representation of a networked system. A brief introduction to this class of models is given in Sect. 9.1. In this chapter we focus on *logistic network models*, which are specially designed to analyze *OpLog* systems and to optimize their design and implementation.

There are two generic types of logistic network models: *visual* descriptive models and *optimization* models. The visual models provide a concise and essentially qualitative picture of an *OpLog* system. The optimization models are mathematical formulas and algorithms that seek best solutions for questions like:

1. What should be the size and content of a certain logistic node?
2. Where to deploy the logistic nodes?
3. How to route the logistic flow?

Chapter 12 discusses this type of optimization models.

A visual model provides a pictorial description of the structure and deployment of an *OpLog* system, and the main characteristics of its employment plan. In particular, it may be utilized to evaluate the operational and structural properties of an *OpLog* system (see Chap. 3, Sect. 3.6). The visual model may also provide means for a quantitative analysis of logistic properties such as *flexibility* (see Chap. 10).

© Springer International Publishing Switzerland 2016
M. Kress, *Operational Logistics*, Management for Professionals,
DOI 10.1007/978-3-319-22674-3_9

As it is shown later on in this chapter, the descriptive and qualitative characteristics of the visual model make it a useful decision aid for the *macro-logistics* phase of the logistic planning process (see Chap. 4). Because of its simplicity and transparency, it may also appeal to military planners who may not necessarily have strong quantitative background.

The objectives of this chapter are:

- Describe the general structure of network models.
- Construct the visual network model.
- Apply the visual model for displaying structural and operational properties of an *OpLog* system.

We start off with a brief and basic introduction to *network flow models*.

9.1   Network Models

A network model is a common and useful tool for modeling situations that range from physical phenomena, like electricity and water supply systems, through operational entities, like distribution and transportation systems, to managerial problems such as job assignment and manpower planning. A network model comprises two parts – a *graph* and a *flow*. The graph constitutes the fix and stable part of the network (the "pipes") while the flow represents the dynamic part (the "flow").

9.1.1   Graph

The graph of a network is composed of points called *nodes* and lines that connect the nodes called *edges*. The edges are directed from one node to another representing the direction of the flow. It is possible (though not very common) to have flow in both directions, in which case the two corresponding nodes are connected by two oppositely directed edges or by an undirected edge. In the rest of this section we focus on directed networks. Each (directed) edge has a *source node* from which it emerges and a *destination node* to which it enters. See Fig. 9.1.

The set of nodes in a graph is usually divided into three subsets: *supply nodes, demand nodes,* and *intermediate nodes*. The supply nodes are the origin of the graph in the sense that they constitute the source of the flow on it. For example, ports of

Fig. 9.1 Directed edge   Source Node   Destination Node

Fig. 9.2 A graph of a
network

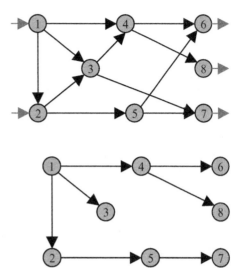

Fig. 9.3 A tree

embarkation are supply nodes in a maritime transportation network. Each supply node generates flow that is distributed throughout the edges, hence the name *supply*. The demand nodes are the end-points of the network graph and the sink of the flow. Each demand node absorbs flow from one or more edges, hence the name *demand*. Combat units who consume resources are examples of demand nodes. A node that is neither supply node nor demand node is called an *intermediate node*. The intermediate nodes constitute the medium between supply and demand nodes. The flow through intermediate nodes is balanced, that is, the total flow on edges that enter such a node is equal to the total flow on edges that leave it. The generated flow at the supply nodes and the need for flow at the demand nodes establish the rationale for the existence of the network. Figure 9.2 depicts a graph of a network.

Nodes 1 and 2 in Fig. 9.2 are supply nodes, nodes 3, 4, and 5 are intermediate nodes, and nodes 6, 7, and 8 are demand nodes. The incoming arrows to nodes 1 and 2, and the outgoing arrows from nodes 6, 7, and 8 indicate supplies and demands, respectively. Notice that an edge is uniquely defined by the (ordered) pair (*source node, destination node*). A sequence of edges such that the destination node of one edge is the source node of the next edge is called a *chain*. For example, the edges (2,3), (3,4), and (4,6) form a chain in Fig. 9.2. If the source node of the first edge in a chain coincides with the destination node of the last edge, then the chain is called a *cycle*. If there are no cycles in a graph and any two distinct chains intersect at most at one node, then the graph is called a *tree*. Figure 9.3 presents a tree that is derived from the graph in Fig. 9.2. Evidently, a tree induces a uniquely defined hierarchy where each node, except for the *root* of the tree (node 1), has exactly one predecessor. The end-points of the tree are the *leaves* – the demand nodes. Nodes 6, 7, and 8 are the leaves of the tree in Fig. 9.3. The hierarchical structure of the *OpLog* system induces a *logistic tree*. This tree is the focus of this chapter.

9.1.2 Flow

The graph of a network can be viewed as a system of pipes – parallel and intersecting – that carry some kind of flow. This flow may be electrons, water, vehicles, messages, or people. The flow is subject to a balancing low which is similar to the Kirchhoff low of distribution of current in electric circuits. That is, the total amount of flow that enters a certain node must be equal to the total flow that exits it. The flow that can run through a certain edge is constrained by the capacity of the edge. In water distribution this capacity is determined by the diameter of the pipes, and in transportation the capacity of the traffic is affected by the quality of the roads and the number of lanes.

A network may carry more than one type of flow. For example, a road network carries several types of vehicles such as public transit, trucks, and private cars. When a network model carries more than one type of flow it is called *multi-commodity network*. The different types of flow on a multi-commodity network are not independent. They share the same edges and the same nodes and therefore their flow is constrained by the capacity of these entities. For example, the storage area at a port of debarkation is limited and therefore different commodities (e.g., arms, ammunition, containers of general supply) may compete for the scarce space.

9.2 Logistic Network Model

We have already seen that the *OpLog* system has a hierarchical structure where a logistic node at a given echelon feeds resources to subordinate units at lower echelons. Specifically, logistic flow is delivered from the strategic bases, plants, depots, and arsenals to receiving points at the rear area of the theater of operations, such as port of debarkation. From there resources are delivered to forward theater bases (typically corps or division logistic units), which distribute the resources to the subordinate combat service support (CSS) units at the tactical level. Figure 9.4 depicts this hierarchy.

The single node at the left of the curved line in Fig. 9.4 is the main *supply node*, which feeds the flow into the logistics network. Note that the representation by a single supply node is notional; in reality there may be several strategic logistic centers that generate flow into the theater of operations. The part of the graph on the right hand side of the curved line represents the *OpLog* system in the theater of operations. Generally speaking, theater facilities and logistic units are intermediate nodes in the network, and battalions and their attached combat service support (CSS) units are the demand nodes – the *customers* or *consumers* (see also Chap. 5). It should be noted, however, that in order to facilitate attainability, theater logistic facilities and CSS units are deployed with an initial load of logistic resources. Thus, at the early stages of an operation, intermediate and demand nodes may also be considered as supply nodes.

Note that the logistic network has the form of a *tree* that is rooted at the strategic level and has its leaves at the tactical level. The number of layers in that tree, that is, the length of a root-to-leaf chain, depends on the number of logistic command levels. For example, if each (operational) command level in the theater of operations also

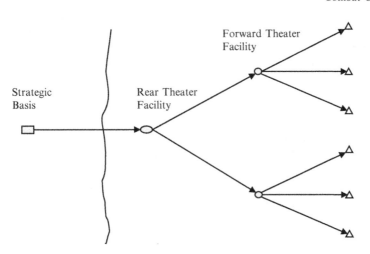

Fig. 9.4 Logistic network of an OpLog system

controls logistic assets, then the number of layers may be as high as five, corresponding to rear theater facilities, forward theater facilities (at the corps level), division,
brigade, and battalions' CSS units. The tree in Fig. 9.4 depicts a three-level
OpLog hierarchy.

Before we present the visual network (VN) model, let us examine more closely
the special properties of a logistic network model.

9.2.1 Nodes of a Logistic Network Model

The nodes in a logistic network model possess three properties that distinguish
them from the nodes in a standard network model introduced in Sect. 9.1. These
properties are:

- Capacity.
- Survivability.
- Dynamics.

Capacity

While nodes in a standard network model are usually dimensionless as they only
indicate end-points of edges, nodes in a logistic network model are capacitated
since they may represent storage facilities (e.g., fuel reservoirs) where flow is accumulated. The larger the capacity of a node the less constrained is the flow that runs
through it because there is more space to store flow. This property necessitates a

slight modification of the flow-balancing rule mentioned above (Sect. 9.1.2) since the total inflow to a certain node may not necessarily be equal to the total outflow. Some flow may remain in the node. In such situations the general balancing rule is preserved by appropriately defining artificial edges that exit the node and virtually release the excess flow.

Survivability

An *OpLog* system operates in a contested environment where logistic facilities and units are subject to battlefield attrition. A logistic node may be damaged by enemy's actions, or even completely destroyed, in which case it is removed from the logistic network. Such a possible predicament must be explicitly represented in a logistic network model by a parameter that indicates the vulnerability of the node and its survivability.

Dynamics

The graph of a general network model is typically stationary. The relative positions of the nodes remain constant over time as they usually represent either virtual junctions between edges in managerial settings such as manpower models, or static entities such as warehouses and stations in distribution or transportation models. Since many of the logistic nodes in the theater are mobile units that may occasionally change their positions – as the operation evolves – it follows that the corresponding nodes in the logistic network model may change their relative position too. This phenomenon implies that the *graph* of such a network model has a *dynamic geometry* – it may change its shape over time.

9.2.2   Edges of a Logistic Network Model

The three properties that characterize the edges of a logistic network model are:

- Capacity.
- Duration.
- Survivability.

Capacity

Edges in a logistic network model correspond to LOCs such as roads, railways, air-routes, and sea-lanes. Similarly to the nodes in the model, edges are *capacitated*. However, unlike the capacity of a node, which is a static attribute measured in terms of storage area or volume, edge capacity is a dynamic attribute that represents the *rate* at which the logistic flow can move through that edge. The capacity of an edge depends on the type, width, and topography of the corresponding LOC, and on the number, capacity, and speed of means of transportation that are assigned to that edge. To simplify the exposition in this chapter we use, from now on, the term *vehicle* instead of *means of transportation.*

The edge capacity is determined by four parameters:

V	Average velocity of vehicles that move on that edge.
Δ	The maximal *nominal density* of vehicles that can maintain an average velocity V. This parameter is affected by the number of lanes and by the minimum safety distance between vehicles.
N	Number of vehicles assigned to the edge.
L	The (geographical) length of the edge.

Note that N/L is the *assigned density* of vehicles on an edge.

The *capacity* of an edge is defined now as:

$$Capacity = Min\left\{\Delta V, \frac{NV}{L}\right\} = V \times Min\left\{\Delta, \frac{N}{L}\right\}$$

Thus, the capacity of an edge is measured by the maximum possible throughput of flow on that edge. It is the product of the velocity of the flow and its *effective* density. The effective density of the flow is the smaller between the nominal and the assigned densities.

Example 9.1
100 trucks are assigned to transport supplies on a road that connects a theater supply depot and a forward logistic facility. The distance is 100 km. The road is poorly paved and has only one lane. The average velocity of a truck on this road is expected to be 30 km/h. Safety distance between vehicles is 100 m. The values of the parameters are $V=30$ km/h, $\Delta=10$ per 1 km, $N=100$, $L=100$ km. In this case,

$$Capacity = V \times Min\left\{\Delta, \frac{N}{L}\right\} = 30 \times Min\{10,1\} = 30 \ trucks \, / \, hr$$

Duration

The *duration* indicates the nominal time it takes a unit of flow (e.g., a truck) to travel from the source node of an edge to its destination node. The distinction made in a logistic network model between the *capacity* of an edge and its *duration* is not common in network analysis. In a standard network model the assumption is that the flow is physically homogeneous and continuous over time (e.g., flow of water in a pipe). In such a situation the length or duration of the edge (pipe) has little importance since, e.g., the travel time of a single molecule of water through a certain pipe is practically meaningless. The significant factor is the feasible *throughput* of the pipe manifested by its physical capacity.

This, however, is not the case in a logistic network since the logistic flow moves through the network in the form of discrete quanta, like trains, trucks, and convoys, and not as a continuous flow. In particular, the "molecules" of the logistic flow are labeled and closely monitored.

Example 9.2

If a certain brigade needs an urgent supply of ammunition, the divisional logistician may be interested to know when the *first* five ammunition trucks (out of, say, 50 trucks) arrive to the division from the corps supply center. In other situations, he would like to know when the *last* transported tank reaches the assembly area.

While the *capacity* of an edge determines the *number* of quanta that can pass through the edge in a unit of time, the *duration* of the edge determines the time each quantum of flow spends en route. Formally,

$$Duration = L / V$$

Evidently, the two properties – *capacity* and *duration* – are not independent; both depend on the length (L) of the edge and on the velocity of the flow (V). The need to distinguish between these two related properties is demonstrated in the following example.

Example 9.3

A logistic unit comprising 480 vehicles has to move from logistic node A to logistic node B. There are two alternative roads – road *I* and road *II* – connecting A and B. The feasible density (Δ) is relatively low on both roads since other traffic (e.g., civilian vehicles) is expected to be heavy on those roads. The physical parameters of the two roads are:

Road	Length (L) (km)	Density (Δ)	Velocity (V) (km/h)
I	80	3	40
II	120	4	40

The *capacity* of *I* is 120 vehicles/h and its *duration* is 2 h. The corresponding metrics for *II* are 160 vehicles/h and 3 h, respectively. Thus, while the *capacity* of road *I* is smaller than road *II* its *duration* is shorter. It follows that road *I* is preferred to road *II* if it is crucial to deploy as fast as possible even a fraction of the logistic unit. If the mission is not complete unless the entire logistic unit arrives at B, then the two roads are equivalent since

$$Accumulation\, time\, on\, I = \frac{480}{120} + 2 = \frac{480}{160} + 3 = Accumulation\, time\, on\, II.$$

Survivability

The everlasting friction at the battlefield, and in particular hostile actions by the enemy, may degrade the capacity of an edge and increase its duration. An artillery barrage or an IED may hit a convoy on the road, and a commando unit may block a crucial passage. Thus, similarly to nodes, *survivability* is an important property of edges. *Survivability* may be measured by various probability parameters such as the probability of reaching the destination within specified time window.

Finally, the dynamic property of the nodes affects the edges too. When nodes change their position, the edges (LOCs) that connect them may be altered too.

9.3   The Visual Network Model

The purpose of the visual network (VN) model is to gain insights on the structure of the *OpLog* deployment and to facilitate a systematic, albeit qualitative, evaluation of its properties. This model is not a technical tool for *micro-logistics* planning (see Chap. 4, Sect. 4.4.2). Rather, it is a visual aid that may enhance the effectiveness of the operations-logistics dialogue during the *macro-logistics* planning stage (see Chap. 4, Sect. 4.4.1).

The VN model is represented by a graphical construct, which may be augmented by quantitative metrics of the type mentioned in Sect. 9.2. Figure 9.5 presents a VN model of a three-level *OpLog* structure. This structure comprises a single rear-theater node (labeled 1), three forward theater facilities (labeled 21, 22, and 23), and nine tactical logistic (e.g., CSS) units (labeled 31,…,39).

The characteristics of the nodes and edges in the logistic network are represented in the VN model by visual features, as demonstrated in Fig. 9.5.

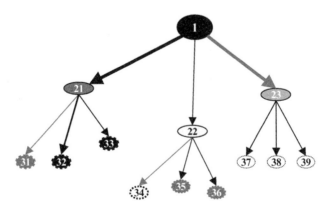

Fig. 9.5 A visual network model

9.3.1 Nodes' Representation

The nodes of the VN model are represented by oval shapes characterized by three visual features: *size, shade,* and *frame.*

Size

The size of the node indicates its *capacity.* The larger is the capacity of the logistic node, the larger is the size of the oval shape.

Shade

The shade of the oval shape represents the *survivability* of the corresponding logistic node. Lighter shade means higher vulnerability to enemy's actions. For example, tactical logistic unit 34 in Fig. 9.5 is more vulnerable than unit 35, and unit 31 is more vulnerable than unit 32. Units 32 and 33, and the rear theater node 1, are relatively safe.

Frame

The style of the frame surrounding the oval shape indicates the mobility of the corresponding logistic node. A solid line denotes static logistic node while a dotted line indicates a mobile node. It can be seen that mobility increases as one moves down the VN tree from the large rear facilities to the forward CSS units attached to the combat units.

9.3.2 Edges' Representation

The edges of the VN model connect nodes and represent lines of communication (LOC). The edges are characterized by three visual features: *thickness, length,* and *shade.*

Thickness

The thickness of the edge represents its *capacity.* Thicker edge can carry a larger amount of flow than thinner one.

Length

The length of the edge in the VN model is proportional to the *time* it takes to traverse the corresponding LOC. Longer edges correspond to longer travel times.

Shade

Similarly to the nodes, the shade of the edge represents the survivability or the risk associated with traveling on the corresponding LOC. A light shaded edge indicates a vulnerable LOC while a dark shaded edge represents safe passage. The possible effects of vulnerability are damage to infrastructure (e.g., severely damaged bridge) or damage inflicted on the flow while passing through the edge (e.g., an IED attack on a convoy).

9.3.3 Implementation

The VN model provides a quick and transparent view of the *OpLog* system in the theater of operations. It visually highlights structural and operational features associated with its deployment. The following two examples demonstrate possible implementations.

Example 9.4
The "width" of the tree in the VN model indicates the dimensions of the *OpLog* system with respect to the number of logistic entities and their deployment. A richer and wider deployment results in a more robust system that contains built-in redundancies. Such planned redundancies may facilitate effective backups among theater facilities. This robustness however is not attained without a cost. A wide deployment may result in inefficient utilization of transportation resources. If transport vehicles are scattered over a large number of disjoint LOCs, their employment may be less flexible and hence less efficient. On the other hand, a narrow deployment enhances the negative effect of bottlenecks or cuts in the logistic flow. In the absence of mutual backups, the *OpLog* system is more vulnerable to congestion and hostile actions. Figure 9.6a presents a wide deployment while Fig. 9.6b presents a narrow deployment.

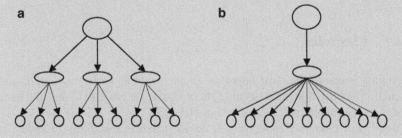

Fig. 9.6 (a) Wide deployment. (b) Narrow deployment

Example 9.5

A necessary condition for obtaining logistic responsiveness is that the *OpLog* system is deployed in accordance to the projected spatial distribution of combat intensity throughout the theater of operations. If the main operational effort is concentrated at, say, the west part of the theater, then the west portion of the *OpLog* logistic network must have larger capacity than the east portion. This property is reflected in the two graphs of Fig. 9.7.

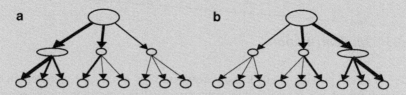

Fig. 9.7 (**a**) Westward oriented OpLog system. (**b**) Eastward oriented OpLog system

The two examples demonstrate a simple – almost trivial – utilization of the VN model for presenting basic structural features of the *OpLog* system in the theater of operations. A more profound use of this model is in presenting the structural and operational properties of an *OpLog* system discussed in Chap. 3.

9.4   Structural and Operational Properties

In Chap. 3, Sect. 3.6.2, we introduced several structural and operational properties of an *OpLog* system. The VN model can visually express some of those properties and thus may facilitate a simple, quick, and clear evaluation of a given *OpLog* deployment. The properties that may be represented by a VN model are *Flexibility, Attainability, Continuity, Simplicity,* and *Survivability*.

9.4.1   Flexibility

Flexibility is one of the most important properties of an *OpLog* system. Detailed discussion and quantitative analysis of this property are given in Chap. 10. Here we look at the visual interpretation of *OpLog* flexibility.

Recall that flexibility in logistics is demonstrated in the ability to update efficiently the quantity, mix, and direction of the logistic flow in the network, according to changes in the operational needs. This ability depends on the geometry of the logistic network, which is, as we have already seen, a hierarchical tree. The flow is running through the tree from its root – the strategic facilities – to its end points, which are the tactical combat service support units. In particular, there are effectively no edges that connect nodes at the same level, which means that there is no significant lateral flow between logistic nodes. For example, notice that the end-nodes in Fig. 9.5 do not have common edges. Excess logistic flow in one node usually does not compensate shortages in another node. This is because such a flow is infeasible due to technical, organizational, and even psychological reasons. A combat unit may only rely on longitudinal support from its "parent" unit – not from its "siblings".

Thus, the ability to effectively redirect logistic flow from one destination to another depends on the *locations* (nodes) where logistic flow is stored, and on the *velocity* of the flow. Logistic assets concentrated higher up in the hierarchy can affect more demand nodes at the tactical level, and therefore manifest higher level of flexibility, than pre-distributed assets. Adequate velocity of the flow is necessary to realize this potential flexibility. These points are further discussed in Chap. 10.

Figure 9.8 presents two deployments of *OpLog* systems. In the system presented in Fig. 9.8a the logistic flow is concentrated at relatively rear nodes. These nodes are connected to the front nodes by short and high-capacity edges. The "range of impact" of the backward concentrated assets is large; it can be directed effectively to practically any demand node according to the emerging demands. Thus, Fig. 9.8a depicts a flexible system. The deployment in Fig. 9.8b is not flexible. The logistic flow is already assigned to the end-nodes thus unexpected changes in the demand pattern may not be adequately sustained.

9.4.2 Attainability

Attainability indicates the logistic independence of the tactical combat units. The higher the attainability, the longer is the time period during which the combat unit is logistically self-sufficient. Attainability is achieved if relatively large amount of resources is allocated to the tactical CSS units before the operation starts. This situation is depicted in Fig. 9.8b. Arguably, high level of *attainability* is usually achieved at the expense of *flexibility*. If attainability is interpreted as the capability to respond fast to logistic demands, then there is another possible way to obtain it. Short, secure, and

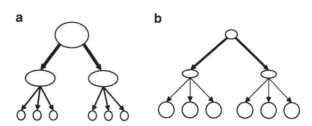

Fig. 9.8 (a) Flexible deployment. (b) Non-flexible deployment

Fig. 9.9 Attainability by velocity

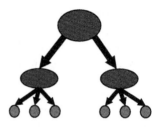

high capacity lines of communication to the demand nodes may provide attainability by "just-in-time" delivery from rear nodes (see Fig. 9.9). In such cases attainability is achieved by trading *mass* of inventory with high and reliable *velocity*. While the former realization of attainability (*mass*) is in discordance with flexibility, the latter realization (*velocity*) is in concordance. When the operation of the logistic support chain is based on high velocity then flexibility is consistent with attainability.

9.4.3   Continuity

Continuity has been defined as the property representing the stability of the logistic flow over time. The flow is stable and uninterrupted as long as the network is not over congested – a situation that may severely reduce velocity. Also, continuity is maintained if no LOC is "cut" by hostile actions or by the elements. The probability for these undesirable effects increases when the capacity and survivability of the logistic network decrease and the duration of the LOCs increases. Thus, adequate continuity of the *OpLog* system is represented in the VN model by dark nodes, and thick, short, and dark edges.

9.4.4   Simplicity

There are several aspects of *simplicity* that apply to *OpLog* systems, not all mirrored in the VN model. One aspect of simplicity is embodied in the number of *interchange points* along the logistic support chain. Interchange points are logistic intermediate nodes in which logistic flow is transferred from one mean of transportation to another. A port of debarkation is one example of an interchange point. Another example is a meeting point between two supply convoys from two different echelons.

Operating and controlling an interchange point is a difficult task – in particular in the presence of battlefield uncertainty and friction. It involves loading, unloading, storing, and traffic control – all of which require careful scheduling and coordination among interdependent entities. Consequently, each such interchange point adds considerable complexity to the execution of the logistic support chain, and therefore simplicity is enhanced when the number of interchange points is minimized.

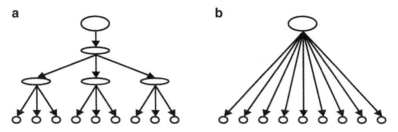

Fig. 9.10 (**a**) Complex OpLog system. (**b**) Simple OpLog system

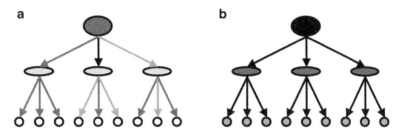

Fig. 9.11 (**a**) Less survivable system. (**b**) More survivable system

In other words, a "direct" logistic support chain is simpler to operate than a multiple-links chain where intermediate nodes add extra delays. This aspect of simplicity may contradict other properties such as continuity. Figure 9.10 presents VN models depicting the notion of simplicity.

9.4.5 Survivability

The survivability of an *OpLog* system is described in the VN model by the shade of the nodes and the edges. Darker shades indicate more secure and robust components of the logistic network. The two graphs in Fig. 9.11 depict this property.

9.5 Summary

Decision-making in complex and uncertain situations is a difficult process that requires analytic skills, well-balanced judgment, and some level of abstraction. Logistic planning is such a complex decision process. Many variables, parameters, and interrelationships must be taken into consideration simultaneously.

Decision support systems (DSS) are models that may aid decision-makers in complex decision problems. DSS models simplify the situation, highlight relevant aspects of it and provide analytic insight. The *visual network* model is a simple, non-quantitative DSS model for logistic planning. It provides visual interpretation of structural and operational properties of an *OpLog* system and therefore may be useful in particular at the *macro-logistics* planning stage where general, sometimes abstract, concepts are discussed and analyzed by both logisticians and operations planners. Such a visual aid may help to transmit ideas, exchange views, and focus the discussion.

An appropriately scaled VN model of an *OpLog* system may be placed as an overlay on a map of the theater of operations, thereby placing the logistic properties in relevant operational context.

Chapter 10
OpLog Flexibility

Field commanders and military scholars recognize the need for flexibility in planning and executing military operations. In operational art the concept of flexibility is imbedded in the tenet of *freedom of action*. At any given time before or during a military operation, the commander seeks to maximize the number of feasible courses of actions. The more the operational options that are available for possible implementation, the larger is his flexibility and his freedom of action. In the decision-sciences literature, flexibility is sometimes defined similarly as the *number of optional alternatives left over after one has made an initial decision* [1, 2]. By increasing the range of optional alternatives, flexibility essentially reduces the number and severity of the operational constraints.

Flexibility in military operations is needed because of the inherent uncertainty that exists in any facet of the battlefield. In the presence of uncertain combat situations, a military force must be capable of responding rapidly and adapting itself effectively to new conditions and circumstances.

Battlefield uncertainty is a result of several factors. The foremost factor is the *enemy* whose continuous objective is to obstruct the actions of the friendly forces. The enemy invests considerable effort to hide his plans and thus to enhance the uncertainty and confusion within the ranks of his opponent – the friendly forces. This effort is confronted by attempts of the friendly forces' intelligence to reveal as much as possible of these plans. Such attempts have never been, and probably will never be, fully successful [3]. Intelligence information is fuzzy, polluted with noise, and, in many cases, it is only partial. Thus, intelligence can provide no more than educated assessments (if not guesses) of the enemy's intentions and plans, and therefore only low-confidence projections of his possible future actions.

Parts of this chapter are adopted from:
Kress, M., "Flexibility in Operational-Level Logistics", Military Operations Research, 5, 1, pp 41–54, 2000.

The other cause for uncertainty at the battlefield is the synergistic effect of two phenomena: environmental and behavioral. On the one hand the environment – the terrain and the elements – impose operational constraints that depend on factors such as road conditions, ground obstacles, weather, and visibility. The type and impact of these environmental factors may change over time in a random manner. On the other hand, the cognitive and behavioral effects of confusion, misunderstandings, and mis-interpretations may have a severe impact on the way missions are executed. The combined effect of the environmental random impacts and the human behavioral confusion leads to a phenomenon called by von Clausewitz the *friction of war* [4].

The uncertainty in the battlefield may lead to altered operational plans and can generate new – sometimes completely unpredictable – combat situations to which the commander must respond effectively and in a timely manner. Field commanders are aware of this unstable, and even chaotic, environment. They usually describe war as the "kingdom of uncertainty." *Flexibility* is an attribute that can mollify the effects of battlefield uncertainty.

In this chapter we review the aspects of flexibility in the context of operational level of war (Sects. 10.1 and 10.2) and discuss the need for flexibility in logistics (Sect. 10.3). The core of this chapter (Sect. 10.4) includes a classification of flexibility into two types – *intrinsic* and *structural*. Methodologies for evaluating intrinsic and structural flexibilities in *OpLog* settings are proposed.

10.1   Facets of Flexibility

Flexibility in combat has several facets. First, flexibility must be integrated in the operational vision of the commander. Schneider [5] defines this quality as *mental agility* – the cognitive ability to react to changes in the combat situation faster than they occur. The second aspect of flexibility applies to the command and control structure, and to the decision-making process associated with it. As an organization, a command post must demonstrate behavioral flexibility manifested in rapid struc-tural and functional adjustments to changing situations. Standard operational proce-dures (SOP) and C⁴I systems must be set such that these adjustments could be implemented effectively and fast. The combined effect of the *cognitive flexibility* of the commander and the *functional flexibility* of his staff facilitate a creative environ-ment in which several alternative courses of actions may continuously be generated and reviewed. These two aspects of flexibility create the *potential* for an efficient response to changes in the battlefield. The *actual* realization of this potential depends on the third facet of battlefield flexibility – *physical flexibility*.

Physical flexibility is derived from the tangible attributes of the force in the the-ater of operations. In manufacturing systems physical flexibility is embodied in the design of production processes, type of equipment used, workforce personnel, and material management. Similarly, physical flexibility (or lack thereof) in military operations is derived from the force size, its mix, and the way it is deployed in the theater of operations. In particular, physical flexibility depends on the layout of the logistic facilities, the choice of lines of communications, the schedule of the logistics support chain, the types of resources, and their allocation among the various units. For brevity we will drop the *physical* part from the term and refer henceforth simply to *flexibility*.

10.2 Flexibility in Military Operations

Before we formally define flexibility in the context of military operations, let us examine this term in a more general setting of *systems*.

Flexibility is an attribute associated with systems [6]. A system is a collection of entities and processes that are united by common objectives. A system can be physical, such as weapon system or audio system, or more abstract, such as health-care system and defense system. An entity in a system may be a system by itself. For example, a computer system is an entity in a manpower system of an organization. A system is said to be *flexible* if it can quickly respond to new constraints, demands, and environmental changes in such a way that its objectives can still be achieved effectively.

A military operation can be viewed as a system. The entities of the system are combat forces, weapons, command and control systems, logistic units and facilities, etc. The processes are fire, maneuver, command and control, intelligence, supply, etc. The commander of an operation commands the entities, initiates the processes, and controls them.

Unlike the flexibility in manufacturing that has some permanent, or at least long-range, effect, flexibility in military operations is temporal – it may change very rapidly over time. A certain deployment of combat forces may exhibit more flexibility than another deployment. Since operational deployments change over time, so does also the flexibility of the force. The imbedded operational flexibility in a certain state of the operation depends particularly on the spatial layout of the force in the theater of operations, the mix of its combat units, the position of the enemy, and the environment. Higher versatility of combat units and weapons enhances the capability of the commander to effectively respond to a wider variety of contingencies. The concept of *combined arms* has emerged as a result of the quest for a higher versatility, and thus flexibility, in employing forces in the modern battlefield. Flexibility is also enhanced when the commander can postpone the decision regarding commitments of units to a particular combat zone as long as possible. Figure 10.1 demonstrates, in simple and generic terms, one aspect of this property.

Figure 10.1a, b depict a rear staging area and three possible forward combat zones where forces may be employed. The lines represent lines of communication. The operational scenario is uncertain and therefore it is not clear what should be the proper deployment of the forces among these three zones. In Fig. 10.1a the entire force is held back at a staging area out from which it can be rapidly deployed in any of the three zones. In Fig. 10.1b the force has been divided and committed to the three zones. As time advances and the battlefield's characteristics and intensities in

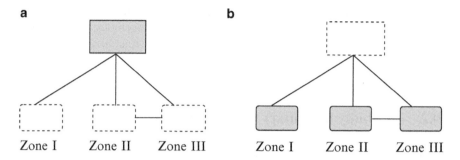

Fig. 10.1 (**a**) Rear deployment. (**b**) Forward deployment

the three zones unfold, the force can be deployed in a much more efficient way in case (a) than in case (b) where force adjustments could be directly accomplished only between zones II and III. Notwithstanding other operational constraints (such as mobility capabilities), it is clear that the posture in Fig. 10.1a is inherently more flexible than that in Fig. 10.1b. It is more robust to possible variability in battlefield circumstances.

The attainment of operational flexibility is affected by the ability of the supporting and sustaining systems to respond quickly and effectively to uncertain demands. In other words – it is affected by *logistic flexibility*.

10.3   Need for Flexibility in Logistics

Operational flexibility may be attained only if the operational plans for the various contingencies can be adequately sustained. To accomplish this requirement, it is clear that the supporting logistic system must be flexible too. Moreover, flexibility in logistics is essential even in relatively stable operational situations where the overall level of uncertainty is low. Within a given operational scenario there is much room for tactical variability that stems from the random effects of combat phenomena such as fire and maneuver. This tactical uncertainty is manifested, among other things, by high variance in consumption and attrition rates, which translate into variable demands for logistic resources (see Chap. 6). It is impossible to project with certainty the demands for the various logistic resources. Specifically, no logistician can be absolutely sure about the quantity of future needed resources, their mix, the time at which they are needed and the location of the points of demand.

The four-dimensional variable that represents demands for logistic resources – *quantity, mix, time,* and *location* – is constantly changing, according to the tactical situations, in a manner that is not completely predictable. The random demands for logistic resources, such as ammunition, fuel, and spare parts may require frequent and unforeseen shifts in their allocations. In order to be able to adequately respond to the uncertain demands, the logistic system must be flexible. The need for flexibility is prevalent in particular if logistic responsiveness depends more on efficient delivery (*velocity*) than on stocks on site (*mass*). When large humps of logistic stocks in combat units are traded for speed and precision in delivery [7] flexibility becomes an essential property to achieve responsiveness. Thus, flexibility is one of the key desired elements of operational logistics [8].

10.4 Defining Logistic Flexibility

Similarly to operational flexibility, logistic flexibility is defined as *the ability to quickly respond and satisfy changing demands for logistic resources*. This definition is simple, clear, and describes reasonably well the nature of flexibility in the logistic context. However, this definition is too general and abstract for any practical analysis. It tells us what are the capabilities that compose logistic flexibility but it can be hardly used to measure, or even to formally identify, these capabilities in a given logistic deployment. The question is: *what are the physical attributes of an OpLog system that generate logistic flexibility?*

There are two main attributes that characterize logistic flexibility:

- *Intrinsic (technical) flexibility.*
- *Structural* and *operational flexibility.*

10.4.1 Intrinsic Flexibility

Intrinsic flexibility is an attribute that relates to the physical components and technical capabilities of an *OpLog* system. This attribute has two aspects: one relates to the *functional interrelationships* among logistic assets (e.g., supplies and means of transportation), and the other applies to the *operational interrelations* between combat units (the "customers") and logistic services (the "providers").

Functional Interrelationships

Logistic assets are divided into two types:

- Direct resources.
- Support resources.

Direct resources, such as ammunition, fuel, food, and maintenance units, are logistics assets that contribute directly to the combat effort. They arm, feed, and maintain the combatants. Logistic support resources, such as means of transportation, handling equipment, storage facilities and command, control and communication systems, are used for processing, shipping, maintaining, and handling direct resources. *Intrinsic flexibility* represents the mutual versatility of the two types of resources – the extent of possible matches between direct resources and support resources. From a functional point of view, one logistic system is intrinsically more flexible than another if, for example, its means of transportation, storage facilities, and handling equipment are more versatile and therefore can handle a wider range of direct resources.

Example 10.1
A support resource that is intrinsically flexible is the Palletized Load System (PLS) [9]. Similarly to the trailer of a semi-trailer truck, the PLS is a transportation concept that is based on the idea of functionally separating between the vehicle and its load. This separation enables to quickly switch from carrying one type of load to carrying another type. Intrinsic flexibility is presented here in the capability to adapt trucks to carry a wide range of direct resources (e.g., different types of ammunition).

Example 10.2
The Movement Tracking System (MTS) [10] enables the logistician to track individual vehicles and cargo throughout the battlefield. In the presence of enhanced visibility of logistic assets, control over these assets is tighter and hence the response to changing circumstances is more effective.

Operational Interrelationships

The second aspect of intrinsic flexibility is the match between the customers – weapons, combat equipment, and personnel – and the mix of direct and support resources that they require. It represents the extent to which customers are interchangeable with respect to a given resource, and resources are interchangeable with respect to a certain customer. Thus, intrinsic flexibility is enhanced if more customers can be served by a certain logistic resource, or more types of resources can support a certain customer. *Example 10.3* presents few cases that demonstrate this facet of flexibility.

Example 10.3
Intrinsic flexibility is enhanced when:

- Certain type of fuel is suitable for a wide range of combat vehicles;
- Maintenance unit can fix a large variety of tanks and armored fighting vehicles;
- A weapon system, such as aircraft, helicopter and artillery piece, can deliver an assortment of munitions.

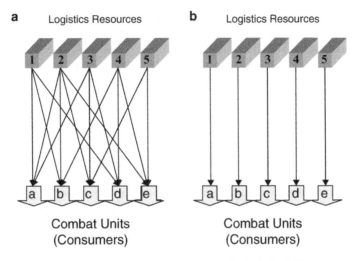

Fig. 10.2 (**a**) Intrinsic flexibility. (**b**) No intrinsic flexibility

Conversely, if a combat unit comprises a large assortment of weapons, and each weapon requires specifically designated and specialized maintenance services, then intrinsic flexibility with regard to maintenance is minimal.

The concept of intrinsic flexibility is similar to the idea of component commonality in Assemble-To-Order systems [11, 12]. A weapon in the theater of operations plays a similar role to the "products" in the Assemble-To-Order manufacturing system. The commander's operational priorities imply "prices" that are associated with mixtures of weapons, and the "common components" are common logistic assets.

Thus, the operational facet of intrinsic flexibility is associated with the versatility of logistic resources. It contributes to the capability to improvise – a basic tenet of operational logistics [13] (see also Chap. 3). Figures 10.2a, b depict graphically the idea of intrinsic flexibility. Figure 10.2a represents a situation where the operational-interrelationship aspect of intrinsic flexibility exists, while Fig. 10.2b represents no such feature. An arrow in the graph corresponds to a possible (physical) match between a customer and a logistic resource. For example, resource number 3 can support combat units a, c, and d in the flexible system (Fig. 10.2a), while it can support only one unit, unit c, in the inflexible system (Fig. 10.2b).

Measuring Intrinsic Flexibility

The *Intrinsic Flexibility Index* (*IFI*) is a quantitative measure depending on the force formation (e.g., combat units, support units) and the set of logistic direct- and support resources. The *IFI* ranges between 0 (no intrinsic flexibility) and 1 (perfect intrinsic flexibility), and it reflects the two aspects of intrinsic flexibility – functional and operational. These two aspects are merged into a single index in the following way.

We define an *essential demand unit* (*EDU*) by an ordered pair (*u,l*). The first entry *u*, *u* = 1,...,*U*, represents a combat unit (e.g., Howitzer battalion, Tow company, Merkava tank battalion). The second entry *l*, *l* =1,...,*L*, represents a *generic* direct resource that may be consumed by the corresponding combat unit (e.g., fuel, AT missiles). For example, the pair (*battalion 123, tank ammunition*) may be an *EDU* if battalion 123 is a tank battalion. It cannot be an *EDU* if the combat unit is an artillery battalion. Let *M* denote the number of possible *EDU*s in a military force.

Let *R* denote the set of all types of support resources (e.g., trucks, warehouses, forklifts, and trailers) and all types of *specific* logistic resources (e.g., 155 mm artillery shells, HE-AP tank rounds, diesel fuel, water, *certain* maintenance unit). A component in *R* is called a *logistic asset* and the number of items in *R* is *K*. Let *k*, *k*=1,..,*K* denote the *k*-th logistic asset in *R*. A logistic asset *k* is said to be *associated* with a certain *EDU* (*u,l*) if it is utilized by the *EDU*. Association is denoted by the symbol →.

Example 10.4
Some associations, such as (*120 mm tank rounds*) → (*Abrams tank battalion 1, tank rounds*) or (*Surgical Company Z*) → (*Infantry battalion, medical*), are self-evident. Other associations may or may not hold. The existence of the association (*Maintenance unit X*) → (*MLRS battery, maintenance*) depends on the qualification and training of the staff at maintenance unit *X*, its equipment, and the spare-parts that it carries.

Support resources in *R* are associated with an *EDU* through the *EDU*'s direct resource.

Example 10.5
The association (*Trucks*) → (*Merkava tank battalion, tank ammunition*) exists because trucks are used to transport ammunition. This reasoning leads to the conclusion that the association (*Trucks*) → more (*Merkava tank battalion, Fuel*) usually does not exist since regular trucks may seldom carry liquids.

Following the discussion so far, we define the *IFI* in the following way. First we compute, for each logistic asset *k* in the set *R*, the ratio between the number of associations it creates with the set of *EDU*s and the number of *EDU*s. This value indicates the versatility of asset *k*. The measure *IFI* is then computed as the average ratio over the entire set *R* of logistic assets. Thus, when a smaller number of logistic assets can cater for a larger set of *EDU*s, intrinsic flexibility is increased.

Formally,

$$IFI = \frac{1}{KM} \sum_k \sum_u \sum_l a_{kul}$$

where a_{kul} is equal 1 if logistic asset k is associated with EDU (u,l), and is equal 0, otherwise.

It can be verified that $0 \le IFI \le 1$. Maximum intrinsic flexibility ($IFI=1$) is attained when each logistic asset is associated with all $EDUs$.

Example 10.6
Combat Units: 10 (dismounted) infantry battalions (*InfBat*), 20 tank battalions (*TnkBat*).

Generic Logistics Resources: machine-gun ammunition (*MGAm*), tank ammunition (*TKAm*), fuel (*F*).

EDUs: (*InfBat, MGAm*), (*TnkBat, TKAm*), (*TnkBat, F*).
  (Here $M = 10 + 20 + 20 = 50$).

Logistics Assets: trucks (*T*), bowsers (*B*). 0.5 inch rounds (*0.5 in*), 105 mm rounds (*105 mm*), diesel oil (*DO*), ($K=5$).

Associations: $T \rightarrow$ (*InfBat, MGAm*), (10 associations); $T \rightarrow$ (*TnkBat, TKAm*), (20 associations); $B \rightarrow$ (*TnkBat, F*), (20 associations); *0.5 in* $\rightarrow$ (*InfBat, MGAm*), (10 associations); *105 mm* $\rightarrow$ (*TnkBat, TKAm*), (20 associations); *DO* $\rightarrow$ (*TnkBat, F*), (20 associations).
  The intrinsic flexibility index in this case is:

$$IFI = \frac{100}{5 \times 50} = 0.4.$$

Suppose now that the trucks and bowsers are replaced by a PLS system that is fit to transport both solid and liquid cargo. In this case,

Logistics Assets: PLS (*P*), 0.5 inch rounds (*0.5 in*), 105 mm rounds (*105 mm*), diesel oil (*DO*) ($K=4$).

Associations: $P \rightarrow$ (*InfBat, MGAm*), (10 associations); $P \rightarrow$ (*TnkBat, TKAm*), (20 associations); $P \rightarrow$ (*TnkBat, F*), (20 associations); *0.5 in* $\rightarrow$ (*InfBat, MGAm*), (10 associations); *105 mm* $\rightarrow$ (*TnkBat, TKAm*), (20 associations);
  and

$$IFI = \frac{100}{4 \times 50} = 0.5.$$

Thus, the introduction of PLS increased the intrinsic flexibility by 25 %.

Example 10.7

Combat Units: 10 tank battalions of type *X1* (*TkBatX1*), 10 tank battalions of type *X2* (*TkBatX2*), 10 tank battalions of type *X3* (*TkBatX3*).

Generic Logistics Resources: maintenance (*MN*), tank ammunition (*TkAm*).

EDUs: (*TkBatXi, MN*), (*TkBatXi, TkAm*), $i=1,2,3$. ($M=60$).

Logistics Assets: maintenance unit of type *Xi* (*MUXi*), $i=1,2,3$; 105 mm rounds (*105 mm*). ($K=4$).

Associations: $MUXi \rightarrow$ (*TkBatXi, MN*), $i=1,2,3$; $105\ mm \rightarrow$ (*TkBatXi, TkAm*), $i=1,2,3$.

Here,

$$IFI = \frac{10+10+10+30}{4 \times 60} = 0.25.$$

If, however, all 30 battalions are of the same type, or each maintenance unit can support all types of tanks, then the three maintenance units are merged into a single logistics asset in *R* and thus the intrinsic flexibility index becomes:

$$IFI = \frac{30+30}{2 \times 60} = 0.5,$$

which is the maximal attainable intrinsic flexibility for that logistics situation.

It should be noted that the value of the *IFI* is affected by the way in which the sets of *EDU*s and logistic assets are set up. When comparing the intrinsic flexibility of two *OpLog* systems these sets must be comparable in terms of content and detail.

10.4.2 *Structural Flexibility*

While intrinsic flexibility is concerned with concrete and practical aspects such as logistic skills, equipment properties, and technical capabilities of logisticians, structural flexibility is more general and less tangible. It applies to the basic design of the *OpLog* system and is heavily depended on the variability of the demand among combat units.

In trying to evaluate structural flexibility one may ask oneself:

What are the structural features of an OpLog system that make it capable to react swiftly and effectively to changing conditions and requirements in the theater of operations?

In order to address this question we utilize the *Visual Network* (VN) model introduced in Chap. 9.

Recall that flexibility is defined as *the number of optional alternatives left over after one has made an initial decision.* Also, similarly to military operations (see Sect. 10.2), flexibility is enhanced when the logistician can postpone the decision regarding commitments of resources to combat units as long as possible. These two definitions imply the following sufficient condition for structural flexibility:

Suppose that two *OpLog* systems – A and B – are equivalent in the sense that they share the same graph in a VN model. The two systems also have the same demand pattern. System A is **more structurally flexible** than system B if the following two properties are satisfied:

- The distribution of the flow capacities over the VN network is concentrated in nodes higher up in the graph of A than in the graph of B,
- The flow velocity on each edge in the graph of A is not smaller than the flow velocity of the corresponding edge in B.

Recall (Chap. 9, Sect. 9.2.2) that edge capacity, length, and survivability affect velocity.

This sufficient condition for structural flexibility is extended later on to a more general case where the two systems do not necessarily share the same graph or have identical demand patterns. Figure 10.3, which is adopted from Chap. 9, depicts the two aforementioned properties. The source and intermediate nodes in Fig. 10.3a have larger capacities than the corresponding nodes in Fig. 10.3b, while the reverse is true with respect to the destination nodes. It can be seen also that the edge capacities in Fig. 10.3a are not smaller than those in Fig. 10.3b, and the reverse is true with respect to their length. The system depicted in Fig. 10.3a is therefore more flexible than that in Fig. 10.3b.

Thus, structural flexibility is manifested by two attributes: *range of impact* and *response time*. If resources located in a certain logistic node can potentially support a larger number of units than the same resources in another node, then the former node has a wider range of logistic impact than the latter and hence it is more flexible. This observation leads to the conclusion that, ceteris paribus, a "concentrated" deployment is more flexible than a "distributed" deployment. That is, resources that are deployed higher up in the hierarchy tree generate more flexibility than resources that are distributed among lower-level nodes.

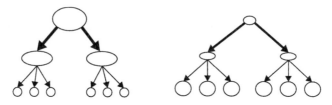

Fig. 10.3 (**a**) More flexibility. (**b**) Less flexibility

The wider range of impact is traded off however with response time (also called lead-time), which is the time it takes to deliver the required resources to the demand nodes. The response time increases as the resources are deployed higher up the tree, and therefore farther away from the demand nodes.

Structural flexibility measures the balance between the two contradicting aspects – range of impact and response time. Arguably, structural flexibility is meaningful only if the demand pattern is subject to statistical variation. If the demands are deterministic and known with certainty, then obviously structural flexibility has no practical relevance since there is no need to *react to uncertain demands*. These observations lead to the construction of the *Structural Flexibility Index*.

Measuring Structural Flexibility

The *Structural Flexibility Index* (*SFI*) is a relative index measuring the embedded flexibility in a given logistic deployment. It is determined by two deterministic (controllable) parameters, and two statistical (uncontrollable) parameters:

Deterministic Parameters:

- *Topology of the hierarchy tree* – the command structure of the force in the theater of operations,
- *Assets' distribution* – the allocation of resources in the various echelons – Battalion, Brigade, Division, Corps, and Command.

Statistical Parameters:

- *Response-times* – the order-and-ship times from each echelon to the customer,
- *Demand pattern* – the statistical distribution of the demands at the demand nodes.

The deterministic parameters are controlled by the commander, who determines the organizational structure of the force, and his logistician, who is in charge of distributing the logistic resources. The statistical parameters are random variables that depend on the combat situation. The randomness of the two statistical parameters implies that the *SFI* must be a probability-based measure. A natural choice for this measure is a function of the probability of satisfying demand. To demonstrate the general idea of the *SFI*, we use a simple two-echelon situation.

Two-Echelon Hierarchy

Consider the two-echelon hierarchy shown in Fig. 10.4. The graph depicts a command structure that comprises three units. Two combat units, $U(2,1)$ and $U(2,2)$, are logistically supported by a third unit $U(1)$ located in the rear area. The allocation of the (direct) resource among $U(1)$, $U(2,1)$, and $U(2,2)$ is x_1, $x_{2,1}$, and $x_{2,2}$, respectively. The effect of the (random) response time is measured by the

Fig. 10.4 Two-echelon
hierarchy

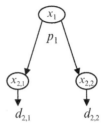

probability that the supply in the rear unit $U(1)$ reaches the customers – $U(2,1)$ and
$U(2,2)$ – within acceptable time frame. This probability, called *response probability*, is denoted by p_1.

Arguably, the response probability is a reasonable measure of effectiveness for
the response rate since it takes into account both the order-and-ship time (the "supply side"), and the acceptable response time by the customers (the "demand side").
The demands for that resource at $U(2,1)$ and $U(2,2)$ are $d_{2,1}$ and $d_{2,2}$, respectively.
The demands are random variables and we assume that the total demand is strictly
positive: $\Pr(d_{2,1} + d_{2,2} = 0) = 0$.

Suppose that the total amount of the resource is X, that is,

$$x_1 + x_{2,1} + x_{2,2} = X.$$

The *SFI* of the system shown in Fig. 10.4 is a function of the probability that the
demands at $U(2,1)$ and $U(2,2)$ are satisfied. To simplify the exposition, we assume
first that the response probability $p_1 = 1$. That is, the response time is adequate with
certainty. In this case it is intuitively clear that maximum flexibility is attained when
the total amount of the resource is pooled in the rear unit $U(1)$, that is, $x_{21} + x_{22} = 0$
and $x_1 = X$. To rationalize and formalize this intuition we proceed as follows.

First let us define,

$$a_{2,j} = Max\{0, d_{2,j} - x_{2,j}\}, \qquad j = 1, 2. \tag{10.1}$$

$$d_1 = a_{2,1} + a_{2,2}. \tag{10.2}$$

Notice that d_1 is the total excess demand by the tactical units that is not satisfied
by local inventories. The probability that the demands at $U(2,1)$ and $U(2,2)$ are satisfied by the resource allocation x_{21}, x_{22}, x_1 is given by the function $R(x_{21}, x_{22}, x_1)$,
which is called *sufficiency probability*. Formally,

$$R(x_1, x_{2,1}, x_{2,2}) = \Pr[Sufficiency] = \Pr(d_1 \le x_1)$$

$$= \Pr\left(Max\{0, d_{2,1} - x_{2,1}\} + Max\{0, d_{2,2} - x_{2,2}\} \le x_1\right). \tag{10.3}$$

Utilizing some elementary probability arguments, it can be shown that the sufficiency probability $R(x_{21},x_{22},x_1)$ is maximized when $x_{11}+x_{12}=0$ and $x_1 = X$. Since we assumed that $p_1 = 1$, it follows that this distribution of resources also maximizes the probability of satisfying demands. Thus, a reasonable measure of structural flexibility for a given allocation x_{21},x_{22},x_1 is the ratio between its sufficiency probability and the maximum possible value of this probability. That is,

$$SFI\left(x_1, x_{2,1}, x_{2,2}\right) = \frac{R\left(x_1, x_{2,1}, x_{2,2}\right)}{R\left(X, 0, 0\right)} \tag{10.4}$$

and clearly $SFI(X,0,0) = 1$.

If the response probability p_1 is less than 1, then the sufficiency probability in the numerator of Eq. (10.4) must be modified. In this case the *SFI* becomes:

$$SFI\left(x_1, x_{2,1}, x_{2,2}\right) = \frac{R\left(x_1, x_{2,1}, x_{2,2}\right)p_1 + R\left(0, x_{2,1}, x_{2,2}\right)\left(1 - p_1\right)}{R\left(X, 0, 0\right)}. \tag{10.5}$$

Note that $R(0, x_{2,1}, x_{2,2})$ is the sufficiency probability when the rear-area unit $U(1)$ is logistically ineffective.

Consider the following two special cases:

Case 1: $x_{21} + x_{22} = 0$, $x_1 = X$. Here the resources are concentrated at the top of the hierarchy and therefore maximum flexibility is degraded only by the response probability p_1. That is, because $R(0,0,0) = 0$, we have:

$$SFI\left(X, 0, 0\right) = \frac{R\left(X, 0, 0\right)p_1 + R\left(0, 0, 0\right)\left(1 - p_1\right)}{R\left(X, 0, 0\right)} = p_1. \tag{10.6}$$

Case 2: $x_{21} + x_{22} = X$, $x_1 = 0$. Here all the resources are committed to the combat units $U(2,1)$ and $U(2,2)$ and therefore the response rate p_i is irrelevant. In this case the *SFI* is just a ratio of sufficiency probabilities:

$$SFI\left(0, x_{2,1}, x_{2,2}\right) = \frac{R\left(0, x_{2,1}, x_{2,2}\right)}{R\left(X, 0, 0\right)} = \frac{\Pr\left(d_{2,1} \le x_{2,1}, d_{2,2} \le x_{2,2}\right)}{\Pr\left(d_{2,1} + d_{2,2} \le x_{2,1} + x_{2,2}\right)}. \tag{10.7}$$

Multiple-Echelon Hierarchy

The above construction of the *SFI* for a two-echelon hierarchy is extended now to the general case where the logistic hierarchy has multiple levels and its structure is not necessarily symmetrical. For deriving the *SFI* in the general case we need the following notation.

Notation

n	Index of a level in the hierarchy, $n = 1, \ldots, N$.
J_n	Number of logistic nodes at the n-th level. We assume, with no loss of generality, that at the top of the hierarchy ($n = 1$) there is only one logistics node, that is $J_1 = 1$.
(n,j)	A logistics node in the hierarchy where n is the level (echelon) in the hierarchy and j is the serial number of the node within the n-th level.
$S(n,j)$	The set of all logistic nodes at level $n+1$ that are supported by the n-th level logistics node (n,j). This set contains all the successors of (n,j) at level $n+1$.
d_{Nj}	Demand at node (N,j). Recall that demands are generated only at the end-nodes (*demand nodes*) of the hierarchy (level N).
p_n	Level n response probability. Formally, $p_n = \Pr[$The response time from level k to level N is *adequate* for $k = n, n+1, \ldots, N$, and is *inadequate* for $k = 1, \ldots, n-1$.]. In particular, p_1 and p_N are the probabilities for perfect response and no response, respectively. Note that in the "no-response" case the combat units (level 3) must rely on their own resources.
x_{nj}	The inventory of the resource at node (n,j).

The excess demand at (N,j) is

$$a_{N,j} = Max\left\{0, d_{N,j} - x_{N,j}\right\}. \qquad (10.8)$$

The total demand that is directed to node $(N-1, j)$ is

$$d_{N-1,j} = \sum_{(N,k)\in S(N-1,j)} a_{N,k}. \qquad (10.9)$$

In general, the excess demand at node (n,j) is

$$a_{n,j} = Max\left\{0, d_{n,j} - x_{n,j}\right\}, \quad n = 2, \ldots, N \qquad (10.10)$$

and the total excess demand that is to be satisfied by the supply at node $(n-1, j)$ is

$$d_{n-1,j} = \sum_{(n,k)\in S(n-1,j)} a_{n,k}. \qquad (10.11)$$

Denote $\underline{x}_n = \left(x_{n,1}, \ldots, x_{n,Jn}\right)$ as the logistic deployment at level n. Then the sufficiency probability at level n is:

$$R\left(\underline{x}_n, \ldots, \underline{x}_N\right) = \Pr\left(d_{n,j} \le x_{n,j}, j = 1, \ldots, J_n\right). \qquad (10.12)$$

$R\left(\underline{x}_n, \ldots, \underline{x}_N\right)$ is the probability that the demands (at nodes (N,j)) are satisfied by the supplies $\left(\underline{x}_n, \ldots, \underline{x}_N\right)$ that are deployed at the various units in levels $n, \ldots, N$. In particular, $R\left(\underline{x}_N\right)$ is the probability that the supplies carried by the combat units themselves satisfy the demands.

The *SFI* is defined now as

$$SFI\left(\underline{x}_1,\underline{x}_2,\ldots,\underline{x}_N\right) =$$

$$\frac{p_1 R\left(\underline{x}_1,\underline{x}_2,\ldots,\underline{x}_N\right) + p_2 R\left(\underline{x}_2,\ldots,\underline{x}_N\right) + \ldots + p_N R\left(\underline{x}_N\right)}{R\left(X,0,\ldots,0\right)} \qquad (10.13)$$

where,

$$X = \sum_{n=1}^{N} X_n = \sum_{n=1}^{N}\sum_{j=1}^{J_n} x_{n,j}.$$

The numerator of Eq. (10.13) is the total sufficiency probability when we also consider the response probabilities.

To demonstrate the use of the *SFI*, consider the logistic deployments shown in Fig. 10.5.

Both logistic systems comprise three levels and six demand nodes. The difference between the two deployments is in their intermediate level. System *A* has two intermediate logistic nodes – each supporting three demand nodes, while system *B* has three intermediate nodes – each supporting two demand nodes.

Assumptions

1. The response probabilities in both deployments are: $p_1=0.7$, $p_2=0.27$, $p_3=0.03$.
2. The demands d_{3j}, $j=1,\ldots,6$, are independent and uniformly distributed random variables between 0 and 200.
3. Within each level $n = 2,3$, the total allocated supply X_n is evenly distributed among the nodes $\left(n,j\right)$, $j = 1,\ldots,J_n$.
4. For each one of the two hierarchies, the *SFI* is computed with respect to three values of X (total amount of supply in the system): $X=500$, 600, and 700.
5. We consider five possible supply allocations to the three levels of the hierarchies:

   (a) *Top* Allocation. The supply is concentrated at the top unit:

   $$X_1 = X, X_2 + X_3 = 0.$$

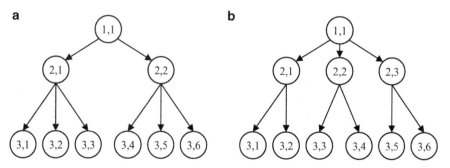

Fig. 10.5 (**a**) Logistics hierarchy A. (**b**) Logistics hierarchy B

(b) **Uniform** Allocation. The supply is evenly allocated among the three levels:

$$X_1 = X_2 = X_3 = X/3.$$

(c) **123**-Allocation. The allocations to levels one, two, and three are proportional to 1, 2, and 3:

$$X_1 = X/6, X_2 = X/3, X_3 = X/2.$$

(d) **012**-Allocation. The allocations to levels one, two, and three are proportional to 0, 1, and 2:

$$X_1 = 0, X_2 = X/3, X_3 = 2X/3.$$

(e) **Bottom** Allocation. The total supply is allocated only to the demand nodes:

$$X_1 + X_2 = 0, X_3 = X.$$

Table 10.1 shows the *SFI* values of the two logistic hierarchies, for each one of the five supply allocations and the three values of total-supply (X). The clear rows present the *SFI* values for logistic hierarchy A, while the shaded rows present these values for logistic hierarchy B.

As expected, the *SFI* values of the two hierarchies are the same for the *Top* and *Bottom* allocations, for any value of X. In these two extreme allocations the topology of the underlying tree is immaterial. Specifically, for any topology, the *sufficiency probability* of the *Top* allocation is

$$R(X,0,...,0) = \Pr(\sum_{j=1}^{6} d_{N,j} \leq X) \tag{10.14}$$

and therefore *SFI*=p_1.

For the *Bottom* allocation the response probabilities are irrelevant and the *SFI* is determined only by the *sufficiency probabilities*:

$$R\left(0,...,0,\frac{X}{6},...,\frac{X}{6}\right) = \prod_{j=1}^{6} \Pr(d_{N,j} \leq \frac{X}{6}) \tag{10.15}$$

Obviously, in our example the *Top* allocation embodies maximum possible flexibility, (*SFI(Top)*=0.7). This may not be the case if p_1 is relatively small. At the other end, the *bottom* allocation has, by design, no structural flexibility at all.

Table 10.1 SFI values

X	Top	Uniform	123	012	Bottom
500	0.7	0.56	0.39	0.17	0.02
	0.7	0.49	0.27	0.07	0.02
600	0.7	0.61	0.48	0.24	0.03
	0.7	0.56	0.37	0.11	0.03
700	0.7	0.67	0.60	0.39	0.06
	0.7	0.64	0.51	0.20	0.06

In this case the *SFI* value does depend on the value of *X*. We observe that the effect of no flexibility slightly diminishes when the total supply *X* increases and, as a result, the situation becomes less constrained. Specifically, *SFI(Bottom)* is 0.02 for $X=500$, 0.03 for $X=600$ and 0.06 for $X=700$.

From Table 10.1 it can be also seen that deployment *A* is more flexible than deployment *B*. Except for the two extreme allocations – *Top* and *Bottom* – where the topology of the graph has no effect, the values in the clear rows always dominate the corresponding values in the shaded rows. The advantage of deployment *A* over deployment *B* ranges between 5 % (*Uniform* allocation and $X=700$) and 143 % (*012*-allocation and $X=500$). In general, as more resources are distributed at the bottom of the hierarchy, and the total amount of resources decreases, the advantage of *A* over *B* becomes more significant. In other words, as the logistic system commits more of its resources to units at lower echelons, and the availability of the resources becomes more constrained, the effect of the hierarchy's topology becomes more dominant.

10.5   Summary

Flexibility is an important *OpLog* property. It introduces some robustness in a situation that is otherwise uncertain and chaotic. The more flexible *OpLog* is, the larger is the spectrum of sustainable contingencies. There are two aspects to logistic flexibility in the theater of operations. One aspect relates to the versatility of logistic resources and equipment. Higher versatility means better chances to cope efficiently with the variability in demands. A simple metric for this type of flexibility – the *Intrinsic Flexibility Index* – has been defined and demonstrated.

The other aspect of flexibility is concerned with the structural and operational features of *OpLog* deployment. The observation that higher flexibility implies better responsiveness is reflected in the measure that has been developed for this type of flexibility. The *Structural Flexibility Index* is a probability-based measure that depends on the topology of the logistic network and the distribution of assets among its nodes. It also depends on the order-and-ship times and on the demand patterns. Notice that the *SFI* also reflects other *OpLog* properties such as continuity and tempo, which are represented by the *response probability* p_n.

Finally, it should be stressed that The *IFI* and *SFI* metrics have very little absolute meaning. Their main purpose is to provide relative measures for comparing the flexibility of alternative *OpLog* systems.

References

1. Gupta SK, Rosenhead J. Robustness in sequential investment decisions. Manag Sci. 1968;15:B18–29.
2. Resenhead J, Elton M, Gupta SK. Robustness and optimality as criteria for strategic decisions. Oper Res Q. 1972;23:413–41.

3. Kovacs A. Using intelligence. Intell Natl Secur. 1997;12(4):145–64.
4. Von Clausewitz C. On war. Princeton, NJ: Princeton University Press; 1976. p. 119.
5. Schneider JJ. The structure of strategic revolution. Novato, CA: Presidio; 1994. p. 51.
6. Mandelbaum M, Buzacott J. Flexibility and decision making. Eur J Oper Res. 1990;44(5): 17–27.
7. Williams N. The revolution in military logistics. Mil Technol. 1997;21(11):50–1.
8. Brabham, MJA. Operational logistics: defining the art of the possible. Marine Corps Gazette; April 1994. p. 27.
9. Haas PM. Palletized loading system: not just another truck. Army Logistician; September–October 1996, p. 14.
10. Weigner HE, Lauden JH. MTS: a success story for battlefield logistician. Army Logistician; September–October 2005, pp 10–12.
11. Gerchak Y, Henig M. Component commonality in Assemble-To_Order systems: models and properties. Naval Res Logist. 1989;36:61–8.
12. Gerchak Y, Magazine MJ, Gamble B. Component commonality with service level requirements. Manag Sci. 1988;34(6):753–60.
13. FM 100-5. Operations. Department of the Army: Washington, DC; 1993, p. 12–3,

Chapter 11
Two Critical *OpLog* Functions

The six main *OpLog* functions were introduced in Chap. 3 (Sect. 3.5). They are:

1. Force accumulation.
2. Logistic deployment in the theater of operations.
3. Management and control of the logistic flow.
4. Medical treatment and evacuation.
5. Prioritization.
6. Logistic forecasting.

Four of these six functions are discussed in other chapters. Specifically, *deployment* and *logistic flow management* are discussed in Chap. 3, analyzed by a visual model in Chap. 9, and optimized in Chap. 12. *Prioritization* is an integral part of the planning process discussed in Chap. 4. Chapter 6 is devoted to *forecasting*.

The remaining two functions – *force accumulation* and *medical support* – are discussed in this chapter. These two functions are critical but in two distinct meanings. Force accumulation (also called *mobilization*) is *operationally critical*. No military operation can start before sufficient forces are accumulated and successfully deployed in the theater of operations. Medical support is *morally critical* because it deals with the life and welfare of human beings. Military commanders have a moral responsibility to secure the life of their combatants and ensure their wellbeing.

These functions also represent, in some sense, two extremes of the *OpLog* spectrum. Force accumulation projects fresh military might from the rear to the front, while medical services deal with attrition and casualties, and the thrust of their actions is usually oriented in the opposite direction – from the front evacuating to the rear.

© Springer International Publishing Switzerland 2016
M. Kress, *Operational Logistics*, Management for Professionals,
DOI 10.1007/978-3-319-22674-3_11

11.1 Force Accumulation

Accumulating combat forces and support units in the theater of operations is critical because it determines the initial conditions of the campaign and therefore also affects its outcome. Mobilizing and building up the military force in the assembly area must be executed fast and effectively, in particular in situations where the enemy has been staging a surprise attack. In such situations time is critical and thus the objective is to reach maximum level of readiness as soon as possible. However, attaining this objective is not simple. Force accumulation (FA) involves transporting masses of different types of forces on limited number of capacitated lines of communication (LOCs). The "friction" generated among military units that compete for limited number of means of transportation and LOCs, coupled with the malevolent environment created by the enemy and the elements, make FA a difficult task.

The objective in planning FA is to design an efficient, effective, and robust transportation plan that takes into account all possible constraints and limitations – both operational and environmental. Solving constrained optimization problems may support planning of FA. Some of these problems are discussed later on in this chapter.

Difficulties in Planning FA

At first glance it would seem that the uncertainty associated with FA is considerably lower than the uncertainty associated with the logistic support chain during operations. The location of the origin (e.g., home bases and strategic-level depots and logistic facilities) and destination points (assembly areas) are well defined, the size and composition of the military force are determined by operational considerations in advance, and the fleet of means of transportation is given. It appears as if all the components of the FA problem are essentially deterministic and subject to very little uncertainty. This apparent determinism is misleading. FA process contains uncertainties too that hinder FA planning.

First, the FA process is inflicted with "friction." People are hastily mobilized, processed, and equipped, and weapons are taken out from storage in a rush to be prepared for deployment. In addition to being conducted under the stress of time, these processes may also be subject to possible attrition by hostile actions of the enemy. Unforeseen predicaments, mechanical failures of equipment, mishaps, accidents, misunderstandings, and delays in the arrival of personnel at the mobilization points are inevitable events that enhance uncertainty and chaos.

Second, the movement towards the theater of operations is subject to random effects – in particular in ground transportation. Mechanical failures in vehicles, traffic jams, hostile activities of the enemy, the effects of the elements and the inherent variance that is imbedded in movements that are controlled by humans, are factors that contribute to that randomness.

Example 11.1

An interesting effect that has been observed in ground transportation is concerned with the internal dynamics among vehicles of moving convoys. This effect, sometimes called the *accordion effect*, is manifested in random expansions and contractions in the length of convoys. This effect affects the average speed of the convoy and its impact increases with the size of the convoy. Specifically, the average speed of a convoy comprising 100 vehicles is considerably lower than the average speed of a comparable convoy of only 3 vehicles.

Planning FA must take into account the embedded uncertainties in this process. These uncertainties, and other characteristics of FA, differ between the two principal FA scenarios:

- Forward Deployment.
- Power Projection.

11.1.1 Forward Deployment

In a forward deployment scenario the theater of operations is located relatively close to the home bases and the strategic logistic facilities. Moreover, certain fraction of the force is usually deployed routinely, at a high level of readiness, as part of the defense layout close to the boundaries of the theater (e.g., international border line). The transition time from peacetime deployment to wartime deployment is relatively short – hours to a few days. In such scenarios FA is executed mainly by ground transportation along LOCs that are no more than a few hundred kilometers long. All of Israel wars, as well as the Iraq–Iran war and the war between Serbia and Croatia are examples of campaigns that evolved from forward deployment situations. Also, the deployment of NATO forces in Europe during the Cold War had been in a forward deployment posture.

Figure 11.1 depicts force accumulation in a forward deployment posture. The width of the lines represents the capacity of the roads (see also Chap. 9). The flow of forces during FA is directed from the strategic source nodes (the rectangles at the left hand side of Fig. 11.1) towards the assembly areas in the theater of operations.

Modes of Ground Transportation

There are two modes of transporting heavy mobile weapons such as tanks and armored personnel carriers:

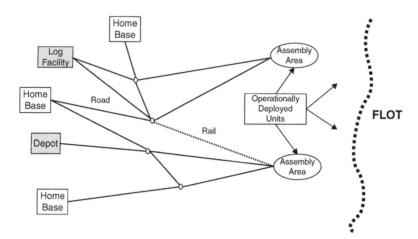

Fig. 11.1 FA infrastructure in a forward deployment scenario

- *Tracked Travel*: the mobile weapons travel independently – on their own tracks or wheels, usually off road.
- *On-Board Transportation*: weapons are carried on-board specially designed trucks called *transporters*, or are transported by trains.

The other parts of the force – personnel, C⁴I equipment, supplies, and service units – are accumulated by *administrative movement* comprising convoys of wheeled vehicles and trains. Arguably, *on-board transportation* is a special case of *administrative movement*.

Tracked travel is typically used for local movements close by to the assembly areas. However, if transporting capabilities are limited, combat units may have to resort to tracked travel for longer distances. Tracked travel is less desirable than on-board transportation because it is usually slower, consumes fuel from the weapons themselves, and may result in mechanical attrition. All these three predicaments negatively affect the readiness of the accumulated combat units. Balancing between tracked travel and on-board transportation is an important issue in forward deployment FA. It can be formulated as an optimization problem solved by a linear programming model [1]. A brief description of such a model is given in Sect. 11.2.2.

Administrative movement during FA may cause severe traffic congestion. Limited capacities of the roads, variable velocities of vehicles within convoys (see the *accordion effect* mentioned in *Example 11.1*) and uncoordinated arrivals of convoys at major intersections may result in long delays. Moreover, stranded convoys on roads are vulnerable to hostile actions by the enemy and therefore their time en-route, when the convoys are exposed to these actions, should be minimized. Thus, proper scheduling of the FA process is crucial for its successful completion. A scheduling-related optimization problem is discussed in Sect. 11.2.3

Convoys vs. Dispersed Travel

Ground transportation during FA is typically executed by long convoys comprising up to few hundreds vehicles. A convoy travels as a unified entity, which is centrally controlled by a commander and a small staff. The vehicles move in a column and no vehicle is permitted to overtake another unless ordered to do so. Moreover, a stalled vehicle – due to accident, mechanical problem, or a hit by IED – may slow down, or even hinder, the advance of the rest of the convoy. The interdependency among the vehicles in the convoy, and the rigid movement scheme that governs their travel, enhance the ability to control the convoy, but at the same time these features also reduce the average speed of each vehicle.

Alternatively, vehicles may be dispatched individually or in small groups. Each vehicle (or small group of vehicles) is assigned a transportation mission (i.e., a route and a destination), which is executed independently of other transportation missions. The advantage of this *dispersed travel* mode over convoys (also called *Platoon Movement*) is higher average speed and thus shorter travel time to the assembly area.

The higher agility of dispersed travel, compared to convoys, is demonstrated in the transition between movement and parking. Vehicles en-route to the assembly area may have to stop occasionally because of operational reasons or for rest. While these transitions are simple and quick for a single vehicle in a dispersed travel that only needs to decelerate to a stop and then accelerate back to its nominal speed, they are time consuming for convoys. The reason is that deceleration and acceleration of each vehicle in the convoy depends on the results of these actions by the vehicles ahead. For example the 99th vehicle in the convoy cannot start moving before the 98 vehicles ahead of it are back on the road. This inevitable delay may greatly reduce the convoy's average speed. Other delays typical to convoys' movement, which are usually absent in a dispersed travel, are those caused by the variance in vehicles' velocity and the congestion at road intersections.

A convoy may be viewed as a chain of operating entities, whose performance is dictated by the weakest link – the slowest vehicle. Slow moving vehicles, and at the extreme – stalled ones – affect the rate of advance of the entire convoy. Moreover, since over-taking is not permitted within and between convoys, fast moving convoys may get stuck behind a slower ones and thus generate a long, slow moving, column of vehicles that may be vulnerable to enemy's hostile actions. The situation can become much worse at road intersections where the passage of a long convoy may occupy the junction for an extended period (hours) and thus hinder the advance of other convoys that reach that road intersection from other directions. Most of these predicaments may be avoided when dispersed travel is adopted since independent vehicle movement reduce transportation constraints and friction, and enhance flexibility in utilizing the roads infrastructure. These properties result in better and more efficient time management of the FA process.

However, the clear time-related advantages of dispersed travel must be weighted against disadvantages due to limited command and control capabilities. A single driver may lose his way or experience a mechanical failure of his vehicle without getting the immediate assistance that is available by maintenance units that escort a convoy. Moreover, dispersed travel creates a state of diffusion in the transportation system where military formations are broken down and fractions of units intermingle among each other. This diffused situation is very difficult to control and thus limits the capabilities to generate an updated and reliable assessment of the FA situation. Lack of such information can have severe operational consequences since crucial projections of accumulation rates may not be available when needed. However, advances in tracking and information technologies may mollify these C[4]I limitations. Combining efficient tracking devices (e.g., GPS) with state-of-the-art information processing systems may facilitate the synthesis of an accurate digital picture of the FA situation even if the travel is dispersed.

> **Example 11.2**
> A problem relevant in particular to dispersed travel is to reassemble the units in the assembly area. The operational dilemma in this case is to determine the point when the accumulated force is transformed from a collection of people, vehicles, weapons, and equipment into a military force ready to fight. A typical question would be: is it preferred to have 30 battalions – each with only 80 % of the force ready for combat – or to have only 24 battalions (80 % of the 30 battalions) that are 100 % mission ready?

Although dispersed travel is potentially more efficient than convoys, it will take some time before such unorthodox method of military transportation is adopted. Only when effective C[4]I systems are fully operational and integrated in the military transportation systems a dispersed travel method may be seriously considered.

11.1.2   Optimizing the Balance Between Tracked Travel and On-Board Transportation

Suppose that N armored vehicles (AV) are to be transported from their home base to the assembly area near the theater of operations. M transporters are assigned to carry out this transportation mission. Transporters are usually a scarce resource ($M < N$) and therefore several tours of transportation (typically, 2–3) may be needed to complete that mission. The transporters load only part of the military unit, transport it to the unloading point, unload it, and then return to carry another part of the unit. This process repeats itself until the entire unit is transported to its destination. The problem is to determine the optimal unloading point for each transportation tour, such that the accumulation time is minimized.

All AVs are loaded at the home base. Point s on the road, $s=1,...,S$, where unloading of AVs is possible is called a *potential transition point* (PTP). Points $s=1$ and $s=S$ are the origin (e.g., home base) and destination (assembly area), respectively. Let,

$n=N/M=$number of tours. (We assume for convenience and without loss of generality, that N/M is integer).

$d_s=$distance between the home base and PTP s.

$VL_s=$average velocity of a loaded convoy (AVs on-board transporters) between the home base and PTP s.

$VE_s=$average velocity of an unloaded convoy traveling back from PTP s to the home base.

$VR_s=$average velocity of tracked travel from PTP s to the destination

$U_s=$Unloading time at PTP s.

$W=$Loading time at the home base.

The values of these parameters depend on the number of vehicles in a convoy. However, since we assume that N and M are given and fixed, the values of the parameters are also fixed for each tour. The travel times are:

- Between the home base and PTP s for a loaded convoy – TL_s,
- Between PTP s and the home base for unloaded convoy – TE_s,
- From PTP s to the destination for tracked travel, – TR_s,

where,

$$TL_s = \frac{d_s}{VL_s}$$

$$TE_s = \frac{d_s}{VE_s}$$

$$TR_s = \frac{d_S - d_s}{VR_s}$$

Finally, let R_i denote the loading start time of tour i. The problem is to determine for each tour its best PTP.

Note that if the PTP of tour i is s then $R_{i+1} - R_i \geq W + TL_s + U_s + TE_s$ must hold because the next tour $(i+1)$ cannot commence before the transporters return empty to the home base from their previous round (i). The accumulation time of the i-th tour is

$$AT_i = R_i + W + TL_{s_i} + U_{s_i} + TR_{s_i}$$

where s_i is the unloading point of the i-th tour. The accumulation time of the entire force is $Max_i AT_i$ and the objective is to find PTPs $s_1, ..., s_n$ that minimize this time. That is, the problem is $Min_{\{s_1,...,s_n\}} Max_i AT_i$. This is a constrained optimization problem (the constraints relate to the inter-loading times $R_{i+1} - R_i$) that is solved using mathematical programming techniques.

11.1.3 Optimizing Convoy's Dispatch Time

A transportation network of convoys has some unique features:

- The flow components in the network – the convoys – have *size*. They are not infinitesimal entities on the transportation graph – as are the individual vehicles in the case of dispersed travel.
- Since overtaking is not permitted, the rate of advance of one flow component on any given edge of the graph may be constrained by the rate of advance of another component that is ahead of it.
- A convoy may be denied passage at a node in the network (road intersection) because it is "occupied" by another convoy that passes through at that time.

Scheduling the dispatch times of the various convoys must take into account these special features, which are not common in ordinary network optimization models. In that regard, FA resembles a typical job-shop problem where several jobs (convoys in our case) must be scheduled on several machines (road segments). We use the following example to demonstrate the types of optimization models that may be applied for optimizing dispatch schedules – schedules that minimizes the accumulation time of the convoys.

Consider the graph in Fig. 11.2. Three convoys – A, B, and C – must arrive, as early as possible, to the assembly area at node 4. Node 1 is the dispatch point (e.g., home base) of convoys A and B, and node 2 is the dispatch point of convoy C. The convoys A, B, and C differ in their length (number of vehicles) and average speed. The problem is when to dispatch each one of the three convoys.

Fig. 11.2 FA network

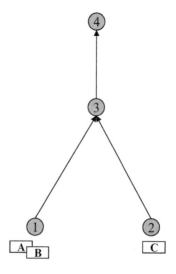

We assume, for simplicity, that there is neither uncertainty nor variability in the scenario's parameters and therefore the schedule of the FA operation is completely determined by three sets of parameters:

1. Dispatch times.
2. Convoys' lengths.
3. Convoys' speeds.

Let,

$X_k(i)$=The time when the first vehicle in convoy k, $k=A$, B, C, starts its movement out of node i. These are the *decision variables* in the problem. Note that at the destination node 4, this variable represents the arrival time to the assembly area.

$T_k(i,j)$ = Travel time of convoy k, $k=A$, B, C, between nodes i and j. The travel time is measured from the moment the *last* vehicle in the convoy leaves node i to the moment when the *first* vehicle of k reaches node j.

$U_k(i)$=Passage time of convoy k, $k=A$, B, C, through node i. The passage time is measured from the moment the first vehicle enters i to the moment the last vehicle leaves i.

$T_k(i,j)$ and $U_k(i)$ are parameters determined by the convoy's length and speed.

Since the graph of the force accumulation network is typically a *tree* that converges at the staging area, and since overtaking of one convoy by another is usually infeasible or not permitted, it is reasonable to assume that the precedence relations among the convoys on a route are maintained throughout the FA process. In other words, if at any segment of the road convoy A is ahead of convoy B then this is also the case for all other road segments on which both convoys are routed to travel.

Define,

$$\delta_{k,l} = \begin{cases} 1 \text{ if convoy k preceeds convoy l} \\ 0 \qquad\qquad\qquad\quad \text{otherwise} \end{cases}$$

Clearly, $\delta_{kl} + \delta_{lk} = 1$. Finally, let M denote a large positive number – larger than the various time parameters T and U of the problem by an order of magnitude.

The scheduling of the convoys is modeled as mixed-integer programming problem. The objective is to minimize the accumulation time. Note that the optimal precedence relation is determined by the binary δ_{kl} variables.

$$Min\, Z$$

st

$$x_k(1) - x_l(1) \geq U_l(1) - \delta_{kl}M, k = A, B, l = A, B, \ l \neq k \qquad (11.1)$$

$$x_k(3) - x_k(1) \geq U_k(1) + T_k(1,3), k = A, B \qquad (11.2)$$

$$x_C(3) - x_C(2) \geq U_C(3) + T_C(2,3) \qquad (11.3)$$

$$x_k(3) - x_l(3) \geq U_l(3) - \delta_{kl}M, \ k = A, B, C, l = A, B, C, l \neq k \qquad (11.4)$$

$$x_k(4) - x_k(3) \geq U_k(3) + T_k(3,4), k = A, B, C \qquad (11.5)$$

$$x_k(4) - x_l(4) \geq U_l(4) - \delta_{kl}M, \quad k = A,B,C, l = A,B,C, l \neq k \quad (11.6)$$

$$x_k(4) - Z \leq -U_k(4), \quad k = A,B,C \quad (11.7)$$

$$\delta_{kl} + \delta_{lk} = 1, \quad k,l = A,B,C \quad (11.8)$$

$$x_k(i) \geq 0, \delta_{lk} \in \{0,1\}$$

Constraints (11.1) determine the earliest possible dispatch time of the two convoys – A and B – that embark from node 1. If, for example, A precedes B then $\delta_{BA} = 0$ and thus $X_{BA}(1) \geq X_{AB}(1) + U_A$, meaning that the start time of convoy B cannot be before the start time of convoy A plus the passage time of convoy A out of node 1. Because M is a very large constant, the other direction is essentially unconstrained. Constraints (11.2) and (11.3) take into account the travel time of the three convoys to determine their earliest possible arrival time at node 3. Constraints (11.4) determine the earliest actual arrival time of each convoy at node 3 due to the delays caused be convoys that arrive earlier at this node. Constraints (11.5) and (11.6) determine, in a similar way to (11.2)–(11.4), the earliest arrival times at node 4. The inequalities in (11.7) are "MinMax" constraints that, together with the objective function (Z), determine the earliest accumulation time.

To illustrate the model, consider the transportation data (in minutes) shown on Fig. 11.3. An optimal dispatch schedule is: $X_A(1) = 0$, $X_B(1) = 30$ and $X_C(1) = 0$, with

Fig. 11.3 Time data for the FA network

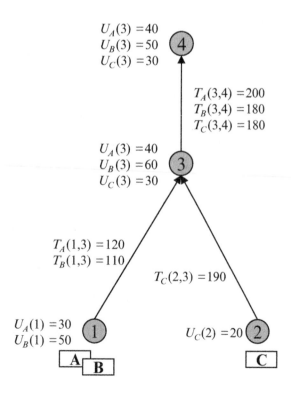

total accumulation time of 510 min. The order of arrival at the destination node 4 is $A \rightarrow B \rightarrow C$. It can be seen that the optimal dispatch schedule is not unique. In fact, the optimal value of $X_C(1)$ can range between 0 and 40. It can be easily verified that such "slack time" multiple optima are expected to exist almost always in this type of problems. This observation leads to the following operational consideration.

While the first priority is to bring the force to its staging area as quickly as possible, another objective is to maximize the survivability of the convoys, which may be subject to hostile actions by the enemy while en-route. Thus, among all optimal schedules that minimize accumulation time we would like to select the one that minimizes the presence of convoys on the road. The latter means delaying the dispatch time of convoys as much as possible. In our example, the optimal solution $X_C(1)=40$ is safer than the optimal solution $X_C(1)=0$.

To capture this secondary objective, we modify the objective function of the problem (Z) into a preemptive optimization setting:

$$Min\, LZ - x_A\left(1\right) - x_B\left(1\right) - x_C\left(1\right) \qquad (11.9)$$

where L is a large positive number. Among all optimal solutions that minimize the total accumulation time Z we select a solution that maximizes dispatch times.

If we modify the travel times of convoy C such that $T_C(1,2)=90$ and $T_C(2,3)=80$, then the optimal dispatch times with respect to the objective function in (11.9) are: $X_A(1)=0$, $X_B(1)=30$ and $X_C(1)=10$, with total accumulation time of 480 min. The order of arrival at the destination node 4 is changed to $C \rightarrow A \rightarrow B$.

This model can be easily extended to take into account also operational constraints such as accumulation priorities. For example, the requirement that convoy A must arrive first at the assembly area (node 4) is represented by the additional constraints: $X_A(4) \leq X_B(4)$ and $X_A(4) \leq X_C(4)$.

11.1.4   Power Projection

In a power projection (PP) scenario the distance to the theater of operations is long – typically thousands of kilometers away from the home bases and the national strategic logistic facilities. Accumulating the force in the theater of operations in such scenarios is done by sealift and airlift. The Falkland War between the UK and Argentina and the Iraq War between the Coalition Forces and Iraq are two relatively recent examples of such operational scenarios. The FA process in a PP scenario comprises five main stages:

1. Moving units from their home bases to ports of embarkation (sea-ports and airports), usually via ground transportation.
2. Loading military units on-board ships and airplanes.
3. Transporting units by air or sea from ports of embarkation to ports of debarkation.
4. Unloading military units at ports of debarkation.
5. Ground movement from ports of debarkation to the assembly or staging areas.

A visual description of this process is shown in Fig. 11.4.

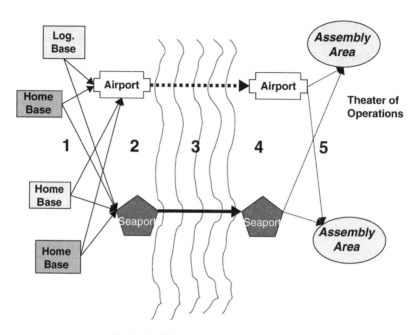

Fig. 11.4 FA in a power projection scenario

Stage 1: From Home Bases to Ports of Embarkation

The movement from home bases to ports of embarkation is similar to force accumulation in a forward deployment (FD) scenario. Convoys of vehicles or trains carry equipment, weapons, and personnel from home bases to ports. In some situations air transportation is possible too (e.g., to carry personnel). This stage differs, however, from FD scenario in two respects.

First, the time factor in PP is not as critical as in FD. Force accumulation in a FD scenario takes days or even hours – in particular when a defending force must be deployed fast to repel a surprise attack (e.g., the Golan Heights during the 1973 war in Israel). On the other hand, FA in a PP scenario may take weeks or even months. The relatively relaxed urgency in a PP scenario is manifested in less acute time constraints than in a FD scenario. The result is less traffic congestion and more organized flow on roads leading to ports of embarkation than the situation on roads leading to assembly areas in a FD scenario.

Second, the convoys traveling from home bases to ports of embarkation are in friendly territory – typically thousands of kilometers from the theater of operations. These convoys are safer than convoys moving towards staging areas in a FD scenario, which may be vulnerable to enemy's artillery, commando, and air attacks.

Stage 3: From Ports of Embarkation to Ports of Debarkation

Airlift and sealift of military forces from homeports to ports at the theater of war are considered strategic operations requiring large numbers of ships and airplanes. Assigning the lift missions to the various means of transportation, and scheduling these missions, are important and difficult planning tasks usually assigned to a special command in charge of strategic mobility. Similarly to the FD scenario, planning strategic mobility heavily relies on optimization models that seek to minimize the time of the operation and maximize the utility rates of the various means of transportation. The THROUGHPUT II optimization model [2, 3] is an excellent example for such a strategic mobility planning aid.

Besides the obvious difference between airlift and sealift regarding the environment of operations – air and water – there are also significant differences in the characteristics of the respective means of transportation. A ship can carry a load that is heavier by two to three orders of magnitude than an airplane. On the other hand, a cargo plane is faster than a ship by more than an order of magnitude. In addition to safety and survivability considerations discussed later on, the tradeoff between airlift and sealift is clear and is summarized in the dilemma: *Transport a smaller load faster or a larger load slower?*

Example 11.3

The "Little but Fast" vs. "Much but Slow" dilemma emerged during operation "Desert Shield" when American forces were transported from the US and Europe to Saudi Arabia. The two major questions were: (1) which cargo to ship and which cargo to fly, and (2) how to prioritize the dispatch times of shipments. The airlift was designated primarily to carry personnel and only little equipment and logistic resources. Almost all the weapons, equipment, and logistic assets were sent by sealift and arrived at the port of debarkation in Saudi Arabia long after the troops' arrival [4]. This difference in logistic tempo resulted in "tooth-to-tail" imbalance at the theater of operations. Note that the entire FA process, which had taken several months, was executed with no hostile interruption or even threat by the Iraqis. Also, it was not seriously affected by operational constraints since the initiative was on the Coalition side. Thus, the question if this imbalance at the beginning of the campaign was justified remains open.

Stage 3 in a PP scenario may be subject to threats and hostile actions by the enemy that may disrupt the FA process. *Example 11.4* demonstrates how Operations Research techniques were utilized to deal with this problem during WWII [5].

Example 11.4

Convoys of supply ships crossing the Atlantic, escorted by warships, were subject to attacks by German U-boats. These subs had managed to sink many of the ships and therefore imposed a grave threat on the supply line from the US to the Allied forces in Europe. A simple analysis of operational data regarding these engagements helped to eliminate the threat. First, data concerning the numbers of supply ships in a convoy, ships that were sunk, escort ships, U-boats in a pack, and U-boats sunk by the escort ships were collected for each incident. Then, basic statistical analysis of these data revealed some functional relations among these numbers, and an appropriate measure of effectiveness, called *Exchange-Ratio*, was defined:

$Exchange - Ratio = \# U - Boats\ Sunk\ /\ \# Supply\ Ships\ Sunk.$

The simple mathematical analysis led to an important operational conclusion, which was to send fewer but longer convoys.

Stage 5: From Ports of Debarkation to Assembly Areas

Delivering military units from ports of debarkation to assembly areas is done in less favorable conditions than the earlier stages. First, the movement of the forces is executed in a foreign, sometimes hostile, territory, and thus subject to disruption and attrition. The roads are not as familiar as at home, and their physical condition may be poor. Moreover, these roads (and other lines of communication) may not be under complete control of the expeditionary force. The movement along these roads may have to be coordinated with local authorities and therefore subject to misunderstandings and even conflict of interests.

Second, the amount of means of transportation available for this transportation mission is limited since they are part of the expeditionary force. This limitation is prevalent in particular at the early stages of the FA process when the priority in the airlift and sealift operations (Stage 3) is set more on combat units than on supporting logistic assets. In such situations transportation at Stage 5 may have to depend on less reliable – both mechanically and operationally – local (host country) assets. In some situations, armored vehicles may even have to travel on their own trucks from the ports of debarkation to the assembly areas. Such a mode of transportation negatively affects the readiness of combat units since it consumes fuel and generates mechanical wear in vehicles. See Sect. 11.2.2.

Stages 2 and 4: Loading and Unloading at Ports

Stages 2 and 4 represent transition points from one mode of transportation to another. These stages, and in particular stage 4, are critical since transshipment capacities are typically limited. These capacities are determined by the available docking spaces, the number and efficiency of the loading/unloading equipment (cranes, forklifts, etc.), and the available storage space in the port. Coordinating between the inflow of cargo into the port and the loading/unloading process imposes a complex managerial problem to the operational logisticians. Poor coordination, in particular in the port of debarkation, may result in congestion, disorder, and long queues of ships (or airplanes) waiting to be unloaded. Besides the chaotic effect of such congestion on the ability to monitor the incoming cargo and to direct it correctly to its destination, the idle ships and airplanes, waiting to be unloaded, create a waste of lift capacity – an asset that is usually in shortage [6].

Proper tuning of the logistic flow at ports is crucial for an effective and efficient FA. This observation is one of the major lessons learned from the Gulf War [7].

11.2   Medical Treatment and Evacuation

In contrast to the other five main *OpLog* functions – force-accumulation, deployment, flow management, prioritization, and forecasting – that directly affect the way an operation commences and evolves over time, the effect of medical services on the operation is indirect and secondary. Prompt medical treatment in the battlefield and fast evacuation of casualties from the front to definitive medical facilities in the rear area have an important psychological effect on the morale of the troops, and a cognitive effect on the commander. But, unlike the supply of fuel and ammunition, medical support does not contribute significantly and directly to the *physical* readiness of the military force.

Moreover, all other logistic functions deal with "large numbers": thousands of vehicles, tens of thousands of combatants, hundreds of thousands of rounds of ammunition and millions liters of fuel. Medical services, in contrast, deal at any given time with relatively small numbers – typically not more than hundreds of casualties theater-wide. Also, medical evacuation generates a flow on the logistic network that is oriented in the opposite direction to the supply flow – from the front back to the rear area.

Thus, medical support during a campaign is a unique logistic function with respect to its effect on combat activities, scale, and characteristics. It is unique also in a deeper sense. Medical is a logistic function that directly and immediately affects human life. Because of the moral commitment to preserve human life, and the considerable attention that modern armies devote to preserve life and welfare of warfighters, medical treatment, and evacuation is considered a major *OpLog* mission despite its relatively small scale.

11.2.1   Principles of Medical Support During Operations

Medical support during an operation is based on two principles:

- Immediate and effective first aid and damage control in the battlefield.
- Fast evacuation to hospitals where definitive treatment is available.

These two principles evolve from two major considerations: operational and medical.

Operational Consideration

Injured soldiers in the battlefield create a burden that limits the agility and combat effectiveness of the combat unit. Although the commander is usually unqualified to treat the injured and therefore is not actively involved in medical aid operations, the presence of injured people in his combat unit is of great concern and it may divert his attention from his combat missions. This is a natural human trait that cannot be completely controlled. Even the toughest and most experienced commander will find it difficult to concentrate on the next combat action when he knows that some of his men are injured and wait for treatment and evacuation.

Thus, the sooner the injured are evacuated from the battlefield, the faster the rest of the unit can carry on effectively with its mission.

Medical Consideration

The medical consideration is more significant. It is based on the fact that good medical treatment requires adequate physical infrastructure and highly qualified and specialized healthcare providers. These two requirements are satisfied at hospitals and medical centers.

Modern medical treatment, in particular for trauma that is prevalent in combat, requires sophisticated instrumentation. Such advanced, physically sensitive, and expensive pieces of equipment are not always available at the battlefield. Even if they are available, they may not be utilized effectively under the constrained battlefield conditions. Moreover, the dust, noise, dirt, and temporariness that characterize battlefield environments are in contrast to the quietness, cleanliness, and stability that are required for an effective medical treatment. Therefore, the physical infrastructure of the medical facilities in the battlefield, even if it is rich and elaborate, is far from providing the ideal conditions for effective medical support. These conditions exist at permanent hospitals.

The most significant medical resource is people – surgeons, physicians, nurses, technicians, and other medical support personnel. Most often, this resource is also quite scarce. The shortage in professionals is acute in particular in critically needed trauma specialists and surgeons. When resources are limited, the most efficient strategy is to pull them together and thus utilizing potential synergies. The synergy created when medical experts from various disciplines (General Surgeons, Neurosurgeons, Orthopedists, Anesthetists, etc.) operate together, coupled with the proper physical environment available at hospitals, provide the best conditions for conducting medical treatment.

Damage Control vs. Fast Evacuation

From a purely medical perspective the first principle – *damage control* – is a *necessity* or a *constraint*. The condition of a casualty may deteriorate very fast if proper medical help is not provided immediately. Therefore, some essential medical capabilities must be available at the battlefield. The other principle – *fast evacuation* – is an *objective*, which is rationalized by the optimal medical conditions that exist in hospitals and other permanent medical facilities.

There is a tradeoff between the two principles. Faster evacuation means shorter delay between the time of injury and the time when definitive medical care is available. The shorter is this delay, the less acute is the impact of the constraint generated by the need for damage control. Consequently, modern military medical organizations have shifted the weight from elaborate battlefield medical services to improved mobility capabilities that facilitate fast evacuation. The idea is to reduce as much as possible the effect of the *constraint* (battlefield damage control) by enhancing the effect of the *objective* (fast evacuation).

11.2.2   The Medical Evacuation Chain

On his way back from the battlefield to a hospital a casualty may pass through several stations at the various echelons. First aid is given at the tactical combat unit and more elaborate surgical treatment may be provided to critically injured casualties at a forward medical unit (typically at the divisional level). These minimal capacity surgical units are designated to satisfy the *Golden Hour Rule* that specifies the allowable time period that can elapse from the time of injury until a (severely injured) casualty is operated upon.

The medical evacuation chain, depicted in Fig. 11.5, comprises five nodes. The closest and most attainable medical help to a freshly wounded casualty is a company medic. This medical node has minimal capabilities and its purpose is to provide prompt (within seconds or at most few minutes) first aid to warfighters wounded in action. The medical node at the other end of the chain represents the ultimate medical

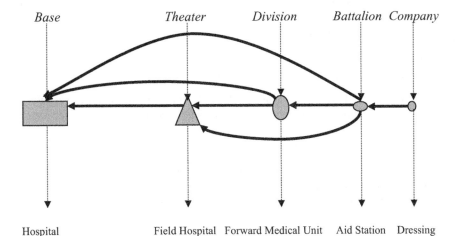

Fig. 11.5 The medical evacuation chain

care – the general (usually, civilian) hospital or medical center. The three intermediate nodes represent various types of medical facilities in the range between the line of fire and the communications zone. The higher the echelon of the node the more enhanced are its medical care capabilities. In some scenarios, forward medical units may be supplemented by small emergency surgical and post-operative facilities.

The geographical distance between a combat zone and a hospital and the battlefield evacuation capabilities (capacity and speed) dictate the number and characteristics of the intermediate medical nodes. While the battalion aid station is indispensable because it is the first medical facility in the battlefield available to professionally treat a casualty, the necessity of the other two – the forward medical unit and the field hospital – depends on the operational scenario. In a forward deployment scenario these two types of medical nodes may be redundant if high-capacity and fast evacuation capabilities are available (see the *Battalion – Base* edge in Fig. 11.5). In a power projection scenario well equipped and staffed field hospitals (e.g., hospital ship) are needed to treat and stabilize casualties before they are transported back to their home country.

The evacuation chain is an abstract representation of the medical organization that extends from the communications zone to the theater of operations. In reality there exists a medical evacuation *network* that is similar, in principle, to the logistic network. The medical nodes at the various levels form a hierarchical tree. The "leaves" of this tree are the company level medics, and the "roots" are civilian hospitals. The edges are lines of communication. Notice that the flow on this network (casualties) is from the front to the rear, which is in the opposite direction to the flow on the logistic network.

11.2.3 Planning Medical Support

The rationale of the medical plan in the theater of operations is represented in Fig. 11.5. It can be summarized by the following guideline combining the two principles presented in Sect. 11.3.1:

Evacuate fast to a medical node as high as possible in the evacuation chain, while providing adequate medical care at the intermediate nodes when needed.

The objective is to utilize, as much as possible, the long edges in the evacuation chain while reducing the number and size of intermediate nodes to a necessary minimum.

The inputs for medical planning are:

• Casualty estimates (classified by type and severity of injury);
• Deployment of combat forces in the theater of operations;
• Availability of medical resources at the various echelons;
• Availability of means of evacuation.

Casualty Estimates

Battlefield casualties generate demand for medical resources. The number of casualties depends on the intensity of combat, and the types of injury and their severity are derived from the combat characteristics. For example, a tank battle is more likely to inflict burns than infantry battle in which casualties are more likely to suffer from wounds caused by penetrating bullets and shrapnel. Forecasting the number, type, and severity of injuries is important for properly allocate the medical resources.

This forecast however is not easy to obtain because of battlefield uncertainties (see Chap. 6). Estimates must take into account historical data and project it on current battlefield circumstances that depend, among other things, on new weapons and tactics. The main challenge is to obtain a reasonable estimate of the total number of casualties, because this number affects the size of the deployed medical support system. It is also desirable to have a good estimate of the distribution of the types of injuries. Such a distribution may guide the medical planner how to determine the mix of medical supplies at the various units.

> **Example 11.5**
> Based on past experience, it is observed that slightly more than 40 % of battlefield injuries are associated with hemorrhage, about 30 % are head injuries and 10 % are multiple injuries. Medical experts, assisted with combat models, may utilize these figures, which represent grand averages over many combat situations, as a basis for projecting casualty-type distributions.

Deployment of Forces in the Theater of Operations

The deployment of forces in the theater of operations affects the geometry of the evacuation network. In particular, the location of the medical nodes is determined according to the location and operational plans of the combat units. Similarly to the logistic network, the geometry of the evacuation network may change over time as deployments and operational plans change.

The casualty estimates and the time-phased deployment plans are the two major factors that affect the demand side of medical services. The projected attrition determines the required capabilities and capacities of medical units, and the deployment plan determines their organizational structure and spatial distribution.

Availability of Medical Resources

Medical resources in the theater of operations range from small medical aid platoons, based on two or three tracked or wheeled vehicles, to a full scale field hospital equipped with up to several hundreds beds and some ancillary facilities such as X-Ray and laboratories. While it is obvious that smaller units are assigned to lower echelons (e.g., medical aid platoon of a battalion) and larger, higher-capability facilities are deployed at higher echelons (e.g., field hospital at the corps level), the actual employment of these resources in the theater must take into consideration the spatial distribution of the projected demands for these assets.

For example, medical coaches – small surgical and trauma units boarded on trailers – are typically corps level assets. These units may however be assigned to a certain division, or even a brigade, as a respond to potential need for surgical capabilities derived from a planned combat mission.

Availability of Means of Evacuation

Effective evacuation depends on the number, types, and deployment of available means of transportation. Recall that the operational goal of the medical support system is evacuating casualties as fast as possible to hospitals. Only necessary medical procedures needed to stabilize the casualty (damage control) should be performed in the battlefield. The fast evacuation goal can be achieved only if large and well-coordinated fleet of fast means of transportation is available for this mission.

The most efficient way of evacuation is by air. Helicopters (e.g., CHINOOK) can carry up to several dozens of casualties, and fixed-wing aircraft can evacuate even more casualties. These means of transportation are fast, and they provide a relatively smooth ride for the casualties. Moreover, if the evacuation from the battalion aid station to the hospital could completely rely on air transportation, the evacuation chain shown in Fig. 11.5 would become redundant. In particular, all the intermediate medical nodes could be eliminated and no tracked or wheeled ambulances would be needed. Unfortunately, this situation cannot be realistically considered because air evacuation is not always guaranteed. Limited availability of aircraft, bad weather conditions, threats of enemy's anti-air fire and other operational, environmental, and technical constraints may hinder the utilization of this most efficient mode of evacuation.

Thus, the medical support in the theater of operations is a mix of medical-aid facilities of various types, ground evacuation vehicles, and air evacuation platforms. Determining the mix of these assets, and their deployment in the theater, is a complex decision process that could be aided by mathematical modeling.

11.2.4   Modeling Medical Support

From a modeling point of view, a battlefield medical system is more complex than the force accumulation process described in the first part of this chapter. Each medical node in the evacuation network is a "service station" that takes in flow (of casualties), treats it according to some priority rules, and then discharges it to a medical node at a higher echelon. The inflow and outflow rates of casualties depend, among other things, on available means of evacuation.

A natural way to model this system is by a queuing network, which is a standard model in operations research. A simplified illustration of an evacuation queuing network is shown in Fig. 11.6.

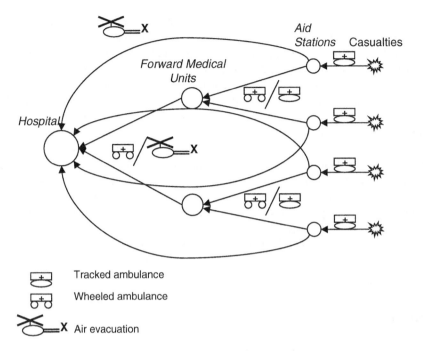

Fig. 11.6 Evacuation queuing network

This type of modeling lends itself to Monte-Carlo simulations. Each medical node is simulated as a multi-server priority queue. The discharge rate is determined by the:

- Number and type of available means of evacuation.
- Number of surgeons, medics, nurses, and other medical assistants.
- Number of beds (or treatment places) and the level of medical instrumentation.

An important planning metrics is the probability that the time it takes to evacuate a severely injured casualty is within the specified *golden hour* – a period within which a casualty must be operated upon in order to have a good chance of surviving. Such network-oriented simulations can estimate this and other metrics.

11.3   Summary

This chapter was devoted to two major *OpLog* missions:

- Force accumulation.
- Medical treatment and evacuation.

The two missions differ in their orientation, scale, and timing. Force accumulation (FA) is oriented from home bases at the rear area to the front, while medical evacuation (ME) is oriented in the opposite direction – from the battlefield back to the established hospitals and medical centers. The scale of FA operations is considerably larger than that of ME. While thousands of vehicles, tens of thousands of people and hundreds thousands of tons are transported to the theater of operations during the FA phase, the number of evacuated casualties during an entire operation can be as little as a few dozens and not more than a few thousands. The exact timing of an FA mission is not as acute as the timing of ME. Mobilizing the Coalition Forces in Saudi Arabia during the Gulf War took more than 90 days [8]. This time scale is larger by three orders of magnitude than the time scale in which evacuation missions are measured.

Despite the major differences between these two functions, many of their typical problems, such as prioritizing, scheduling, routing, and locating are similar. The common modeling tool for FA and ME, as well as many other *OpLog* functions, is the *logistic network* model. Proper utilization of this model can greatly improve the effectiveness and efficiency of executing these missions.

References

1. Kress M. Efficient strategies for transporting mobile forces. J Oper Res Soc. 2001;52:310–7.
2. Morton D, Rosenthal RE, Teo-Weng L. Optimization modeling for airlift mobility. Mil Oper Res. 1996;1(4):49–68. Winner, Rist Prize of the Military Operations Research Society, 1997.
3. Rosenthal RE, Baker SF, Lim T-W, Fuller DF, Goggins D, Toy AO, Turker Y, Horton D, Briand D, Morton DP. Application and extension of the THROUGHPUT II optimization model for airlift mobility. Mil Oper Res. 1997;3:55–74.
4. Stucker JP, Kameny IM. Army experiences with deployment planning in operation desert shield. Santa Monica, CA: RAND, Arroyo Center; 1993.
5. Morse PM, Kimball GE. Methods of operations research, vol. 46. Cambridge: MIT Press; 1951.
6. Hewish M. Logistics war. Jane's Int Defense Rev (Oct. 2001):28–33.
7. Schrady DA. Combatant Logistics Command and Control for the Joint Forces Commander. Naval War College Rev. 1999;LII(3):49–75.
8. Pagonis WG. Moving mountains: lesson in leadership and logistics from the gulf war. Cambridge: Harvard Business School; 1992.

Chapter 12
Optimizing Logistic Networks

The term *logistic network* was defined and discussed in earlier chapters. It was shown to be a natural abstraction of an *OpLog* system. In Chap. 9 the logistic network *model* was defined and a visual version of that model – the VN model – was presented as a descriptive decision aid. The logistic network model was described as a multilevel *tree* where each level corresponds to a certain military echelon.

While the descriptive VN model is an adequate representation of the logistic *deployment* in the theater of operations, it does not capture the dynamic nature of its *employment*, which is manifested by the logistic support chain. Also, the VN model is only descriptive – not prescriptive. It neither generates nor quantitatively evaluates alternative deployments.

To model the time-phased flow of logistic resources during a military operation, and to facilitate optimization of possible deployment plans, the basic tree model is modified and expanded such that three issues are explicitly addressed:

- Dynamics.
- Uncertainty.
- Optimization.

First, the hierarchical tree in the basic logistic network model is expanded over time to capture inter-temporal effects that result from an evolving scenario. Second, the imbedded uncertainty regarding logistic demands at the tree's end-points is explicitly captured. Third, the expanded network model is utilized to develop a mathematical model that optimizes *OpLog* deployment and employment while accounting for uncertainties. The model, called *Logistic Inter-Temporal Network Optimization* (LITNO), is the subject of this chapter.

© Springer International Publishing Switzerland 2016
M. Kress, *Operational Logistics*, Management for Professionals,
DOI 10.1007/978-3-319-22674-3_12

12.1   Decision Problems

The long-term employment of an *OpLog* system depends on effective and efficient execution of the logistic support chain. This chain starts at the strategic level and ends at the combatants – the "customers" of the logistic support chain. While this chain is the main supplier of logistic resources, the combat forces cannot totally rely on it. Some organic logistic capabilities must be present in the theater at the beginning of the operation to enable a certain level of logistic independence. These capabilities include supplies, services, storage capacity, and means of transportation.

Logistic independence is needed because of two factors:

- Lead-time (order-to-ship time).
- Demand uncertainty.

If logistic response was instantaneous (lead-time = 0) then the fact that demand is uncertain would be irrelevant; realized demand would immediately be satisfied. On the other hand, if demand was deterministic and known in advance, the supply chain could be planned accordingly and lead-time will have no effect. The fact that neither assumption is true necessitates careful planning addressing two main questions:

- *Deployment* – How much logistic assets to pre-position at the various echelons of the logistic support chain?
- *Employment* – how to route and schedule the logistic support chain?

12.1.1   Deployment

Determining the deployment of logistic resources at each echelon has two aspects. The first aspect concerns the resource itself – its quantity and distribution across echelons. For example, a typical question in this context would be: *how much ammunition should a tank battalion carry with it*? The answer depends on ammunition consumption rate, lead-time of ammunition resupply from a higher echelon, and the risk the commander is willing to take regarding possible ammunition shortage.

The second aspect refers to handling requirements for resources at each echelon. Specifically, the operational logistician is concerned about the number and type of transportation vehicles to be deployed at each logistic node. The allocation decision depends on the needs of the logistic support chain, and in particular, on the balance between the "pull" and "push" supply methods. A "pull"-oriented method, where customers are responsible for transporting resources from higher echelon, implies a larger deployment of vehicles at the receiving end (e.g., battalions). A "push"-oriented support chain, where the suppliers are responsible for transportation, implies a larger deployment at the supplying end (e.g., corps or division).

12.1.2   Employment

Employment of the *OpLog* system is manifested in the execution of the logistic support chain. The decision variables in this process are *routes* on the logistic network, *flow* of logistic assets, and *time*. The execution of the logistic support chain involves selecting routes for moving resources, determining the batches of logistic assets to be delivered from one logistic node to another, and scheduling the dispatch of these batches.

The two problems – deployment and employment – are modeled and solved by the LITNO model, which is discussed next.

12.2   LITNO's Basic Concepts

Recall that the *OpLog* system has a hierarchical structure where logistic facilities at a certain echelon feed resources to subordinate units at lower echelons. Specifically, logistic flow is delivered from strategic bases, depots, and arsenals, through the communication zone, to receiving points at the rear area of the theater of operations. The receiving points are gateways to the theater and they typically comprise ports of debarkation or major theater logistic bases. From these gateways, resources are delivered to forward bases (typically corps or division logistic units) within the theater of operations. The latter logistic nodes distribute the resources to subordinate combat service support (CSS) units at the tactical level (brigades and battalions). Figure 12.1, which is similar to Fig. 9.4 in Chap. 9, is a *basic logistic network* model that depicts this hierarchy.

The single (rectangle) node at the top represents the logistic source at the strategic level, which supplies logistic flow to the theater. The intermediate nodes correspond to logistic facilities at the operational level – rear area theater facilities and forward logistic units – which may be further split to several sublevels (see *Example 12.1*).

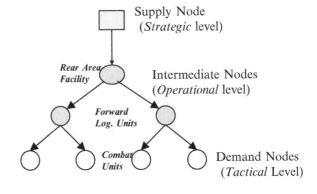

Fig. 12.1 Logistic network

The destination nodes are the brigades' and battalions' CSS units, which are placed at the lowest level of the organizational hierarchy. They constitute the demand nodes of the logistic network.

12.2.1   Inter-temporal Network

While the type of graph in Fig. 12.1 is adequate for representing logistic *deployment* in the theater of operations (see Chap. 9), it does not capture the dynamics of its *employment*, expressed by the *logistic support chain*. To model this dynamics, we expand the basic network in Fig. 12.1 to create an *inter-temporal network* (ITN).

The nodes of an inter-temporal network (ITN) are created from the nodes of the basic network by duplicating them for each time period of the planning horizon. The edges of the ITN reflect the inter-nodal directions of the flow in the basic network and the inter-temporal relations among the nodes. A three periods ITN, based on the three lower levels of the basic logistic network in Fig. 12.1, is shown in Fig. 12.2. The notation used for constructing the LITNO model is based on the network in Fig. 12.1.

Each node in the ITN is of the form (x,t), where x, $x = 1,\ldots,7$, is the identity of a certain *logistic node* in the underlying basic logistic network (e.g., the logistic node $x=1$ corresponds to the rear area facility in Fig. 12.1, and $x=7$ corresponds to a combat unit), and t, $t = 1,\ldots,3$, indicates a time period.

The set of logistic nodes $\{1,\ldots,7\}$ is partitioned into three disjoint subsets Y_1, Y_2, Y_3 according to the levels of the nodes: $Y_1 = \{1\}$, $Y_2 = \{2,3\}$ and $Y_3 = \{4,5,6,7\}$. An edge in the ITN is of the form $[(x,t),(x',t')]$ where $t \leq t'$ (no flow goes back in time).

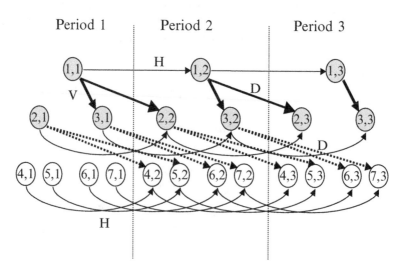

Fig. 12.2 Inter-temporal network

The edges in the ITN of Fig. 12.2 also satisfy the condition that If $x \in Y_i$, and $x' \in Y_j$, then, $i \le j$. This condition reflects the direction of the edges in the basic logistic network in Fig. 12.1, which is top down.

Type of Edges

- *Horizontal Edge* is of the form $[(x,t),(x,t+1)]$. The flow on a horizontal edge (labeled by H in Fig. 12.2) stays in a certain node x from one time period to the next. It represents inventory that stays in a certain location. For example, the edge $[(1,1),(1,2)]$ is a horizontal edge. Horizontal edges only exist for nodes sharing the same logistic node x. That is, if x, $x' \in Y_i$ for some i then the existence of $[(x,t),(x',t')]$ implies $x = x'$ and $t' = t+1$. This means that there are no *transshipment* edges within a certain level. For example, there is no edge $[(2,1),(3,2)]$ in Fig. 12.2. This assumption is explained later on when the LITNO model is constructed.
- *Vertical Edge* is of the form $[(x,t),(x',t)]$. A vertical edge (labeled by V in Fig. 12.2) carries flow that moves from one level to a lower one within a time period. For example, the edge $[(1,2),(3,2)]$ is a vertical edge. Vertical edges represent fast modes of transportation.
- *Diagonal Edge* is of the form $[(x,t),(x',t')]$, $t' > t$. A diagonal edge (labeled by D in Fig. 12.2) represents a flow from one node to another in a lower echelon across at least one time period. For example, the edge $[(3,1),(7,2)]$ in Fig. 12.2 is a diagonal edge. Since the time resolution is arbitrary, we may assume that all nonhorizontal edges are diagonal, i.e., we assume that there are no vertical edges.

12.2.2 ITN of the Logistic Support Chain

The ITN is a visual representation of the structure and time-dependent dynamics of an *OpLog* system. The design of the ITN depends on the length of the operation and its time resolution.

The size and intensity of the operation determine the number of logistic nodes (X), levels (n), and edges in each period. The length of the operation and its time resolution determine the number of time periods (T). The ITN is utilized for optimizing the deployment and employment of an *OpLog* system. The resulting optimization model is called *logistics inter-temporal network optimization* (LITNO). To set the LITNO model within a relevant and realistic *OpLog* context, we make the following assumptions:

- The first level of the ITN corresponds to the logistic gateway nodes in the theater of operations. That is, if $x \in Y_1$ then x corresponds to a rear area facility such as port of debarkation or major theater logistic base.

- To simplify the exposition of the LITNO model we assume that the logistic gateway node is unique, that is $|Y_1| = 1$.
- If the scenario comprises T time periods then the number of time periods in the LITNO model is $T+2$. The first and last time periods correspond to the logistic baseline and end-state, respectively (see Sect. 12.2.3).
- No "lateral" or transshipment flow is allowed between distinct logistic nodes within a certain level. Formally, if x, $x' \in Y_i$ for some i then $[(x,t),(x',t')]$ implies $x = x'$ and $t' = t+1$. This assumption is based on the operational observation that logistic support is almost always provided from higher echelons. For example, incidences where one brigade provides significant logistic support to another brigade are the exception, rather than the rule.

Example 12.1
A typical logistic deployment in the theater of operations comprises four levels:

$Y_1 = \{$Ports of debarkation, major theater logistic bases$\}$
$Y_2 = \{$Corps logistic units$\}$
$Y_3 = \{$Division logistic units$\}$
$Y_4 = \{$Brigade/battalion CSS units$\}$

To simplify the exposition we adopt from now on a three-level structure.

Figure 12.3 presents a three-level (three echelons) LITNO model that comprises three periods. Time period $t=0$ is the baseline period and $t=4$ corresponds to the end-state. Notice that we assume here that the lead-time between the first and sec-

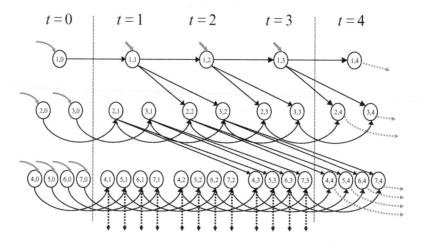

Fig. 12.3 LITNO model

ond echelons is one time period, and the lead-time between the second and third echelons is two periods.

Next, we describe the LITNO model – as shown in Fig. 12.3 – in more detail.

12.2.3 Time Periods

The base-line period ($t=0$) corresponds to the time period prior to the beginning of combat operations. It represents the logistic situation of the forces at the staging area. Time periods $t=1,2,3$ correspond to the active combat phase, and $t=4$ corresponds to the logistic end-state after the operation is over. The outflow from the end-state nodes represents operational requirements regarding logistic readiness at the end of the operation.

Time resolution is a key parameter in LITNO. It is determined by operational and logistic considerations that reflect typical time parameters of various activities such as movement, transportation, and unloading. The time resolution is usually determined according to the frequency of the logistic "pulses," or the *tempo* (see Chap. 3), of the logistic support chain. A typical length of a time period at the operational or tactical levels is between 24 h and a week.

12.2.4 Nodes and Edges of LITNO

Similarly to the notation in Sect. 12.2.1 regarding the ITN, we adopt here the following classification of nodes:

- Y_1 = Set of logistic nodes at the top theater level (rear area facilities). These are the *supply nodes* in the underlying logistic network. Recall we assume that $|Y_1|=1$.
- Y_2 = Set of intra-theater logistic units and facilities. These are the *intermediate nodes* in the underlying logistic network.
- Y_3 = Set of logistic nodes at the bottom of the command hierarchy. These are the customers of the *OpLog* system – the *demand nodes*.

The set of supply nodes (x,t) is divided into two subsets. The first subset comprises *external* supply nodes, where $x \in Y_1$ and $t=1,2,3$. The inflow to an external supply node comprises resources that arrive to the theater at time period t from the strategic level. This inflow is exogenous to the *OpLog* system. The external inflow is depicted in Fig. 12.3 by the thick short gray arrows at the top of the graph.

The second subset comprises *internal* supply nodes, which are of the form $(x,0)$. The inflow to an internal supply node represents pre-positioned resources at a logistic node x. These resources form the supply *baseline* of the *OpLog* system.

The internal inflow is depicted in Fig. 12.3 by the curved gray arrows at the left-hand side of the graph. Note that internal supply nodes appear at all levels.

The intermediate nodes are of the form (x,t), where $x \in Y_2$ and $t=1,2,3$. These nodes correspond to intermediate logistic units during the operation. The intermediate nodes in Fig. 12.3 are $(2,1)$, $(3,1)$, $(2,2)$, $(3,2)$, $(2,3)$, and $(3,3)$.

Similarly to the supply nodes, the demand nodes are also divided into two subsets. The first subset comprises *combat* demand nodes, which are of the form (x,t), $x \in Y_3$, $t=1,2,3$. The outflow in these nodes is the consumed resources by combat units (Recall that Y_3 is the lowest level in the hierarchy). The combat outflow is depicted in Fig. 12.3 by the vertical dotted arrows at the bottom of the graph. The second subset of demand nodes includes nodes of the form $(x,4)$ that represent the logistic end-state – resources that are left over at unit x at the end of the operation. The end-state outflow is depicted in Fig. 12.3 by the curved, dotted arrows at the right-hand side of the graph.

12.2.5   The Flow

Many types of logistic items flow through the logistic network. Supplies like ammunition, fuel, and spare-parts move in the LITNO model downwards – from higher echelons to lower echelons – while human casualties and damaged equipment are evacuated in the opposite direction – from lower echelons to higher echelons. The latter observation implies that edges of the type $[(x,t),(x',t+1)]$, where $x \in Y_j$ and $x' \in Y_{j-1}$ may also exist in the LITNO model.

The various types of flow, which compete for limited transportation capabilities, generate a *multicommodity flow* on the network. Many problems, such as deploying resources, scheduling transportation, and coordinating deliveries, are associated with such a multicommodity network.

To simplify the exposition of the LITNO model we assume here a single logistic commodity. The model can be extended to handle multiple commodities, sharing common means of transportation, at the expense of higher complexity.

12.3   Objective, Constraints and Decision Variables

To put the model in a concrete context, from now on we use the term *ammunition* to denote the supply flow under consideration. The optimization problem is concerned with optimizing the deployment and employment of ammunition in the theater of operations.

During a military operation, combat units consume ammunition and therefore generate demands that must be satisfied. These demands are uncertain; they are not known in advance and depend on the evolving scenario. In addition, the end-state inventory requirements (at time period $t=4$), which are determined by operational readiness requirements, must be satisfied too. The problem is how to optimally deploy the supply of ammunition in the various echelons, and schedule its delivery.

12.3.1   The Objective

A natural objective of LITNO is to minimize a certain *cost*. Similarly to the commercial world, the military supply chain incurs inventory, handling, and transportation costs that are measurable and thus could be used in a quantitative objective function. However, the military context also includes operational consequences – mission success or failure – that are not readily quantifiable. How would one quantify the "want of a nail?" In other words, how do we measure the cost of inadequate logistic responsiveness realized in operational outcomes?

One way to handle the incomparable logistic and operational costs is to remove the operational cost from the objective function and set some operational goal in terms of probabilities for satisfying demands. Specifically, we assume that the total logistic cost comprises of transportation and storage costs, and the goal is to minimize this total cost such that demand is satisfied with some pre-specified probability. The requirement for satisfying demand takes the form of a *constraint* described in the next subsection (Sect. 12.3.2). Thus, the objective function is purely economic and is of the general form:

$$\textit{Amount of ammunition shipped} \times \textit{Per unit cost of transportation}$$
$$+\textit{Amount of ammunition stored} \times \textit{Per unit cost of storage}.$$

12.3.2   The Constraints

There are three types of constraints in the LITNO model:

- Demand constraints.
- Flow-balance constraints.
- Safety-stock and capacity constraints.

We assume from now on that the flow of ammunition is measured in terms of truckloads.

Demand Constraints

The demand constraints represent the need for ammunition by the customers at the various time periods. A demand constraint is of the form:

Total inflow of ammunition into demand node $(x,t) \geq$ *Demand at* (x,t)

There are two sets of demand constraints. The first set relates to on-going demand during the operation and therefore it applies to the demand nodes $(4,1), (4,2),...,(6,3)$, $(7,3)$ in Fig. 12.3. The demands are unknown in advance; they are random variables with some known probability distribution. The demand values are simulated in LITNO from the given probability distribution so that operational requirements of the type: "at least 90% of the time the demand is satisfied" could be explicitly specified in the optimization model. This point is elaborated later on. The second set of constraints relates to the end-state requirements and therefore it applies to all the logistic nodes x's at $t=4$. These requirements are based on tactical and operational plans and readiness requirements. Therefore these constraints are deterministic, unlike the on-going demand.

Flow-Balance Constraints

As in any network flow model, the flow-balance constraints are technical features in LITNO guaranteeing that the total flow is preserved. Any quantum of flow (truck-load of ammunition, in our case) entering a node must exit it one way or another. No flow is "lost" and no flow is "gained" during the passage through the node. A flow-balance constraint is of the form:

Total inflow to node $(x,t) =$ *Total outflow from node* (x,t).

Safety-Stock and Capacity Constraints

The purpose of the *safety-stock* constraints is to secure a certain level of readiness. All units x must maintain, at all times, a minimum supply of ammunition for unforeseeable contingencies. That is,

$$Flow\ of\ ammunition\ on\ edge\ \left[(x,t),(x,t+1)\right]$$
$$\geq Safety\text{-}Stock\ in\ x\ at\ time\ t,$$
$$\forall x \in Y_j,\ j,t = 1,2,3.$$

On the other hand there may be storage capacity constraints, which have the form

$$Flow\ of\ ammunition\ on\ edge\ \left[(x,t),(x,t+1)\right]$$
$$\leq Storage\ capacity\ in\ x,$$
$$\forall x \in Y_j,\ j = 1,...,n.$$

Limited transportation capacity constraints are of the form:

$$Flow\ of\ ammunition\ on\ edge\ [(x,t),(x',t')]$$
$$\leq Transportation\ capacity\ between\ x\ and\ x'.$$

12.3.3   Decision Variables

The decision variables are capacities and flow values on the various edges of the network, including inflow and outflow edges.

The focus of attention is the inflow, which is assumed to be equal to the capacities at the various logistic nodes at time period $t=0$. These variables represent the *OpLog* deployment at the beginning of the operation, and the objective is to find the values of those variables that satisfy logistic responsiveness requirement at a minimum cost. See more details in Sect. 12.4.1

12.4   LITNO's Formulation

In this section we present a formal description of the LITNO model. In general, LITNO can accommodate an arbitrary number of echelons, units, and time periods, and it can represent variable and time-dependent lead-times between echelons. However, the model presented here is restricted in size. It only has three echelons (as in Fig. 12.3) and the lead-times are fixed – one time period between any two adjacent echelons (unlike Fig. 12.3). These restrictions are made only for expositional convenience.

12.4.1   Notation

Parameters

$D^s(x,t)$	Demand at destination (customer) logistic node x ($x \in Y_3$) at time t according to (simulated) demand scenario s, $s=1,...,S$. Recall that demands are unknown in advance and are simulated in the model based on past data. The larger the number of simulated scenarios S the more robust is the optimal solution of LITNO.
$S(x,t)$	Safety-stock in x at time t.
$T(x,x')$	Transportation capacity from logistic node x to x'.
$D_e(x)$	End-state requirement at node $(x,4)$.

$$\beta((x,t),(x',t')) = \begin{cases} 1 & \text{if flow is possible from node } (x,t) \text{ to node } (x',t') \\ 0 & \text{otherwise} \end{cases}$$

The parameter $\beta((x,t),(x',t'))$ specifies the hierarchy in the *OpLog* system and the feasible lead-times. For example, in Fig. 12.3 $\beta\big((2,1),(4,3)\big)=1$ (node 2 is a supplier of node 4 and the lead-time is two periods), but $\beta\big((2,1),(6,3)\big) = \beta\big((2,1),(4,2)\big) = 0$.

$C_T(x,x')$:	Cost of transporting a truckload of *ammunition* from node x to node x'. For simplicity we assume that this cost is independent of the time when it is incurred. $C_T(1)$ is the transportation cost of the exogenous flow into logistic node 1.

$C_H(x)$:	Cost of storing a truckload of *ammunition* in node x during one time period. Here too, for simplicity, we assume that the cost is independent of the time when it is incurred.
$C_K(x)$:	Cost of unit capacity at logistic node x. This is a fixed cost of establishing inventory infrastructure, while $C_H(x)$ represents the variable cost of handling inventory.
p	Probability that demand is satisfied. This is a mission-specific parameter representing the commander's accepted risk level.

The values of these parameters are determined based on the operational plan and the projected scenario.

Decision Variables

$w(x)$	Capacity of logistic node x. For the various logistic nodes, these are the crucial decision variables; they determine the initial inventory in each logistic node and also the capacities of those nodes.
$u^s((x,t),(x',t'))$	The flow of ammunition (number of truckloads) between nodes (x,t) and (x',t') in scenario s. In particular, $u^s((x,t),(x,t+1))$ represents the flow on a horizontal edge. This flow is constrained by the corresponding logistic flow capacity $w(x)$
$u^s(1,t)$	The exogenous inflow into node $(1,t)$, $t=1,2,3$ in scenario s. These variables represent the supply of ammunition from the strategic level to the top-echelon logistic node (theater facility) at the three different time periods.
z_s	A technical binary decision variable that indicates if the demands corresponding to scenario s, $s=1,\dots,S$, are satisfied. If $z_s = 0$ then the demands must be satisfied. If $z_s = 1$ then the demands may or may not be satisfied. See Sect. 12.4.3

12.4.2 Objective Function

The objective is to minimize the total cost of the operation – establishing capacity, transportation and storage of ammunition. The cost function comprises four parts: (1) capacity cost, (2) cost of delivering the exogenous flow to the theater of operations, (3) cost of intra-theater transportation, and (4) storage (holding) cost. Formally:

$$\underbrace{\sum_x C_K(x)w(x)}_{\text{Capacity cost}}$$

$$+ \underbrace{\frac{1}{S}\sum_{s=1}^{S}(1-z_s)\{\sum_{t=1}^{3}C_T(1)u^s(1,t)}_{\text{Transportation cost of exogeneous flow}}$$

$$+ \underbrace{\sum_{t=1}^{2}\sum_{t'=2}^{4}\sum_{j=1}^{2}\sum_{x\in Y_j}\sum_{x'\in Y_{j+1}}\beta((x,t),(x',t'))C_T(x,x')u^s((x,t),(x',t'))}_{\text{Intra-theater transportation cost}}$$

$$+ \underbrace{\sum_{t=1}^{T}\sum_x C_H(x)u^s((x,t),(x,t+1))\}.}_{\text{Storage (holding) cost}}$$

The last three terms in the objective function are averaged over the S scenarios.

12.4.3   Constraints

Recall that there are three sets of constraints:

- Demand constraints.
- Flow-balance constraints.
- Safety-stock and capacity constraints.

Demand Constraints

The demand constraints represent operational requirements derived from the scenario and the commander's acceptable level of risk

Combat Operation (Ongoing) Demand

$$\underbrace{u^s\big((x,0),(x,1)\big)-w(x)=0}$$

The initial supply in each logistic node
is equal to the predetermined capacity

$$\underbrace{u^s\big((x,t-1),(x,t)\big)}+\underbrace{\sum_{x'\in Y_2}\sum_{t'=1}^{t}\beta\big((x',t'),(x,t)\big)u^s\big((x',t'),(x,t)\big)}+\underbrace{D^s(x,t)z_s}=\underbrace{D^s(x,t)}$$

Supply that stayed over   Supply arriving from higher echelon   Demand in
from the previous period   s-th simulated
                                                                                                            scenario

$$t=1,2,3,\ x\in Y_3, s=1,...,S.$$

$$\underbrace{\sum_{s=1}^{S}z_s-(1-p)S\le 0,\ z_s\in\{0,1\}.}$$

Demand must be satisfied in at least
a fraction p of the scenarios

End-State Requirements

$$\underbrace{u^s\big((x,3),(x,4)\big)+\sum_{x'\in Y_{j-1}}\beta(x',t'),(x,4))u^s\big((x',t'),(x,4)\big)+D_e(x,4)z_s\ge D_e(x,4)}$$

A "satisfied" scenario must also satisfy the end state requirements

$$s=1,...,S, x\in Y_j, j=1,2,3$$

Balance Constraints

The balance constraints are equations guaranteeing that the *principle of conservation of mass* is satisfied. The total flow that enters a node must equal to the total flow that emerges.

1. **Top Echelon**

$$\underbrace{u^s(1,t)}_{a}+\underbrace{u^s\big((1,t-1),(1,t)\big)}_{b}-\underbrace{u^s((1,t),(1,t+1))}_{c}$$

$$-\underbrace{\sum_{t'=t}^{4}\sum_{x\in Y_2}\beta\big((1,t),(x,t')\big)u^s\big((1,t),(x,t')\big)}_{d}=0,\ ,t=1,...,3, s=1,...,S.$$

Inflow
a – Exogenous supply.
b – Supply that remains from the preceding period.

Outflow
c – Supply that stays to the next period.
d – Supply sent to subordinate units.
2. **Intermediate Echelon**

$$\sum_{t'=1}^{t} \underbrace{\beta\big((1,t'),(x,t)\big)u^s\big((1,t'),(x,t)\big)}_{a} + \underbrace{u^s\big((x,t-1),(x,t)\big)}_{b} - \underbrace{u^s\big((x,t),(x,t+1)\big)}_{c}$$

$$-\sum_{t'=t}\sum_{x'\in Y_3} \underbrace{\beta\big((x,t),(x',t')\big)u^s\big((x,t),(x',t')\big)}_{d} = 0, t = 1,2,3, s = 1,\ldots,S.$$

Inflow
a – Supply delivered from the higher (top) echelon.
b – Supply that remains at the node from the preceding period.

Outflow
c – Supply that stays at the node to the next period.
d – Supply sent to subordinate units.
3. ***Bottom Echelon*** *(Combat Units)*
   The balance constraints at the bottom echelon are essentially the demand constraints shown above.

Safety-Stock and Capacity Constraints

Safety-stock constraints apply to the flow on the horizontal edges (see Sect. 12.3.2).

$$u\big((x,t),(x,t+1)\big) \geq S(x,t), \qquad t = 1,2,3.$$

The capacity constraints apply to both storage facilities and means of transportation. For the logistic nodes (i.e., horizontal edges) the capacity is optimized within LITNO, and for the inter-echelon transportation (diagonal edges) the capacities are determined by the available means of transportation, which are exogenous to LITNO. Thus,
Node capacities:

$$u\big((x,t),(x,t+1)\big) - w(x) \leq 0, \qquad t = 1,2,3.$$

Transportation capacities

$$u\big((x,t),(x',t')\big) \leq T(x,x'), \qquad t = 1,2,3.$$

LITNO can be implemented and solved in any commercial optimization software package such as GAMMS.

12.4.4   *Extensions and Modifications*

The basic LITNO model presented above may be extended and modified in several directions.

More Types of Supply

The single supply (ammunition) in the current model can be extended to include several types of supplies (e.g., rations, spare-parts) that share common means of transportation. The basic structure of the LITNO model is not changed but the size of the problem may be increased considerably.

Optimizing Deployment and Employment of Means of Transportation

Means of transportation are not explicitly modeled in the current version of LITNO. The effect of these assets is implicitly modeled by imposing capacity constraints on the flow in the network. In reality, optimizing the employment of means of transportation – allocating trucks to the various logistic nodes and scheduling their operation – could enhance the efficiency of the logistic support chain. Incorporating means of transportations in LITNO will require, in addition to the balance constraints, a set of coupling constraints that connect the flow of supplies with the means of transportation that carry it.

12.5   Summary

Many design and operation problems associated with *OpLog* may be modeled as an inter-temporal network. In this chapter we modeled the design of a logistic support chain as an ITN. The resulting logistic inter-temporal network optimization model was described in detail. Typical real-world LITNO models may comprise several thousands (and perhaps even tens of thousands and more) of variables and a comparable number of constraints. However, commercial optimization software can easily handle problems of this size on standard personal computers. Although it is formally and rigorously constructed as a mathematical model, the main utilization of LITNO is not as a prescriptive "black box" tool but rather as a robust guide for efficient deployments of logistic assets in the theater of operations. The optimization model translates scenario-dependent uncertain demand profiles, operational parameters such as safety-stocks, transportation capacities, and delivery lead-times to a minimum cost deployment, and as such could also be used for sensitivity and "what if" analyses.

Index

© Springer International Publishing Switzerland 2016
M. Kress, *Operational Logistics*, Management for Professionals,
DOI 10.1007/978-3-319-22674-3

CPI Antony Rowe
Eastbourne, UK
January 08, 2020